THE NORTH APENNINES AND BEYOND

THE NORTH APENNINES AND BEYOND

WITH THE 10TH MOUNTAIN DIVISION

by Harris Dusenbery
Illustrations by Wilson P. Ware
Maps by Armand Casini

Binford & Mort Publishing
Portland, Oregon

The images on the front cover
are the Combat Infantryman Badge
and the 10th Mountain Division
Shoulder Patch.

This work is dedicated to the 992
of my comrades in arms who died in 1945
on the field of battle in far off Italy

THEY FACED THE FOE AS THEY
DREW NEAR HIM IN THE STRETCH
OF THEIR OWN MANHOOD AND
WHEN THE SHOCK OF BATTLE CAME
THEY IN A MOMENT OF TIME AT THE
CLIMAX OF THEIR LIVES WERE
RAPT AWAY FROM A WORLD FILLED
FOR THEIR DYING EYES NOT WITH
TERROR   BUT   WITH   GLORY...

THEY RECEIVED EACH FOR HIS
OWN MEMORY PRAISE THAT WILL
NEVER DIE AND WITH IT THE
GRANDEST OF ALL SEPULCURES A
HOME IN THE MINDS OF MEN.*

*From Memorial Panels No. 1 and No. 2 at the American Military Cemetery,
Florence, Italy. Quotation from the *Funeral Oration of Pericles*, reported by
Thucidides, and translated by A. E. Zimmern.

CONTENTS

SKETCHES, MAPS AND PHOTOGRAPHS

Wilson Ware's Sketches

Armand Casini's Maps

Listed by the dates of the military actions

Photographs

A BRIEF HISTORY OF
THE 10TH MOUNTAIN DIVISION

In the great cataclysmic events of World War II a single Army Division has but a tiny influence over the outcome of this greatest of all wars, but from the point of view of a rifleman within a Division, it appears to be a huge, mysterious organism that can project enormous power. As a former cell in this great organism that I proudly call the 10th Mountain Division, I can only view it with love and respect for the men with whom I served. Within this context I shall strive for objectivity, acknowledging my perspective from within the 1st Battalion of the 86th Mountain Infantry from October 1943 to October 1945.

As Athena sprang from the head of Zeus, the 10th Mountain Division sprang from the head of Charles Minot Dole, but not instantaneously as Athena. The Division's gestation and birth involved a long and persistent labor. Back in the 1930s Dole was in the insurance business in New York and was an avid weekend skier. Injured in a skiing accident and seeing an unmet need, he led in founding the National Ski Patrol System to aid injured skiers on the mountain slopes.

In the Russo-Finnish War of the winter of 1939–40 the Finns on their skis showed remarkable ability to contain far superior Russian forces for several months. From this and the war going badly for the Allies in Europe Dole saw the need for army troops trained for mountain and winter warfare.

With great resolution and tenacity Dole pursued his vision with the highest elements of the Army staff including Chief of Staff General George C. Marshall. In the winter of 1940–41 elements of a few Army divisions were given some ski training and work was continued in developing proper equipment for mountainous and Arctic conditions.

In November, 1941 the 1st Battalion, 87th Mountain Infantry Regiment was activated at Fort Lewis, Washington, and subsequently the full Regiment was established there.

In 1942 after the Army decided to activate a full mountain division, Camp Hale was constructed in the Rocky Mountains of Colorado near Tennessee Pass at over 9200 foot elevation. After the Camp was completed near the year's end, the 87th Regiment was moved there, and within a few months the 86th and 85th Regiments were activated.

For the first time in its history the Army used the services of an outside organization, the National Ski Patrol System, for recruitment. It rounded up men experienced in skiing and mountaineering for the new division. Artillery and other units necessary for an Army division were added and on July 19, 1943 the 10th Infantry Division (Light) was activated at Camp Hale. It had nine-man squads rather than the twelve-man squads of a regular division. Artillery was armed with the 75mm mountain howitzer that could be broken down and carried by mule pack with mules having been made an essential part of the Division's transportation. Training at Camp Hale was carried on through the winter of 1942–43.

In the summer of 1943 the 87th Regiment was detached for the Kiska invasion in the Aleutian Islands. The landing was made on August 15th, a few days after the

Japanese forces had pulled out. It gave the Regiment experience in making a landing and occupation under arduous conditions. The 87th did not return to Camp Hale until December. The rest of the Division continued mountain training through the summer and fall.

Winter and high altitude tactical training at Camp Hale for all units of the Division went on during the winter of 1943-44. Winter training ended in April, 1944 with the end of D-Series, which were exercises for the whole Division in the high mountains around Camp Hale. They lasted for three weeks without our returning to barracks. They were military maneuvers at times in extreme cold and at others under blizzard conditions at elevations from 9,000 to 12,000 feet. It was final proof that the men of the 10th Division had lived up to their reputation as ski troopers and could perform in the most arduous of conditions. For a personal account of the D-Series experience see my book, *Ski The High Trail*.

In April of 1944 Minot Dole inquired of General George Marshall why he had not committed the 10th Division to combat. Marshall replied that he did not want to commit the Division without a specific mission in a place where our mountain training would be needed.

Much to the chagrin of the mountain trained "Ski Troopers," the Division, still named the 10th Infantry Division (Light) was transferred in June, 1944 to Camp Swift on the hot plains of Texas east of Austin. There what we called flat land training began. New elements were added, squads were increased to twelve men and the Division became more like a regular infantry division. The landings in Normandy occurred just before the Division left Camp Hale. With the Allied successes during the summer and fall of 1944 the men of the 10th began to wonder whether the Division would ever be committed to combat in Europe. Talks about landing in Norway became less frequent. Routine infantry training continued through the summer and fall. In November of 1944 things began to happen. The Division was finally renamed the 10th Mountain Division. The Army decided to commit it to the Italian Campaign, and General George P. Hayes took command of the Division. Brigadier General David L. Ruffner was the Division Artillery Commander. Regimental commanders were Colonels David M. Fowler of the 87th, Clarence M. Tomlinson of the 86th and Raymond C. Barlow of the 85th.

In December the 86th Mountain Infantry Regiment was sent to Italy and the rest of the Division followed in January. Battalions of the 86th first entered into the front lines on January 8, 1945. The front was a snow bound area of the North Apennines and both sides were maintaining a defensive posture under severe winter conditions with snow three feet deep in many areas. By the end of January units of the 87th and 85th Regiments and the Artillery had seen action. Battalions were rotated in and out of the front lines at frequent intervals.

Back at Fifth Army Headquarters ideas were circulating about how to use this new Division that had been trained for mountain warfare. Mt. Belvedere and the ridges extending to the northeast were commanding heights overlooking Highway 64, the western approach through the Apennines to Bologna. Army Command recognized the strategic importance of these heights and had twice before tried to take Mt. Belvedere. The Fifth Army assigned the taking of these heights to the 10th Mountain Division. A precipitous ridge that the soldiers soon began to call Riva Ridge lay to the west and south of Mt. Belvedere and offered complete observation by the Germans on all approaches to that mountain. The generals decided that Riva Ridge had to be taken first.

The 1st Battalion of the 86th Mountain Regiment, reinforced by F Company, by stealth took Riva Ridge on the night of February 18–19. That is the action covered in

Part II of this book. The 87th and 85th Regiments and the 3rd Battalion of the 86th attacked Mt. Belvedere on the night of February 19 and by the 24th had taken and consolidated defensive positions on Mt. Belvedere, Mt. Gorgolesco and Mt. Della Torraccia.

Army Headquarters ordered a second phase of the advance. It began on March 3, 1945 and was completed two days later. The main objectives, Mt. Grande d'Aiano, the town of Castel d'Aiano, and Mt. Della Spe were captured after strong resistance by the Germans and heavy losses by the 10th Mountain Division. The Army decided that we had driven a salient deep enough into the German lines and ordered a halt. These new objectives were consolidated and the Division settled down to a defensive mode with battalions again being rotated out of the lines into rest areas in the Arno Valley.

All winter the Fifth Army had been working on plans for a Spring offensive to break through the mountain lines into the Po Valley and all of northern Italy. The decision was made to make the major thrust in the IV Corps area west of Highway 64 and to have the 10th spearhead the attack. After two days delay because of fog in the Arno Valley airfields the 10th on the morning of April 14th attacked straight north from Castel d'Aiano and Mt. Della Spe. The fighting was fierce and the 10th had its highest daily casualties by far, but with constant pressure it succeeded in breaking through the German main line of defense within three days. German prisoners numbered in the hundreds. The mine fields had been passed and the Germans were on the run.

On April 20 with the three Regiments abreast the Division broke out into the Po Valley and the race for the Po River was on to try to make a river crossing before the Germans could organize a defense line there. On April 22 units of the Division reached the Po and on April 23 the 87th Regiment crossed first in hand paddled assault boats encountering artillery and mortar fire but crossed with relatively few casualties for a major river crossing. By the 24th all three Regiments were on the north side and awaiting the completion of a bridge to get vehicles and tanks across the Po River.

On April 26th the 86th Regiment reached Verona and Bussolengo and the 87th passed through and went on to Lake Garda. Large numbers of German troops were fleeing toward the Brenner Pass up the west shore of the lake and our Division was ordered to cut them off.

For the next few days the Division rotating regiments fought its way up the east shore against at times strong enemy resistance. We reached Torbole at the north end of the Lake on April 29th and German resistance in the area decreased rapidly with the German army surrendering in Italy on May 2.

On May 14th the Division moved back into the hot Po Valley southeast of Brescia, but on May 19 it was moved to the Yugoslav border as a dispute arose between Yugoslavia and Italy over the location of the border. Again the 10th Mountain Division found itself in beautiful mountains this time in the Julian Alps and again patrolling with loaded weapons. Within a few days things settled down, patrolling ended and training resumed. The troops enjoyed the peaceful stay there. Duties were light and leaves were frequent.

In July the 10th Mountain Division was ordered back to the United States for training for the invasion of Japan. Near the end of July the Division sailed for home arriving in the first half of August. Men were given 30-day leaves. The Division reassembled at Camp Carson, Colorado. Japan had surrendered and men were being transferred and "ruptured ducked" by the hundreds every week. Officially for the Division the end came on October 20th but some units were not deactivated until November. In a way it was a sad ending to a unique army Division, but as individuals the men were happy to be going home. What a great sound that phrase has "going home"!

But this glorious emotion was for the living. Our hearts went out to our dead, to the 992 comrades in arms who died on the field of battle, and can appear in their homes only as memory. They served their country well and we will never forget them.

We faced enemy artillery, mortar fire, small arms fire and crossed fields with mines in the thousands. We advanced with stealth and with verve and daring. We lost few as prisoners of war but our wounded numbered 3080. The 10th Division's casualties were a significant percentage of all Fifth Army casualties during the 114 days we were engaged in combat on the Italian front. We took the high ground and we always held it.

In the article "Counting Costs of Elite Forces" appearing in the November 1985 periodical *ARMY* the authors Lt. Col. Gary L. Bounds and Maj. Scott R. McMichael name the 10th Mountain Division as one of the elite units of World War II. They considered many elite units, the British Commandos, The American Rangers, the Airborne divisions, and in later years the Green Berets. One characteristic they found was high casualty rates. They pointed this out as also being true of the 10th Mountain Division in their fighting in Italy.

Units of the Division were in combat from January 8, 1945 when the 86th Regiment entered the lines as part of Task Force 45 to May 2, 1945 for a total of 114 days. Most of that time we were merely holding defensive positions or pursuing a beaten and retreating enemy. More than three-fifths of our casualties, killed and wounded, occurred during the twelve days of our three major attacks. The first was the seizure of Riva Ridge and the Mt. Belvedere to Mt. Della Torraccia ridge. That action lasted for six days, from the evening of February 18 to February 24. A second phase was started on March 3 and ended on

March 5 with the capture of Mt. Grande d'Aiano, Castel d'Aiano and Mt. Della Spe. It was competed in three days. The Division was selected to spearhead the Fifth Army breakthrough of the German lines. That our most costly action lasted from April 14 to 16, also only three days. Those were the twelve days of trial and suffering and victory for the 10th Mountain Division.

Perhaps we deserved to suffer the most casualties. We were the new kid on the block. The British Eighth Army had been fighting the Germans since 1940. Many elements of the American Fifth Army had fought in North Africa before the Italian invasion and had been at this fighting game since 1942. They number their combat experience in months and years: we of the 10th Mountain Division number our combat period in days. In spite of their many losses over the years the German Army we faced in Italy in 1945 was still an army with excellent weapons and years of experience fighting defensive battles. They were surprisingly efficient in the use of their limited resources. We men of the 10th have pride in what we accomplished on the Italian front, but we must never forget the many other divisions and supporting units of the two great armies stretched from the Ligurian Sea to the Adriatic across the mountains of the North Apennines. It took them all to defeat the Germans in Italy.

Today a new 10th Mountain Division exists in the U.S. Army at Fort Drum, New York. It is classified as a light infantry division and has trained for fighting in the mountains, deserts, tropics, cities or wherever needed. Units of it have seen duty in Somalia, the Persian Gulf, Haiti and Bosnia. It probably is the type of military unit that is best suited for meeting our nation's needs in the 21st century. The infantry will still be "Queen of Battle."

PART I
ITALIAN DIARY

INTRODUCTION

This diary covers the period from when I sailed with the 86th Mountain Infantry for Italy on December 10, 1944 on the SS *Argentina* to the time I sailed home from Italy on July 26, 1945 on the *Westbrook Victory*. During my service there I was classified as a Scout-Observer in the S-2 Section of the 1st Battalion, 86th Mountain Infantry. For the last three weeks of the War, I replaced our Battalion Intelligence NCO, who was hopitalized with Hepatitis.

During the War soldiers were not permitted to keep diaries. I compiled this diary in 1946 several months after I was discharged from the Army. My wife, Evelyn, had kept all my letters. On the basis of those letters, some notes I made in Italy after the war, maps and unit records I brought back from Italy and from memory I was able to write this diary which I believe is an accurate account of my experiences in wartime Italy.

A few years later I added my copy of our Battalion Journal for the Riva Ridge Operation to it. This document that I call the Battalion Journal is a log of messages received by radio and telephone. It is included in Part II of this book. I had photocopies made of my diary and the journal and over the years have sold many copies to veterans of the 10th Mountain Division.

I have now rewritten the diary and corrected a number of errors in getting it ready for inclusion in this book as Part I. More importantly I have included twelve sketches drawn by Lt. Wilson P. Ware, our Battalion S-2 (Intelligence Officer). Now after these many years, I thank him for his permission to use them. These sketches suddenly stop as Lieutenant Ware was seriously wounded by one of those ubiquitous mines that our Division so often encountered. This was on April 15, 1945 during our breakthrough of the German lines just northeast of Rocco Roffino. He was out of the war but faced months and months of hospitalization. The Battalion truly missed him in our dash across the Po Valley.

Wilson Ware was born and raised in New York City. He attended Yale University and earned a liberal arts degree in 1936, after which he studied at the Yale School of Drama for two years. Before the War he skied and climbed mountains. He served in the 87th Mountain Infantry at Fort Lewis, and in the 10th Mountain Division at Camp Hale, Camp Swift and Italy.

After the Division moved to Camp Swift he recruited me, a rifleman in C Company, for training as a Scout-Observer in his S-2 Section of our Battalion Headquarters and trained me for those duties. From then on I was closely associated with him up until he was wounded in Italy near the end of the War. He was a superior officer but even more for me he was a superb gentleman.

After the War he lived in Connecticut and had a career in the practice and teaching of architectural design. He died in 1997 and will be long remembered by those who knew him for his compassionate heart.

Armand Casini served in and Regimental Headquarters of the 86th and in 10th Division Headquarters. Shortly after the war he drew the artistic sketch maps that I have included in the Diary. They cover the Division's operation and advances from the initial attack on Riva

Ridge and Mt. Belvedere to the final surrender in Italy on May 2, 1945.

These maps have been used many times in books and articles about the 10th Mountain Division and also in the pamphlets prepared for our reunion trips to Italy. They are familiar to most veterans of the Division and they are so popular because they give such a beautiful and concise summary of our combat operations.

After the War Casini became an award winning architect with the firm of Skidmore, Owings and Merrill, and in a 40-year career he worked on many important buildings in California, elsewhere in the United States and in other countries. He died in 1995, but he will be long remembered by the men of the 10th Mountain Division for these maps.

I thank all my 10th Mountain Division comrades who over the years have provided me with a wealth of information about the Division. I particularly want to thank my wife, Evelyn, who proofread the manuscript and who for more than fifty years has understandingly stood by me with my passion for the 10th Mountain Division.

Finally I thank Pamela A. Henningsen of Binford & Mort Publishing for her dedication in improving this book through the stages of publication.

I
OCEAN CROSSING
10 DECEMBER TO 23 DECEMBER

10 DECEMBER 1944

I boarded our transport, the former passenger liner, SS *Argentina,* at 2:30 A.M. at Newport News, Virginia after a short train trip from Camp Patrick Henry. With the S-2 Section I climbed down to my berth at the bottom of the forward hold and went to sleep. Most of us were up in time to see the ship get under way at 8:00 A.M.. Hampton Roads was full of ships coming and going. We went down stream rapidly; other ships followed, and as the bay widened out the ships took on a convoy formation. We crossed the bar and felt the Atlantic swell heave the ship. We were on our way to an unknown destination. The Navy patrol vessels on our flanks reminded us of the enemy submarine danger. The land dropped rapidly behind us. We watched it for hours and how we hated to see it drop below the horizon in the bright afternoon sun. In the evening we got word that our S-2 Section was scheduled for KP tomorrow.

11 DECEMBER 1944

Eight of us from the S-2 Section spent all morning peeling spuds. We did not keep track of how many bushels of potatoes we peeled. We speculated on whether we were peeling enough for the 5,000 troops aboard our ship and decided that there must be others also peeling spuds somewhere on this great ship. We agreed that doing this was better than doing nothing. Through the afternoon the Section peeled on, but I was assigned to washing the tremendous pots and pans. That was worse, but as consolation I did have a porthole to look out. Two seventeen-year-old boys who had just joined the merchant marine were helping and complaining all the time. What a life!

12 DECEMBER 1944

KP again from noon to 8:00 P.M., still on pots and pans. The ocean was rougher and I had a touch of sea sickness. I took a pill that had been given us at Patrick Henry. It helped and I got through the day OK.

13 DECEMBER 1944

Washing, brushing teeth and showering in cold salt water isn't any fun. I had KP again, but after a couple of hours in the galley I got sea sick. I spent the rest of the day in my bunk which is simply chicken wire stretched over a wooden frame. I skipped the evening meal.

14 DECEMBER 1944

With no KP, I spent the day reading an Agatha Christie mystery. We are required to wear our life jackets everywhere we go. A water-proof flashlight is attached to the jacket. We get a mimeographed news bulletin every day, and at noon one of the crew broadcasts a news report over the public address system. Part of the time he plays music. We have movies every afternoon on the forward part of the promenade deck, but my turn has not yet come around. In the evening I went back to the fantail watching the sun set and our wake bubbling us along on our way to war in Europe or Asia.

15 DECEMBER 1944

Men who have been on transports before tell us that we are lucky to have three meals a day. Usually on crowded troop transports only two are served. We now are having fine weather and it seems very warm for December. I spent some time today up in the bow watching the flying fish dart away from the prow. We saw some porpoises and in the Section we had a big argument over whether they were porpoises or dolphins. We did not have a dictionary to settle it. Dickson as usual was in the thick of it. Most of the Section are still on KP. They like it because they get more and better food. I started reading Canby's biography of Walt Whitman.

16 DECEMBER 1944

I spent most of the day reading the biography of Whitman. It is good. For men on their way to a fighting front the war news from Europe is definitely not good. There is no chance of it being over before we get there. We are not allowed on deck after dark so it means long hours below in the stuffy hold. I have been shaving every other day and taking a salt water shower every third day.

17 DECEMBER 1944

For an Atlantic crossing in mid-December the weather has been very good. A warm south wind has been steady sometimes blowing at gale force. We have whitecaps and a choppy sea. I finished Henry S. Canby's biography of Whitman. It is a provocative book that I enjoyed thoroughly. I can only read on deck as my bunk is too dark for reading. Life on a troop ship is crowded and monotonous, but my reading keeps me occupied and my mind off the war.

18 DECEMBER 1944

Our good weather is still holding and I have no detail today. I am still reading my way to that unknown destination.

19 DECEMBER 1944

Shortly after noon we saw a Liberator bomber, probably a naval patrol craft looking for German submarines. The rumor has it that we are in the vicinity of the Azores, but we have no official word of where we are bound. The weather has been so mild that many of us think we are on our way to the Mediterranean.

20 DECEMBER 1944

I saw a movie this afternoon but took little note of it. Afterwards a band played on the aft promenade deck. The trip seems to be passing far too rapidly because we are not anxious to get to wherever we are going. The war news from Europe continues to be bad. In the evening we get the announcement that tomorrow morning we will pass through the Strait of Gibraltar. There is a lot of speculation tonight about where we are bound. Southern France and Italy are most commonly mentioned, but a few kill-joys bring up the possibility of going on through the Suez Canal to Burma. Our convoy formation has remained the same all the way. We have one passenger ship to starboard and two to port. About eight or ten ships including some tankers are visible astern. Usually we can see three Navy patrol vessels out on the horizon ahead of us and one on each flank. We hear that we are in a fast convoy, but this is our eleventh day at sea.

21 DECEMBER 1944

I was up early to watch our passage through the Strait of Gibraltar. Many men were on deck right after breakfast watching for the landfall. Before 9:00 A.M.

land was sighted off to the northeast. It was the mountainous coast of Spain. Here was our first view of a continent engulfed in war. The land loomed higher and higher, and then more land ahead of the ship was sighted. Lower, it was Africa. Nearing the Strait we could see the white buildings, villages and towns in Spain and more over on the African side. We were at the meeting of two continents. The gleaming city of Tangier rose above a line of frothy surf and over on the Spanish side on higher ground was Tarifa. So this is Europe and Africa! The land is brown and dry and few trees break the monotony of the terrain. The many houses are almost all painted white or built of white stone.

Just before entering the Strait a flight of RAF fighter planes from Gibraltar flew over buzzing our ship just above the masthead. They tore past at blinding speed welcoming us as comrades in arms to Europe. They appeared to be painted black with RAF circles on the wings and tails. I thought they might be lend-lease Corsairs.

We could not see any pillar-like land formations, but here in the Strait we were between the Pillars of Hercules. I thought of ancient Greek legends, of Roman triremes, and of Moorish galleys. It thrilled me to realize that we were now entering the historic Mediterranean Sea. We were an American convoy bearing thousands of soldiers and untold gallons of gasoline for the fighting fronts, and in our closed formation our five Navy escorts were still with us.

We looked hard and long for the Rock of Gibraltar. When we finally found it we were disappointed. From the middle of the Strait it did not look like the pictures emphasizing its rugged strength. It was long and low and insignificant in comparison to the hills of Spain rising up behind it. After Gibraltar, now early afternoon, the Strait widened out into the Mediterranean. Gone was the ocean roll, and the blue water sparkled with a new brightness.

Soon five of our ships changed course for the northeast and our escort vessels dropped behind us. The *Argentina* picked up a faster rhythm in her engines and parted company with the convoy. We sailed east within sight of the coast of Africa. It was a wonderful afternoon with a mild breeze blowing from the west. The sun was bright and warm.

I was nearing the end of a voyage that I wanted to go on and on, not that it was a pleasure cruise, but it was certainly better than the war that lay ahead. I went up to the bow and watched the flying fish dart away through water and air from the onrushing ship.

After dinner I went back to the stern and watched one of the loveliest sunsets I had ever seen. The blue Mediterranean surpassed my expectations. I thought often that afternoon of its history and its past glory. Now it is but a sideshow in the great European war but one in which men die in mortal combat so its glory cannot be less.

Shortly after dark we passed the lights of a city. A crewman told me that it was Oran. I went below for two or three hours and then returned to deck for a last look around before going to bed. Here in the Mediterranean we could be on deck at night. We were passing another city that was a blaze of lights sloping from the water level up to high hills. The crew said that it was Algiers. The night was warm; it was hard to believe that it was December.

22 DECEMBER 1944

Today was beautiful, steaming across a smooth, blue, warm sea. It would be fine sailing for a small yawl. In the afternoon we were served in our long mess lines a Christmas dinner of turkey and all the fixings. It was later announced that our destination was Naples. For the first time most of us knew that we would be fighting in the mountains of Italy.

Later in the afternoon we sighted Italy. We had another gorgeous sunset. We were heading toward a signal light flashing on the mainland shore. At dusk we passed just south of the Isle of Capri, and many of us thought of the popular song of that name. Our ship passed between the Isle and the mainland and headed north across the Bay of Naples.

The temperature fell as we approached land and soon after dark a strong cold east wind came up. It was penetratingly cold blowing across Italy out of the heart of the Balkans. We passed two small sail boats making their perilous way across the bay through the storm. In my wool uniform I stayed out on deck to watch the anchoring just outside the inner harbor. We had arrived and I went below for what I hoped would be a good night's sleep.

23 DECEMBER 1944

Mt. Vesuvius looked cold and quiet in the morning sun. The east wind still blew and it was not comfortable on deck. The city of Naples, badly bomb damaged, was spread over the hills to the north.

We raised anchor and steamed slowly into the inner harbor which contained many bomb damaged and sunken ships. We tied up to a badly damaged pier. The whole port operation appeared to be a makeshift affair. Some of the piers were merely platforms built on the hulls of capsized ships.

Unloading 5,000 men from a troop transport takes hours of standing in line. Eventually we were loaded into trucks and taken to a new debarkation center in a school west of the city in a suburb called Bagnoli. The buildings were fine new ones but every window in them had been blown out or possibly had never been installed. We were assigned rooms and told we would have to sleep on the floor and it was cold marble. This would be worse than a bivouac, but we were able to take hot showers for the first time in two weeks. No passes were issued. This does not feel like the Christmas season. Little of the Christmas spirit is in evidence. The Red Cross Club has a tree and decorations, but to us it appears very superficial in this bleak war theater we are now entering.

II
PREPARING FOR COMBAT
24 DECEMBER TO 6 JANUARY 1945

24 DECEMBER 1944

Last night a few of the men bought liquor from some Italians who sneaked into our area. One man in the Battalion was sent to the hospital because the stuff he drank had gasoline in it.

We each have one blanket. I put my overcoat and all the extra clothes I had on the floor as padding for a bed. The stone floor was still mighty hard and I did not sleep at all well. Day and night it seems colder in our building than outdoors. We are getting our meals from a field kitchen in the courtyard and we eat standing up.

25 DECEMBER 1944

This morning we got word that we are leaving and none of us seem to be sorry about it. This does not seem like Christmas even though we had a turkey dinner in a new mess hall where we sat down to eat.

In the afternoon we completed departure preparations. We rode in army trucks for a short distance to a train siding where we loaded into box cars, twenty-five men and all their gear in each car. We heard that our Battalion was going to Livorno by train while the 2nd and 3rd were going by ship. Our train pulled out at 4:00 P.M. east through Naples and up over hills to the interior. We passed many wrecked railroad cars, stacks of ammunition in open fields and damaged buildings along the way. Traveling by rail gives one a concentrated picture of the ravages of this war because rail lines are a prime bombing target. This was one of the first troop trains to make this trip.

With all our baggage in the car and twenty-five men there was not room enough for everyone to stretch out at one time so we spent the night lapped over each other. At least it was warmer that way. It was a cold night and we had no heat in the car. We all wore our overcoats for warmth. Our train speed was slow.

26 DECEMBER 1944

The next morning we were winding through mountainous valleys passing ruined towns. The fortress-like character of the stone towns was the first thing that struck me, how well they suited the defense.

We passed by what we thought was Cassino. We were all thankful that we did not have to fight through that bloody battle. In the afternoon we came through the Alban Hills out onto the plain of Rome, past the great Roman Aqueduct along the Appian Way and into Rome itself. We were in the west part of the city and I did not recognize any historic buildings. We were in the railway yards for about an hour. The only food we were having was cold C-rations and we were getting tired of them. A few of the fellows managed to trade C-rations for bottles of *vino*. The train finally started north along the coastal route and again we had a poor sleep, but after being hardened from going through a cold winter in the Colorado Rockies it was not too bad.

27 DECEMBER 1944

When I woke up the train was stopped. We have a C-ration breakfast and wait and wait some more. Being the S-2 Section we do some checking. We find that we are in Cecina and cannot proceed because of a train wreck ahead of us. We are right on the coast. The Mediterranean is blue and calm this morning, but the air is cold and the east wind continues.

About 10:00 A.M. a convoy of trucks come for us. We load up with our equipment and ride north on the coast highway. Going through Livorno we see considerable bomb damage. Barrage balloons ride over the harbor at Livorno or Leghorn as it is more commonly called by us Americans. The concrete pillboxes along the Arno River make us glad we didn't have to fight through here. Passing a miles-long supply depot we see mountains of C-rations stacked forty boxes high. That doesn't make us too happy, but the huge quantities of trucks, artillery pieces and tanks give us the feeling of strength and a realization that we won't have to win the war all by ourselves. The convoy passed a fighter field. A flight of P-47s took off on some unknown mission. At this field I saw the P-63 Black Widow night fighters for the first time. We were glad to see air support this far north.

We ride through the west side of Pisa. It is a factory district and has been badly damaged. We all look for the Leaning Tower but cannot see it from our route. The convoy stops at a Redeployment Depot two or three miles northwest of Pisa. We have no accommodations except a large open field. In this we set up our tents in even rows. We all curse this order as we think we are too close to the battlefront to be so G.I. We would make a good strafing target. We are furnished with straw so we do have some comforts, and B-rations taste good after the Cs for three days. We spend the day making our bivouac as comfortable as possible and dig slit trenches. Blackout orders are in effect in the bivouac area. You can tell we are a new outfit and everything is really G.I.

28 DECEMBER 1944

Our Battalion Motor Pool is being set up and Lieutenant Ware learns that he is being assigned a Jeep. I am picked to be the driver. I spend most of the day at the motor pool learning how to service a Jeep.

In the evening I went out for a walk with two men from the S-2 Section. A mile or two out we encountered a guard at a small bridge. It was a dark, isolated spot and he had a small fire burning. He was cold and lonely and wanted to talk. He has been in the infantry and seen lots of fighting in Africa and Italy. He is now recuperating from wounds, but his troubles seem to be mental rather than physical. He can't bear the thought of being sent back to the front. In his condition he would be useless as a front line soldier. It made us realize what a tough job a rifleman has, and we left him a sober group agreeing among ourselves that here was one permanent casualty. That man's fear is his whole life now, and it will take a long rehabilitation for him to get over it. We walked slowly back to camp and crawled into our pup tents. I have difficulty sleeping not because of my bed of straw but because I cannot shed from memory the fear in his eyes.

29 DECEMBER 1944

Today I went out with Lieutenant Ware in the Jeep on a reconnaissance of the roads in the area. We wanted to get some mileage figures for a battalion march tomorrow. It gave me some experience with the Jeep.

In the evening some of us hitched a ride into Pisa. It was a beautiful moonlit night and we went to see the Leaning Tower. The Cathedral and Tower were beautiful, but I thought the Baptistery was best. In the moonlight it looked like a jeweled crown with perfect proportions. From there we went to an off-limits bar and had on Italian soil our first *vino rosso*. We got a ride back to our camp before midnight.

30 DECEMBER 1944

I am not sure whether it was last night or this morning that the Battalion and Regiment received orders to move. Anyway I drove Captain Krumm in a convoy with other officers to survey possible sites for the bivouac. The area was located right along the coast about twelve miles south of Livorno in the vicinity of Quercianella. It was a rough section of country and we did a lot of driving looking for enough level areas. It was a picturesque region with a high rugged coastline and some nice villas overlooking the sea. We saw two islands far out on the horizon and a ship convoy headed into Livorno harbor. After much discussion among the officers they decided on various sites right along the highway. In the afternoon we drove back to Livorno and the officers conferred with PBS officials on the location. It was agree that we would move there tomorrow.

31 DECEMBER 1944

We broke camp in the morning and by late afternoon the S-2 Section had set up an eight-man pyramidal tent in a garden about twenty yards above the coast highway. We had a fine view of the Tyrrhenian Sea. We installed the heating stove that came with the tent. We were even furnished straw to stuff in our mattress covers. and we had folding army cots. This was real luxury compared to pup tents.

In the evening for our New Year's celebration the Section shared one can of shrimp, two cans of tomato juice, and a few candy bars and lemon drops; alas! no *vino*. I wrote a letter home by candle light. As we were to get up at 6:30 A.M. we went to bed without seeing the New Year in.

1 JANUARY 1945

We spent most of this New Years Day making our bivouac more comfortable. It was cool and sunny, and with the hills behind us we were out of the east wind. Getting wood for our stove was the big problem. We spent hours scrounging for a supply and then we had to guard it from our fellow soldiers.

2 JANUARY 1945

This region lives up to its *old world* name. I was impressed with how much stone has been used in the buildings down through the centuries. In my Jeep back in the hills today I saw several old ruins not from this war but from hundreds of years ago; some of them appeared to be survivals from Roman times.

The days have been clear, dry and cool. The temperature generally goes down to freezing at night. The climate and geography remind me of parts of California. We are more comfortable now than we ever have been on bivouac in Colorado or Texas.

Kurt Honberg has been carting a three-pound can of coffee around ever since leaving the ship. Today he traded it to an Italian for two bottles of Cognac. Dickson thinks he has another can in reserve.

We have a shortage of candles and no daylight hours to ourselves. It is difficult to find time for reading and letter writing. Besides a crowded tent with conversation, arguments and fights going on over one's head is not conducive to such activities. Also Sergeant Anderson came into our tent to take a sponge bath because we have a stove and his tent does not.

3 JANUARY 1945

In the motor pool this morning we had a lecture on Third Echelon Maintenance. I spent the rest of the day lubricating the Jeep and waiting around for something to happen.

We have a fine view of the shoreline and the ocean from our tent. The sunset this evening was spectacular. It seemed so peaceful here. Since moving back we can no longer hear the big guns at the front. After dark we spent the rest of the evening in our tent reading, writing and arguing.

4 JANUARY 1945

Sergeant Matthews and three of us in the S-2 Section went on a road reconnaissance in the Jeep into the hill country back of our bivouac area. We drove through the hillside town of Monte Nero overlooking the Livorno district. It felt good to get out of camp and on our own to see more of the countryside.

5 JANUARY 1945

The companies are making conditioning marches and the various units are doing some training. We don't have any idea how long we will be here. It is a comfortable spot and we all hope it will be a long time.

6 JANUARY 1945

The A & P platoons have been working with mines and clearing some fields left by the Jerries. Today the 3rd Battalion set off an S-mine and I hear that several of our men were killed and many more were wounded. That news certainly set our stomachs to churning.

In the evening our Battalion made a ten-mile conditioning march. It was pitch dark and on our way back we were marching down a narrow road. Linwood "Duke" Wellington of our section had his rifle riding crosswise on top of his rucksack. Captain Krumm came walking up the road in the opposite direction. In the dark Duke's rifle knocked him off the road and down a ten-foot embankment. We heard some cussing but we kept right on marching. I don't think Captain Krumm ever knew what he had run into.

III
TASK FORCE 45
7 JANUARY TO 13 FEBRUARY

6 JANUARY 1945

This Sunday we find out that we are going to move, and an advance party goes tomorrow. We are not told where. I am to drive Lieutenant Ware, and I have to haul a trailer which I have never done before.

I get a brief practice handling the trailer. We get the vehicles gassed and ready to go and most of our personal packing done. We have lots of speculation about where we are going, but we all fear that wherever it is will be worse than what we have here.

7 JANUARY 1945

After breakfast the convoy assembled in the motor pool. We were told that we were going to the front as part of Task Force 45. We left at eight o'clock driving north through Livorno and Pisa. Out of Pisa we were on the autostrada, a straight four-lane highway with overhead crossings. It was perfectly level going east up the Arno River. After some time we left the autostrada and headed north toward the mountains.

At one road junction we stopped for about half an hour. In a small store we bought wine and filled our canteens. Because of the War, bottles are very scarce in Italy. We also bought some dried figs and nuts. The store had for sale straw sandals and bread which they would only sell to civilians on ration tickets. This was all the stock they had.

After miles of winding precipitous road far up into the North Apennine mountains we came to the Light Line. This is a line about ten miles back of the front lines beyond which complete blackout is observed and vehicles cannot use their lights at night. We passed through San Marcello and drove along a winding road that parallels the front for several miles. We crossed a pass of the Apennines and descended a few miles to Poretta Terme. This is the first of the mountain towns that shows much damage. It is full of soldiers and military traffic. We stopped here for about an hour while our officers try to get clearance to proceed to our destination. The names here mean nothing to me. Some soldiers on the street tell us that we are within artillery range of the enemy and that they shell Poretta Terme quite regularly.

This being winter there are a couple of inches of snow on the ground. We get orders to put down our Jeep tops and fold and cover the windshields forward so they will be less visible to the enemy. We put chains on all four wheels.

About 1:30 in the afternoon we get clearance to proceed. Poretta is a smoky town and we soon learn the reason why. Some two miles north at Silla we turn left toward the mountains and come to a smoke generator placed right next to the road. Hugh clouds of smoke billow out from it and the wind blows the dense smoke directly across the road. What a traffic jam as the vehicles inch their way through it! When I get into it the smoke is so dense I cannot see the wire bar that is welded to the middle of the front bumper. This is a heavy vertical steel bar about five feet high designed to protect the Jeep riders from decapitation by wires strung across roads at night by the enemy.

SMOKING THE VALLEY, SILLA BRIDGE

Sergeant Matthews gets out of the Jeep and tries to guide me through, but I cannot see him. A truck driven by a Brazilian backs into my Jeep and nearly shoves us off the road. After much honking it stops in time, then proceeds and we manage to follow it through the smoke. It takes about ten minutes to make that hundred feet. We curse the Army for putting the generator so close to the road, but we know little of the "big picture."

From there we start climbing. The shell craters are more frequent, and in two places we have to make detours around bridges that have been zeroed in by German artillery and are shelled frequently. MPs at these places

CONVOY

W.WARE/45

tell us to hurry through. The Front is now crawling skin
on the back of my neck.

The snow gets deeper as we go higher into the mountains. At Lizzano in Belvedere we stop for a time to get
further clearance. Here we are much closer to the Front.
I do not see the bustle there was at Poretta and few
soldiers are visible. From here we look right across the
valley to Mt. Belvedere which is occupied by the
enemy. We finally get our clearance and go on three
miles up to Vidichiatico which is our destination and
will be our Battalion CP.

We are relieving the 900th Anti-Aircraft Battalion that
was converted on short notice to infantry. The several
tanks and tank destroyers in town are from the 1st
Armored Division. I park the Jeep and trailer. Sergeant
Matthews and I are put up in the Albergo Alberto with
some of the men we are relieving. They tell us of the shortage of infantry and how tough it is here on the Front. They
are a happy bunch to be going back.

8 JANUARY 1945

We have two feet of snow here in Vidichiatico, but
the streets are pretty well cleared. I have no assignment
during the day so I explore the town, being careful not to
show myself to the enemy watching the town from Mt.
Belvedere. We are not expecting the Battalion until early
tomorrow morning.

In the evening well after dark I am sent down to
Lizzano with two assignments, the first being to intercept
Major Espey and tell him to check in at the telephone
switchboard and the second being to make sure that C
Company stops here at Lizzano as it will be our reserve
company.

I have no trouble driving the Jeep without lights on
the rutted, snow-covered road to Lizzano. Since the companies are not expected until midnight or after, I wait in

the switchboard room where it is warm. I hear some war experiences from the men we are relieving. They admit that they now have a soft job. During the evening it is very quiet with no sound of artillery or small arms fire. A patrol of a dozen Partisans on foot go by. It is a cold night out there to go looking for the enemy.

About eleven o'clock the traffic begins to pick up going both ways so I have to get out on the road and check every vehicle going up to find out who they are. It is a cold, dark job without any lights in town or on vehicles. I finally locate Major Espey and give him the message, but I get further orders to stay out on the road and check the companies as they come through to see if they know where they are going and tell them if they don't know. The men are marching up with heavy packs from Silla or Poretta. It will be late before they get to their assigned sectors I stay out on the road for several hours during that long, cold night.

The artificial moonlight does little to dispel the gloom. We have many searchlights back of Poretta out of artillery range of the enemy. They shine their beams at an angle into the sky over the Front. They are supposed to reflect light from the clouds down to the ground and increase our ability to see at night but not help the enemy who would be looking into the light. It still is what I would call a dark night out here on the main street through Lizzano in Belvedere. It seems the Germans do not suspect a relief is being made and the night is quiet.

9 JANUARY 1945

After 3:00 A.M. and the last of our Battalion has passed through Lizzano except C Company which is remaining here, I am able to drive back to Vidichiatico. I sleep in a real bed until noon. The S-2 Section is installed on the second floor of the Albergo Alberto. From the back windows of the hotel we look right over the valley to the enemy on Mt. Belvedere. We are green and we know it. Caution is the word.

10 JANUARY 1945

We have not yet established a Battalion OP (Observation Post). We spend the day getting our accommodations in shape. Apparently we are waiting for the line companies to settle into their positions.

1ˢᵗ BN. CP VIDICIATICO   WWAREᴀˢ

11 JANUARY 1945

This is another day of watchful waiting for us. Patrols are being sent out, but mobility is hampered by deep snow.

12 JANUARY 1945

I wasted away the day talking with my fellow section members and waiting for something to happen. After dark I drove Lieutenant Ware from Battalion Headquarters in Vidichiatico the few miles out to Able Company's CP at Querciola to orient a patrol. Out here we are within five hundred yards of German positions. The doorways and windows of the first floor are sandbagged, and the men are much more cautious than they are in Vidichiatico. It is only our second day at the Front, and I feel such an attitude makes good sense and is to be expected. We have to learn what it is like by first hand experience before we know when we can relax and when we should be alert to danger.

The doorway to Able CP behind a curved sandbag wall was covered with three blankets. We went through a double draped blackout chamber that kept the light from escaping as we entered.

The CP was a little room not much more than ten feet square. The radio and switchboard were located through an arched doorway in a smaller adjoining room. Both rooms were dark, cold and smoky. It did have a fireplace, but the tiny fire seemed to give off no heat, just smoke. Two burning candles seemed to have little effect in their feeble light penetrating the darkness. I swear that it was lighter outside in the moonlight. The two small rooms were crowded with about ten men; the company commander, one of his officers, a commo sergeant, and other hangers on. Lieutenant Ware exchanged pleasantries with the captain. I found a place for my Tommy Gun in a corner where about ten other weapons were stacked. I found a seat on a sack of potatoes.

Word was sent out over the telephone for the patrol to come in to the CP for orientation. Within a few minutes a second lieutenant, a sergeant, and several men came in. They could just barely squeeze in, and probably a man or two was sticking part way out the door. I heard the guard outside softly tell someone to douse the light. Out here, when in the open, we all talked with hushed voices.

Lieutenant Ware using a 1:25,000 map showed the men where they were to go and where they might make contact with the enemy. He also let them study two aerial photos of the terrain they were to go over. He repeated the instructions as to objectives that were given more generally over the telephone earlier in the day. For security reasons the definite objectives of patrols were not given over the phone but were delivered in person as close to the time of departure as possible. The orientation was finished and the patrol left to get ready. They were not to leave for an hour, this giving time to alert our outposts about the patrol.

Soon after they left a call came in on the phone from one of the outposts that they had sighted someone moving out in front of them. All outposts were alerted. The CO took the phone and talked personally to the man at the outpost. On another phone he called Battalion Headquarters to see if any other patrols might be out in this sector. He got a negative answer. He checked on the map for the position our patrol should be and then gave the order to shoot anything that moves in front of the outpost. I felt the great tension in the room. After a few anxious minutes a call came in from the outpost reporting that the BAR man has killed one Partisan and wounded another. An aid man was cleared through the outposts to see what he could do. The switchboard operator called the Battalion Aid Station for an ambulance. The alert was canceled. Lieutenant Ware and I drove back through the moonlit, snow-covered landscape two very sober soldiers, thinking what a hell of a way to be introduced to combat, shooting two men from our own side.

13 JANUARY 1945

We had snow falling most of the day, and in the evening I drove Watzek and two others from the section out to Querciola. The snow was falling so fast I could hardly see beyond the hood of the Jeep. Part of the time I had a man walking out in front to find the road and guide me. We needed our chains on all four wheels and I drove in compound low through about eight inches of snow. Part

of the time it was falling at the rate of several inches an hour. I ran off the road about six times and we lost much time digging out of drifts. With no top or windshield it was a pretty miserable trip, especially considering that I was not averaging more than a mile an hour. It got so bad that we finally stopped at Bulldog, a position half a mile south of Querciola. We hiked on in to Querciola through the blizzard of snow. At least we felt fairly safe from German patrols. Our mission was to check on possible locations for an OP, but the weather was so bad that we couldn't do much more than talk to some of the A Company men about possible locations. On our return to Vidichiatico in the early morning hours it was not snowing so much. We

CROSS OF THE FORTY CHILDREN   WWARE45

made an uneventful and faster trip, that is relatively fast. We still had all that snow to drive through and our tracks were completely buried in the new fall. We were a tired bunch when we finally fell into bed back at Vidichiatico.

14 JANUARY 1945

This morning we of the long night ride slept late and had breakfast in bed. Dickson, a pal of Watzek, brought it up to us. This is Sunday and it has been just like any other day for so many days that I no longer think of it as a special day. The days just go on and on one after another without a break, and I am afraid it will continue like this until the War is over. Not having Sundays makes one more aware of the steady, ceaseless flow of time.

15 JANUARY 1945

Today was bright and clear. I did a little maintenance work on the Jeep. Later I walked through the village watching children play and trying to pick up snatches of conversation to see if I could recognize any Italian words. I have been studying my Italian Sentence Book and hope I am beginning to learn a little of the language.

We set up our Battalion OP out at Querciola today. Because of my driving job I will stay in Vidichiatico. I will drive out from time to time to keep the men supplied with 10-in-1-rations. Here in Vidichiatico we are getting B-rations, which are cooked in our Field Kitchen. It is set up in the parking lot right next to our hotel. I believe it serves all the Headquarters Company men who are located here.

16 JANUARY 1945

Evelyn sent me a gold ring which came in the mail today. It was too large so this afternoon I took it down to the village jeweler to have it sized. He was a little hunch-backed man, and he spoke no English. I showed him the ring, put it on my finger, and said "*anche grande.*" He looked at it. Talking Italian which I did not understand at all, he picked up a little bottle and had me smell it. I finally understood that he needed alcohol to heat the ring. I went to the Battalion Aid Station and got an ounce or two and incidentally some aspirin and cough medicine for my cold. I took the alcohol to the jeweler and he measured my finger for size. He gave me a receipt and with the aid of my Sentence Book I learn I can get the ring day after tomorrow.

17 JANUARY 1945

Nothing to do today. I checked over the Jeep. Gas, oil, radiator water, battery, and tires were all O.K. I read most of the day.

18 JANUARY 1945

This morning three of us from the S-2 Section were invited into their home by an Italian family to have some coffee. A daughter, Albina, had learned a little English at school perhaps and from the American soldiers. Our troops have been in this area for at least three months. A fire was burning in the fireplace, and I was impressed with the hollow poker which they used to blow through to aid the fire. The coffee was quite sweet. I wondered where they got the sugar. It is very scarce here in Italy and of course rationed back home. Our limited conversation got around to where I was from. They had never heard of Oregon. I made several attempts to explain where it was. The one that satisfied them was that Oregon was north of Hollywood.

I went back to my hunch-backed little jeweler in the afternoon and got my ring. It fitted perfectly. I asked him *"Quanto Costa?"* and he answered *"Cento lire."* At official exchange rates 100 lira is one dollar in US money. I gave him a 100 lira bill and then offered him a package of cigarettes. He took the cigarettes and gave me back the money saying there was nothing he could buy with it.

In my PX rations I get the equivalent of a pack of cigarettes a day. They are worth a dollar a pack on the black market in Naples but much less up here on the line where the supply is greater and the demand less.

19 JANUARY 1945

During the evening I took the Jeep out to Querciola. It was an uneventful trip in the dark. I have never turned on the headlights in this Jeep since I started driving it.

This seems to be becoming my milk run. We do not have a continuous front here but rather a series of strong points. The road lies just behind some of these strong points, Tigers II, Tigers I, Tigers, Panthers, Bears, and Lions, and we feel it is reasonably safe from German patrols because their outposts are about a kilometer or two away from the road.

20 JANUARY 1945

The *Stars and Stripes* we got this morning brought news of the Russian offensive reaching the German border in Silesia. The Russians have achieved a real breakthrough, and it is hard to tell where the Germans will be able to stop them. We all hope that the Germans don't have the reserves to do it, but I am afraid the next hundred miles will be harder for the Russians than the last hundred. Here in the deep snows of the North Apennines we all hope the Russians can sweep on to Berlin and end the War before we have to do any real fighting.

I had started reading an English translation of Dante's *Divine Comedy*, but now Dickson has it out at the OP and I don't know when I'll get a chance to go on with it. I am now reading a book called *Great Poems From Chaucer to Whitman*. It's a good selection and I'm enjoying the poems. Our S-2 Section seems to be specializing in the classics, at least good literature. I know I want to read only the best. Contrary to previous reports comic books seem to be scarce here.

Tonight the Partisans gave a dance in the basement of the Albergo Alberto. They had two accordions and a clarinet for music, and there were about five men for every woman. I looked in for a time and found it very crowded and stuffy inside. The *vino* was poured freely. Everyone seemed to be having a good time and oblivious of the fact that the enemy was not far off.

DAWN, PATROL, ROCCA CORNETA

21 JANUARY 1945

The day was very quiet on the Front and I took it easy. I did a little reading and studied some Italian in the morning. In the afternoon I cleaned by rifle and Tommy Gun. I now have both weapons. I carry the M1 rifle as Scout-Observer in the S-2 Section and the Tommy Gun as Jeep Driver. I also wrote a letter to Evelyn.

22 JANUARY 1945

During the day I had little to do. I checked into the CP from time to time. I am sure I have been gaining weight. I get plenty of good food from our field kitchen in the parking lot next door and I get little exercise. I still have a head cold, but it does not bother me too much. It's like most colds. The medicine I am using has no effect.

Today Battalion Headquarters decided to change our OP from Querciola to Plinardo. In the evening Sergeant Matthews, Watzek, Beck and I loaded five spools of wire into the Jeep trailer and drove out to Plinardo to lay a telephone line from there back to our CP in Vidichiatico. The Communications Section would ordinarily be assigned this job, but they were too busy replacing lines broken by enemy artillery fire so we were doing it ourselves. It was a bright moonlit night and very quiet.

Plinardo was our most exposed position but only lightly held. It was the farthest away from our main defense points and the position most nearly surrounded by the enemy. It looked directly down on the Germans in Rocco Cornetta, but on the left flank the Germans looked down on Plinardo from a high precipitous ridge with our maps showing strange Italian names along it and on the right were the Germans on Mt. Belvedere.

We got started laying wire about nine o'clock. The wire was simply laid on the ground or on hedges alongside the road. The reel holding the spool was mounted on a frame on the back of the Jeep. I drove and a lot of it was stop and go. We had some trouble unreeling the wire because it had to be passed over the trailer, which we had to have to carry the extra spools of wire. Each spool held one-half mile of wire. We were green at the job so it went slowly. We felt lonely and exposed out there on the Front during those long night hours. It was oh so quiet. We rarely heard even the sound of distant artillery. The bright moonlight gave us plenty of light to see what we were doing. We kept our weapons close at hand because we knew that an enemy patrol could spot us from a long distance. We got back to Vidichiatico at one o'clock shortly after starting our fifth spool. We had a long day and were glad to get that job done.

23 JANUARY 1945

Today the weather was clear and cold. In the morning I drove Major Espey to visit an Italian family about half way down the road to Lizzano. After waiting in the Jeep for a while, I was invited in to sit by the fire. I had no knowledge of what our mission was and was thankful for the invitation to come in out of the cold. My conversation was limited. A woman asked me if I came from California. I told her Oregon and she looked a little disappointed. I'm afraid she had never heard of the place. I was served a glass of the best wine I've so far had in Italy. A little blue-eyed, yellow-haired boy two or three years old sat wide-eyed all the time and stared at my Tommy Gun. I thought he must be just the age of my son, David. We like the friendly people here in the mountain villages. They welcome us into their homes quite generally and generously.

Major Espey and I went on to Lizzano and had lunch in the OSS quarters. They get around. China plates, table linen, and a waitress to serve the meal was an unexpected pleasure. Some lucky people can have luxury at the Front, but it is all comparative. The outposts have it the worst, some being only dugouts in the snow, and the units farthest to the rear have the best conditions. We returned to Vidichiatico before dark. I have driven my Jeep around enough during the day in full sight of the Germans to feel that they do not think a single Jeep is significant enough of a target to spend artillery ammunition on. With their constrictions on ammunition they are probably right. Better to save for more advantageous targets when the real battle begins.

This evening the Section started in on our fortnightly beer ration which arrived today. It is beginning to snow and the temperature is moderating. We are glad we don't have to go out tonight. My greatest fear in driving the Jeep is encountering a German patrol at night. I have been doing quite a bit of night driving, some of it alone.

"PLINARDO" W.WARE/45

24 JANUARY 1945

We are still following the Russian offensive very closely, and we eagerly look forward to new editions of the *Stars and Stripes*. The offensive has reached the point where the loss of East Prussia and Silesia is certain, at least as production centers for the Germans. The Russian offensive will certainly make Germany a more vulnerable and less formidable foe.

25 JANUARY 1945

Now most of my trips are out to Plinardo and it is not as far as Querciola. I took out rations tonight. We have a good set up there, and the telephone line we laid is working O.K. I marvel at how a sound powered telephone can convert the sound waves to minute electric waves and send them for miles over a copper wire. The Italian family living at our OP cook our meals. Observing enemy held areas is the only function we have during the day, but during the night the men of our small section pull long hours of guard duty as Plinardo is practically undefended. Honberg has picked up Italian rapidly and he sure is handy to have around.

26 JANUARY 1945

This was a long hard day because I had to take the Jeep back to Porretta Terme and get it serviced at the Battalion Motor Pool. I had to get up a 5 A.M. to make the trip back in the dark as they are more sensitive about daylight Jeep traffic back there. A cold rain fell all day and it was disagreeable driving the Jeep without benefit of a top or windshield. I got back to Vidichiatico for a late dinner.

27 JANUARY 1945

Today I got a shave and a haircut from an Italian barber. He took his time and was careful and gave me a better haircut than I get at home. I gave him a pack of cigarettes in payment as the shopkeepers all seem to prefer anything to money. The cigarette shortage has not reached our Section yet. The few who smoke have all they want and there are always surplus cartons around, which we can use as money with the local people.

28 JANUARY 1945

The telephone line to our OP went out today probably from an artillery shell. In the evening we spent two hours or so looking for a break in the line and finally located it after tracing the line nearly all the way in from Plinardo. We should have started at the Vidichiatico end. It is a very simple procedure with a sound-power telephone.

29 JANUARY 1945

Our battalion has been relieved by a Battalion from the 87th, but Lieutenant Ware has secured permission for our Section to stay at La Ca while the Battalion goes to a rest area in the rear. That is O.K. with us because we will be pretty much on our own—anything to get out of the G.I. conditions that we are afraid will exist in the rear area.

We moved out to La Ca in the evening and settled down for a nice, restful stay at the Front in a tiny, friendly mountain village that is off by itself and too isolated to be bothered by either the Germans or our own troops. We are sitting pretty.

30 JANUARY 1945

Someone in the 87th must have become nervous about our being out at La Ca. Today we were ordered back to Lizzano and installed in new quarters. I am living in a private home with Sergeant Matthews. Our hostess, I can't call her landlady as the army pays no money for rooms, moved out of her own bedroom for the two of us. She now sleeps in the kitchen. Her name is Issa and she has two boys, one three, named Lucciano and the other seven. He is staying with relatives. Her husband has been gone for three years and she has not heard from him for eighteen months. She feels sure he is a prisoner of war. The kitchen is the only warm room in the house. Issa somehow managed to buy a new pair of shoes for Lucciano for 1,000 lira.

In the afternoon we did some recreational skiing on the slope up by the school house. It was in plain sight of the German positions over on Mt. Belvedere, but we didn't mind as long as they didn't mind. It was good fun.

31 JANUARY 1945

Today we got orders to rejoin our Battalion. Issa gave Sergeant Matthews and me a dinner before we left. She had her sister over and brought out her best wine for the occasion. We had a good noodle dish. Lucciano ate with us. We had a good time even though they spoke little English and we knew little Italian. We hated to leave, but orders are orders. We drove back to San Marcello and found our Company there.

1 FEBRUARY 1945

Today we were assigned to an area about ten miles northwest of Lucca. Back here there is no snow. It is warm and the roads are muddy. The countryside is green and it reminds me of the Willamette Valley in winter time.

We finally get settled in our country estate. Our Section is on the third floor sharing rooms with the Commo Section and we are very crowded. Our Battalion officers have moved into a villa presided over by a countess so they say.

2 FEBRUARY 1945

The sun is shining today. Our field kitchen is set up in the back yard of our villa and we are getting good food.

In the afternoon the S-2 Section moved to another house two hundred meters to the north. We have beds on the third floor and much more room. This is real luxury.

3 FEBRUARY 1945

Our regiment is now in Corps reserve north of Lucca. We are all in houses and have good accommodations. Today we are having a warm winter rain that feels just like home. Yesterday's paper brought news that the Russians are forty-five miles from Berlin. Their taking Berlin will probably not be the end of the war, but I believe it will be close to it. If the Russians take Berlin and our American forces take the Ruhr, we can begin sending troops home, I hope. For the troops here in Italy the War just goes on as if nothing is happening up north.

4 FEBRUARY 1945

I learned today that I am to have an additional job. It has no official title but is sort of a battalion map clerk. I will have to order, catalog, file, and issue all maps that are needed by the Battalion. That means I have to keep up on planned operations and get maps ordered from Regimental HQ ahead of time for proper distribution to the companies. At present we are using or maintaining for planned operations about a hundred different maps so it promises to be quite a job. I've got to figure out a way store all our maps and aerial photos. Old ammunition boxes might serve as good containers.

5 FEBRUARY 1945

We are still resting. The country around here is highly developed and quite beautiful. All available soil is tilled, and the hillsides are terraced. The roads, through centuries of use, in many places have worn down six to ten feet below the level of the surrounding fields. There are some handsome villas in the vicinity owned by wealthy people from Florence and other cities.

Some of the men brought in fresh eggs last night for which they paid 20 lira each. I soft boiled one. It was small. It made just one good sized spoonful, but it certainly tasted good. The Army eggs we have been getting are powdered. When scrambled are they rubbery!

6 FEBRUARY 1945

It has been over a month now that I have not slept on straw and it is not because of no straw. I have had mattresses and part of the time real beds.

The Section went out on a conditioning hike today, but I had to work in Battalion Headquarters. I am still driving the Jeep but now spend most of my time working on maps for the Battalion.

There is plenty of wine here in this part of Italy even in war time, and I am having it every day. This good life won't last long.

7 FEBRUARY 1945

This morning we had fried eggs and bacon for breakfast. It was certainly better than army rations. Our semi-monthly beer ration of six bottles per man came in today.

My new job has been keeping me very busy working all day long and evenings so I have not had time to read anything since leaving the Front. I hope my work will let up next week.

Sergeant Anderson is making a sand-table model of a mountainous piece of terrain. It is not finished yet and the location is still kept a military secret from me.

We had roast chicken tonight, the second time this week. I know we should not buy additional food from the people, but sometimes we do.

8 FEBRUARY 1945

More work on maps. It has been raining frequently, and I have an inside job. I am filing maps in 60 mm mortar cases and in two 105 artillery shell boxes.

9 FEBRUARY 1945

Now that the sand-table model is finished, I think I know what it is. I have not heard anyone who might be in-the-know say.

Today we went into Lucca to a Shower Unit for showers and a complete change of clothing. It feels good to be really clean again. Lucca is a fine city and I would like to spend more than a few hours there.

10 FEBRUARY 1945

It is evening. Some of the boys are sitting around a table lighted by three candles. Watzek is reading the Easton, Pa. *Times*; Wellington, the *Reader's Digest*; Beck is writing letters; and Dickson and Taylor are arguing the proposition of whether a church minister can get any fun out of life. I am letter writing with one hand and drinking grapefruit from a can with the other. Strangely there is no wine bottle on the table. Later Dickson, Taylor, Watzek and Wellington are joined in the Catholic Church argument. In this section we never lack a subject to argue about. We have an "expert" on every subject.

Our PX rations came yesterday. I got one can of grapefruit juice (now being consumed), one can of peanuts, three little packages of pretzel sticks, four Milky Way bars, four Mars bars, four cigars, and one carton of cigarettes. Our beer ration came some days ago.

Stars and Stripes did not come in today, but a report is circulating that the Russians are twenty miles from Berlin. I hope so. If true it means the German army in the east has disintegrated and War will soon be over.

11 FEBRUARY 1945

This has been a quiet Sunday for me. I got up late and spent a couple of hours at headquarters filing aerial photos. In the afternoon I read the Sunday paper. It brought no news of the Russians crossing the Oder before Berlin. I guess that was a false report I heard yesterday. I really look for the Russians to stop and consolidate for a few weeks before renewing the drive. It's hard to predict about them as the German commanders have undoubtedly learned the hard way.

I found time to read a few chapters from the New Testament that Mother recently sent me. No mail came today.

12 FEBRUARY 1945

The January issue of the *Reader's Digest* arrived today. It reads better over here than it did at home, perhaps reminding us of the simple pleasures of home life.

13 FEBRUARY 1945

It was warm today and I saw some flies for the first time. Spring must be coming. The roads are still muddy from our recent rain. No letters from home now for several days.

A few days ago the Regiment was alerted for a move and possible action reinforcing the 92nd Division, but it was soon canceled. The 442nd Combat Team is over there to the west helping out.

IV
WE TAKE THE SUMMITS
14 FEBRUARY TO 5 MARCH

14 FEBRUARY 1945

This morning we got word that an advance party was going up to the Front a few days ahead of time to get things ready for our scheduled operation. Most of us did not know the timing or what was coming off.

On the way back to the Front our small convoy stopped at a store. About all that I could see to buy was wine, dried figs, nuts, wooden soled, canvas-topped shoes and sandals, reed fans, and bread which was rationed. Some of our men bought figs and nuts. I bought a canteen full of *vino* for 70 lira. That price seemed quite high. Wine seems to be one product that is available in unlimited quantities. Ordinarily a package of cigarettes will buy a liter of wine.

Our Battalion Headquarters group pulled into the tiny mountain village of La Ca after dark.

15 FEBRUARY 1945

Sergeant Matthews and I are living with an old woman, 72 years old if we understand her Italian correctly. We refer to her as Grandma and share our C-rations and 10-in-1-rations with her which she prepares. It is nice to have a soft bed to sleep on and hot water to shave with.

Patrols are being sent out at night to explore the long, steep escarpment to the west of us that we call Riva Ridge.

We are checking approach and climbing routes. We know the Germans are well dug in along the top.

Grandma's son has been taken away by the Germans for forced labor. She is always talking about how brutal the Germans were. *"Tedesci, bruta, bruta,"* she keeps repeating. She tells about their shooting twelve villagers picked at random because the village harbored some Partisans. La Ca is so small that we think she is talking about some neighboring village.

16 FEBRUARY 1945

The last reconnaissance patrol was scheduled for this evening. Lieutenant Ware picked me and Sergeant Thompson from B Company who has been on other patrols on Riva Ridge. We are to make a final survey of a potential mule trail up from Pianacci.

A low overcast put the top part of the Ridge in the cloud layer, ideal conditions for a daylight patrol. Lieutenant Ware decided to start out at 4:30 P.M. instead of waiting for dark. Sergeant Thompson carried a Tommy Gun and Lieutenant Ware his favorite burp gun. He thought we should have an M-1 rifle along so I borrowed one. This was to be purely a reconnaissance patrol of just the three of us. We hoped to avoid any contact with the enemy. We went from La Ca at a rapid walk down the trail to Farne and then on to Ca di Julio and across the Dardagna River flowing at the base of Riva Ridge on a stone bridge to Pianacci. We inquired there as to whether any Germans had been down recently, and the people denied seeing any. The mule trail takes off from there and goes up a gorge for a few hundred yards to a farm house. We stopped and again inquired. The farmer said he had not seen any Germans for some time and invited us in for some wine. Lieutenant Ware declined as he wanted the mission to be accomplished before dark if possible. We could tell the condition of the trail much better in daylight, and we would be safe from enemy observation as long as the cloud cover held.

We went on up the trail. At one place where the trail rounded a steep bluff, the rock had fallen away badly, leaving little of the trail. We recognized this as a danger spot for pack trains and put it down as an early repair job for the Pioneer Platoon. This trail would be our major supply route as it was the only one which mules could get up. We went on to a high shoulder which was about two-thirds of the way up and included the steepest parts of the trail. From where we stopped it was a straight, even rise up to the top of this ridge at this point called Mt. Cappel Buso, less than half a mile away. We saw no signs of the Germans and heard nothing. We stopped to rest for a few minutes and then hurried back to get as far as possible before dark. It was just about dark when we crossed over the river to Ca di Julio. We took the long pull in the dark up to La Ca more slowly. I felt greatly relieved to be able to put down my rifle and empty the grenades from my pockets. The preliminary work was done; now all we had to do was move into position and wait for D-day and H-hour.

17 FEBRUARY 1945

Last night our snow plows cleared the road into La Ca. I thought it was a foolish thing to do, giving the Germans another clue that we were up to something.

Today we got ready to move. It was decided that I would leave the Jeep at La Ca and would pack down to Farne after dark with Sergeant Matthews. For the Ridge operation, La Ca was to become our Regimental Headquarters and Farne was to be our Battalion CP. The advance parties were arranging billets in various buildings. The order was that every man had to stay indoors tomorrow during daylight hours.

We got down to Farne early in the evening, found our billets and then began setting up the CP, arranging tables for maps, locations for telephones, radios, etc. all in preparation for our first major action.

Farne was a busy place most of the night with the line companies moving through to their billets in other villages. We got to sleep after midnight, but that was all right because we have all of tomorrow to sleep in if we want to.

18 FEBRUARY 1945

This was our day of waiting inside. I woke up about noon and ate my C-rations. In our S-2 Section billet we read, talked, argued and got restless, but we did stay inside. This was our first offensive action, and this objective of the 1st Battalion of the 86th Mountain Infantry was said to be the most rugged piece of terrain yet assaulted in the Italian campaign, which for nearly two years now has consisted of taking one mountain ridge after another. We knew that surprise was our only hope for success.

As soon as it was fully dark Sergeant Matthews and I went to the CP. The town came alive. The Communications Section began stringing telephone lines out to the companies. At 7:30 the line companies moved out toward their assigned objectives on Riva Ridge.

I was up all night. My main job was recording messages as they came over radios and telephone and in spelling Sergeant Matthews in keeping the Battalion Journal. We watched the progress of the companies intently, and I could not have gone to sleep it I had wanted to. All Companies were on their objectives well before daylight.

19 FEBRUARY 1945

After being up all night I got about four hours sleep the next morning and went back on duty recording the Journal. It was too exciting to be away from the progress

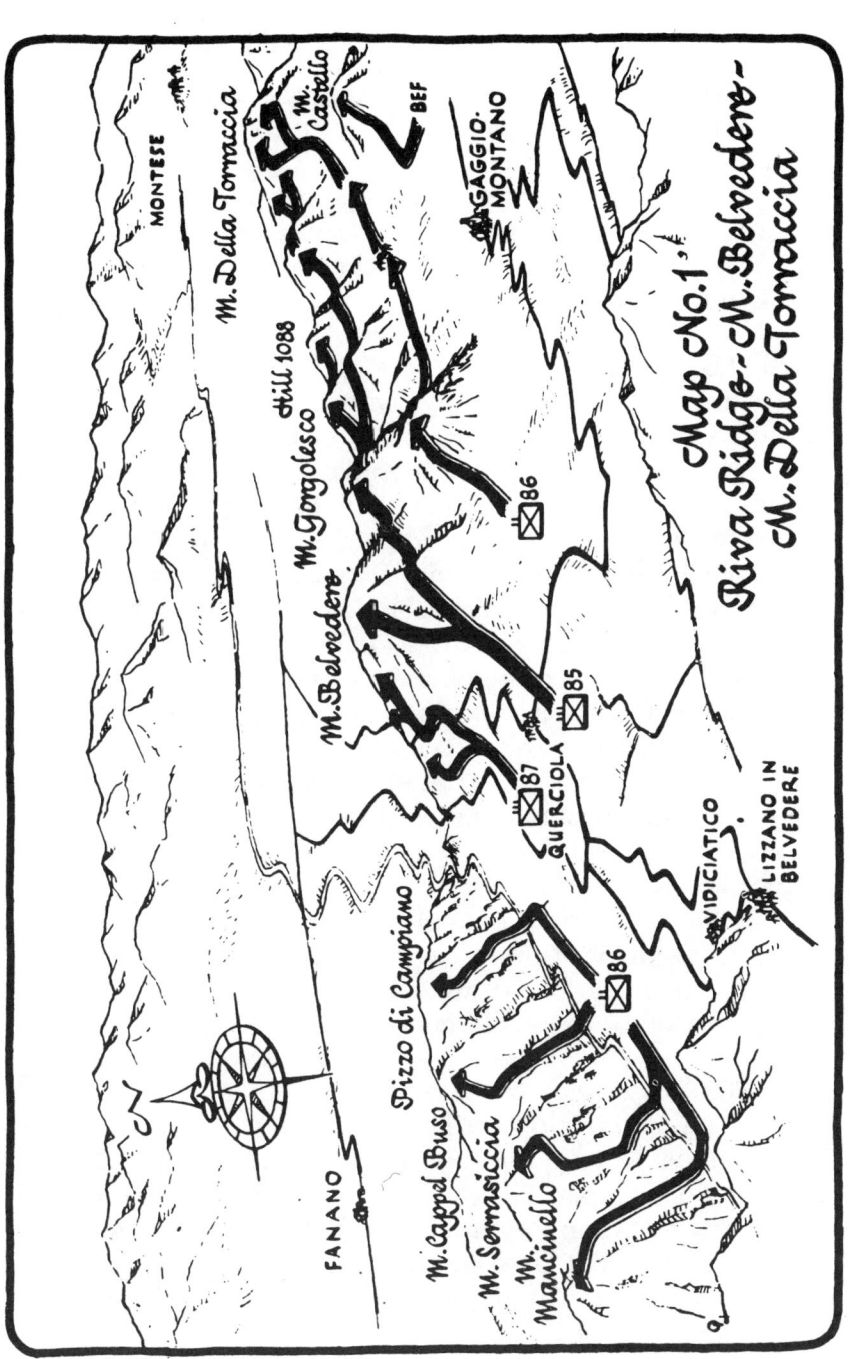

MONTESE

M. Della Torraccia

M. Castello

BEF

GAGGIO-
MONTANO

Hill 1088

M. Gorgolesco

M. Belvedere

⊠ 86

⊠ 85

⊠ 87
QUERCIOLA

VIDICIATICO

LIZZANO IN
BELVEDERE

⊠ 86

Pizzo di Campiano

M. Cagged Buso

M. Serrasiccia

M. Mancinello

FANANO

Map No. 1.
Riva Ridge – M. Belvedere –
M. Della Torraccia

reports for long. All was going well, and we appeared to have achieved a complete surprise on the enemy. I spent all day in the Battalion CP.

The engineers are having trouble punching a road across a slide area just east of Farne, and we don't like that. The land is so unstable that the bulldozers get bogged down in the muck.

20 FEBRUARY 1945

I managed to get some sleep between 3:00 and 6:00 A.M. The night and morning were relatively quiet.

Just after 1:00 P.M., C Company sent two platoons against enemy units entrenched on Ridge X which is just northwest of their positions on Mt. Serrasiccia. Most of us in the CP went out to watch the attack. We saw a squad of our men advancing along the skyline of the ridge that towers above Farne. They made good progress and in twenty minutes took their objective capturing or killing all the Germans. One man looking through glasses at one spot reported that he saw a German soldier driven off a cliff and fall for a hundred feet or more. We could see our men on the round promontory of Ridge X waving their weapons after taking it. We down here are as happy about it as they are.

We saw many flights of P-47s strafing and bombing the German positions from Mt. Belvedere to Mt. Della Torraccia as the rest of the Division was engaged in the hard battle for those summits.

21 FEBRUARY 1945

Since the action has quieted down I got more sleep last night. During the day some enemy artillery shells landed in an open field just beyond our CP. In the early afternoon I went out with two other men to inspect the craters and see if we could get an azimuth reading. They were nearly circular and it would be very difficult to get an accurate reading on the direction from which the shell came. We didn't even try. We heard another round coming in and hit the ground. The shell landed about a hundred feet out from us. We beat it back to the shelter of the buildings, good, solid, stone, Italian buildings. This was enough investigating for us.

Apparently the Germans are trying to shell Farne, but because of the height of Riva Ridge they can't quite get their shells in at even the highest angle of fire.

News came this afternoon that we are to be relieved by the 10th Anti-Tank Battalion, a unit we had never heard of at Camp Hale. A few of us wonder if it is too early to leave because we don't know anything about this unit. Perhaps they were organized after we were stationed at Camp Swift. We think there still could be some real fighting on the ridge. We wish them luck and are glad to be relieved.

During the night the relief was accomplished, but we are leaving some platoons on Riva Ridge to help the new units for one more day.

22 FEBRUARY 1945

This morning I hiked up to La Ca, got the Jeep and drove it around via Vidichiatico to Farne. The units along the way didn't like my driving through their area in daylight. They were afraid I would attract enemy artillery fire, but we need the Jeep and trailer to haul out our Battalion CP supplies.

The slide area had not yet been cleared. I left the trailer at the slide. I took a two mile detour around the slide area over the worst road I ever hope to drive. We used the Jeep to haul the CP supplies from Farne to the slide. We packed them across the 100-yard wide slide area on our backs and loaded the trailer. Fortunately the Germans are no longer firing their artillery on this area. They are too busy over on Mt. Belvedere. I drove the Jeep back around the rugged detour and hooked up to the trailer where I waited for Lieutenant Ware and others to get ready to go. While waiting I watched our P-47s with bombs, rockets and machine guns work over the enemy north of Rocca Cornetta and Mt. Belevedere where the fight still goes on with the 85th and 87th Regiments.

Finally we pull out in convoy and drive back through Vidichiatico, Lizzano, and Gaggio Montano to our reserve area about a mile and a half west of Gaggio.

In afternoon I have to drive back to La Ca to pick up some things we left there and bring them around to our new area. Gaggio is being shelled steadily. I cannot take the short road west through Querciola as it is tied up with traffic supporting our Mt. Belvedere operation. I had no problems going to La Ca and getting our stuff. On my way back a barrage comes in when I am a half-mile below Gaggio. All traffic stops as the drivers seek shelter behind a stone retaining wall. This shelling lasts for about ten minutes. It lets up and we proceed at breakneck speed to get through Gaggio. As I drive through Gaggio another barrage comes in. This time I wait in the shelter of a building for fifteen minutes. A Medic who goes to the aid of a wounded man about one hundred yards down the road is killed. We cuss the enemy and wait for a lull in the shelling. Then I speed out of there mighty glad that I am not stationed in Gaggio.

23 FEBRUARY 1945

I shaved this morning, the first time in three days. I spend the morning out in the sun on a warm grassy slope taking it easy. We got our PX rations and mail. Evelyn sent me a Union Pacific calendar which reminds me how good home is. I have it hanging on the trunk of a large deciduous tree, probably beech, of which several are in our area. Birds are singing and it seems like spring on this warm day even though the calendar tells us it is still winter.

TORRACCIA

Higher up in the mountains the snow still looks deep and cold, but it must be melting fast today. War can be pleasant at times and the pleasure in simple things is emphasized by the ordeal that has gone before.

24 FEBRUARY 1945

We have a noisy bivouac because batteries of 105 howitzers and tanks are right south of us, and by right, I mean within a hundred yards. At all sorts of odd hours they fire over our heads, especially at night. Unpleasant though it is to have shells cracking past a hundred feet over head, it makes us feel good to have all that fire power on our side.

We are still in reserve with not much for us to do but wait. On orders from the Company Commander we dug slit trenches today, why after being here for two days I do not know. So far no shells have hit our area. The Germans no longer have observation on this area and probably do not know our Company is here, but from our artillery firing they must have a good idea where our artillery is even if they cannot see the source.

25 FEBRUARY 1945

We are still in reserve and having another day of rest. We heard over the Armed Forces radio today that the 10th Mountain Division was mentioned for the first time as being in action in Italy. Of course we remembered that Axis Sally welcomed us to Italy within a couple of days of our arrival, before we left Naples as I remember. The Germans have known about our being here all along. At the fighting front a basic rule of military intelligence is to assume that the enemy knows of any action or proposed action within twenty four hours. With lives on the line, one has to be ready for any eventuality.

26 FEBRUARY 1945

Here it is my birthday, but birthdays mean nothing over here where for so much of the time one day is just like another. The weather is mild for February and again we have bright sunshine. We are rather enjoying camping in the open for a change.

The S-2 Section received orders to set up an outpost and observation post on the promontory in front of our bivouac area. In the afternoon I drove the boys up a rocky creek bed as far as I could get the Jeep with their equipment. I am staying down below.

I stopped by Charlie Company to say hello to my former buddies. I found out that Sgt. Morgan Desmond, my squad leader all through our long winter of training at Camp Hale, Colorado, was killed on Riva Ridge. It was in the action taking Ridge X in which my old squad was heavily involved. and they suffered several casualties. Des was a great guy. My thoughts went back to the fateful circumstances in the summer of 1944 at Camp Swift that separated me from the doomed squad.

27 FEBRUARY 1945

The Communications Section has a radio and sometimes I get a chance to hear it. This evening I heard some opera music, records broadcast by a Fifth Army station. I got the War news too, and it is still good.

28 FEBRUARY 1945

Today I drove Lieutenant Ware in the Jeep up near the top of Mt. Della Torraccia over a very bad road. In some places the ruts were two feet deep, but luckily I stayed out of them. This is now our new front line, and our Battalion is scheduled to make an attack from here tomorrow.

While Lieutenant Ware was conferring with Lieutenant Colonel Hampton, our Battalion Commander, I distributed operation maps to the companies. My job is now over for this attack. I was sent back to the motor pool with orders to bring the Jeep up with the CP supplies when we take our objectives.

The weather is still pleasant and mild even at night. This evening a quarter moon is shining in all its splendor.

1 MARCH 1945

With plenty of leisure today I wrote Evelyn a long letter telling her something of the men in our S-2 Section. Sgt. James Matthews is an Irish Catholic from New York

City. He is a pretty fair leader, but his Irish temper gets in the way once in a while. We all like him though. He does have a tough section to manage.

Kurt Watzek is about twenty or twenty-one and he was born in Vienna. His parents had money and an established business in New York. They moved to New York just before Hitler took over Austria. Kurt is interested in engineering, but he will argue on any subject.

He pals around with Robert W. Dickson, about twenty-three, also from New York. Watzek started calling him "Genius" and now we are all doing it. Genius is a smart fellow and he studied physics at Dartmouth, that is before, as he claims, he was kicked out of school. It's all very vague, and some of us are skeptical. He was in the 87th Regiment and went to Kiska. He is an only child and both his parents are famous chemists so he has his handicaps.

Norman Wightman came from New York too. His father runs or works for a big printing business that among other things prints the overseas edition of *Newsweek*. He's another only child. He hasn't been to college but is still young and is considering going into the ministry.

Kurt Honberg is the only Jew in the Section. He is about twenty-eight and was born in Munich. He came to the U.S. in 1937 and went into the hide business in Boston. His parents and an older brother, a physician, are living in England. Kurt is easy to get along with and we all like him.

Linwood Wellington, whom we often call Duke, is from Caribou, Maine. He is an excellent skier and is interested in camping, fishing, and the outdoors generally. He is about twenty-four and has been up and down the ladder, having been a squad leader and a platoon sergeant. He has had his troubles in the army and now is a plain private like the rest of us. He is plenty smart, reads good literature and is New England to the core. For some reason he reminds me of Ralph Waldo Emerson.

Charley Beck is twenty, from New York state, and the fellows say that he is too much in love with his girl. He is 6 foot 4 inches tall and has a hard time getting army clothes that fit him. He does not enter much into our arguments. His dad owns a garage in White Plains, New York. Charley is toying with the idea of being a gunsmith after the war. Honberg rates him along with me as being the only gentlemen in the Section. I quote from him "Charley never gives anyone a hard time."

The other two in the Section are Cliff Taylor and "Mac" Maccaluso who only joined the Section a few weeks ago. They had been in our Regimental Intelligence and Reconnaissance Platoon. They wrecked a Jeep and were accused of being drunk while overturning and demolishing said vehicle. For punishment they were sent down to the 1st Battalion and our section got them. Mac is from up-state New York, and Cliff, I believe, is from Providence, Rhode Island.

I have a tough time holding out for the West against this bunch of Easterners. The guys are crazy!

2 MARCH 1945

After spending last night over a chicken coop where I didn't like the smell, I moved into a hay mow where other drivers are sleeping. Six letters from home arrived today.

In my now quiet waiting I have the feeling we are sitting on a sideshow here in Italy while the main attraction is going on in the Rhineland and Pomerania. The papers bring news of the continued advances of the First and Ninth Armies toward the Rhine. With Cologne and Dusseldorf under artillery fire we should see a marked drop in Germany's war production. We are waiting anxiously for the Germans to quit, but it does not look as if they are going to. Certainly the war in Europe cannot be considered finished until the Allies and Russians meet, and then there still may be some mopping up in the Mountain Redoubt of southern Germany and western Austria. We fear that task may fall largely to the 10th Mountain Division.

Fortunately we are having clear, dry days and the snow is going fast. The nights are still cool, but it feels like spring is on the way even here in the mountains.

Time magazine has started printing an edition over here and we get the magazines in our PX rations. Plates are flown over and it is only a few days late. The poor guys who have subscriptions get theirs about two months late.

3 MARCH 1945

A little snow fell last night, just enough to cover the ground white. The morning is raw and blustery, but by afternoon the sun is warm with only a few scattered clouds in the sky. The snow has all melted.

According to a story in *Stars and Stripes* we are enjoying the mildest winter in Italy in thirty years and also the driest. In this part of Italy they ordinarily get five inches of rainfall in each of February and March. This year we got less than an inch in February. I hope March is the same. Rain makes miserable fighting.

Torger D. Tokle, the famous ski jumper, was killed in A Company's attack on Mt. Della Torraccia.

4 MARCH 1945

Today we moved the Battalion Motor Pool about two miles further west from Gaggio Montano. Back here in this reserve area we are well aware that the battle still goes on for what we will soon find out is for Mt. Grande d'Aiano, Castel d'Aiano and Mt. Della Spe.

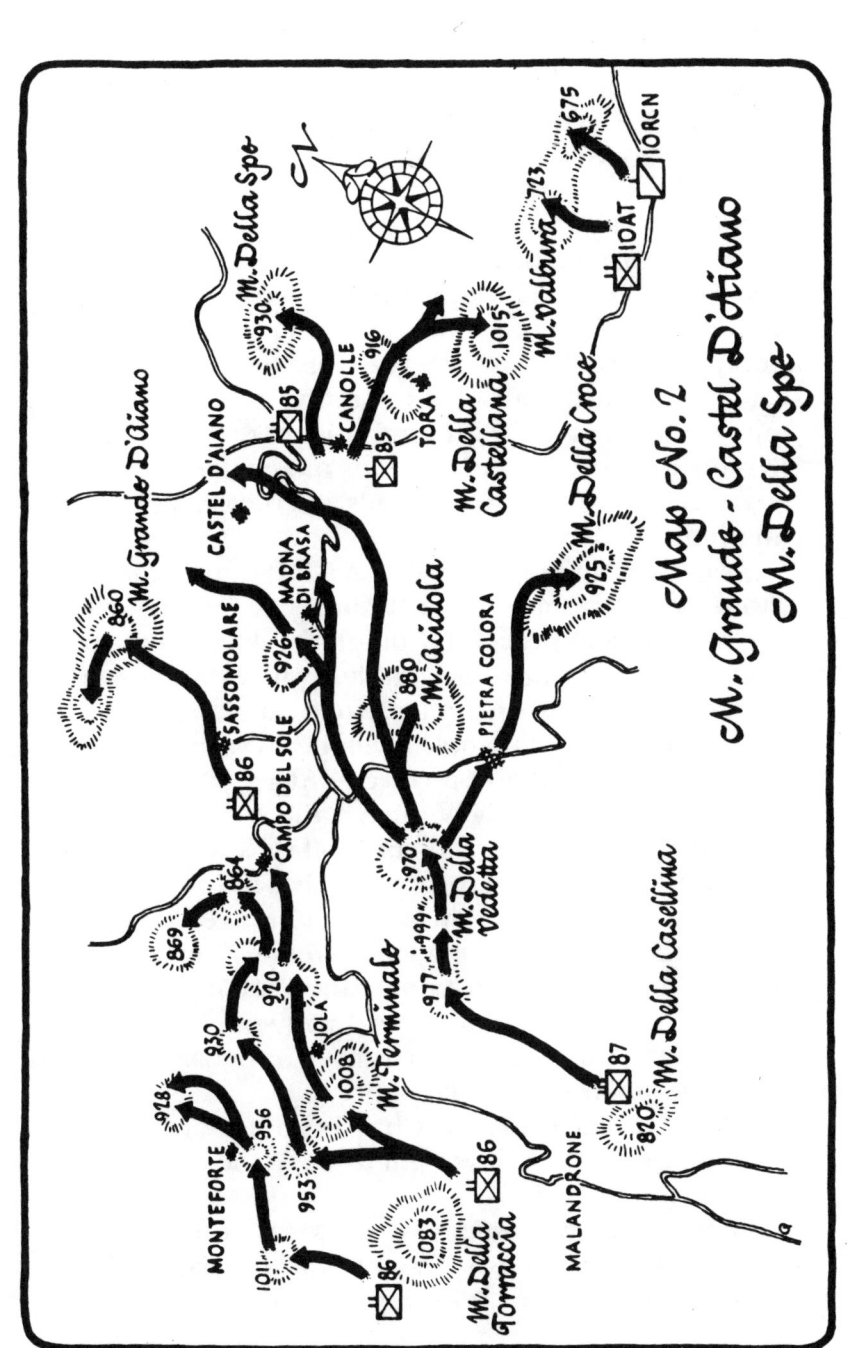

Map No. 2

M. Grande - Castel D'Aiano

M. Della Spe

Late in the day we hear that Lieutenant Colonel Hampton, our Battalion CO, was wounded this morning in the capture of Sassomolare.

5 MARCH 1945

This morning the motor pool got orders to move forward again. We went in convoy over steep mountain roads and passed streams of prisoners coming back. They were a sorry looking lot with some walking wounded, but they seemed glad to be out of the fighting. The roads were jammed with military traffic and tanks of the 1st Armored Division were everywhere. In this mountainous country the tanks have to stick to the roads and they can certainly jam up traffic.

We located the motor pool in a little valley meadow with a small stream flowing through. At first it seemed very pastoral and peaceful. I did not realize it that afternoon but just over the ridge a mile away was the town of Montese which was a German strong point.

I started to dig a foxhole in good soil with few rocks. When I got it well dug, I received orders to move out of that section of the meadow, such is the army.

Later in the afternoon on orders I took the Jeep up to the Rear CP at Sassomolare. It was only a mile or so to the north. I made the trip at dusk. When I arrived there was lots of excitement. Less than ten minutes before an 88 shell had hit a building just under the eves. It blew a hole through the foot-thick stone wall and sent a shower of stone chips down on some twenty Headquarters Company men, but not a man was hurt.

We speculated that if it had been a foot higher, it probably would have gone right through the roof causing many casualties.

After dark I was ordered to try to take the Jeep up to the Forward CP on *Sasso* (Rock) *Baldino*. Sassomolare, the Mt. Grande ridge and the valley between had just been captured today after heavy fighting. I had two men with me. In the black smoky valley all we could see were fires from a few buildings burning in the distance. We inched along in the darkness over a narrow, muddy and rocky road. We passed a Tank Destroyer that had slipped off the road and mired down nearly on its side. There was just barely room to get the Jeep past it. The going got so tough that we decided we would never make it in the dark. I don't think we made over two hundred yards in half an hour. In turning around we wrapped a newly laid telephone wire around a wheel and broke it. When we got back to the CP the Commo men were mad at us but relieved to learn that the break was so close. A few men went out on foot and soon had it repaired.

I slept in the Rear CP in Sassomolare on a good straw bed. I slept soundly though several rounds of artillery and mortar fire that hit the village during the night. Several buildings were blazing and an old straw pile right next to our building was also burning. Stone buildings make a secure foxhole and one that doesn't have to be dug.

VITORINO

WWARE/45

V
HOLDING OUR GAINS
6 MARCH TO 5 APRIL

6 MARCH 1945

This morning I was asked to try to take my Jeep through to the Forward CP. No vehicles had yet been taken in there, all supplies had been packed in by mules during the night. My mission was to find a route into the CP, passable with Jeep and trailer, that we could use for bringing in ammunition and supplies. I was provided with a guide and at the last minute Lieutenant Danoff announced that he wanted to go with us. He had a man with him so that made four of us in the party.

We started out at 9:00 A.M. and the route we took was marked as a mule trail on our maps. It was the poorest of roads but it was easier going in the daylight than it had been in the dark last night. For a good part of the way we were in plain view of the enemy. I had been assured that the route had been cleared of mines by our engineers.

We spent some time wandering around in the valley floor looking for the way. Some of the houses and barns were still burning from yesterday's attack, and we were not sure that all houses had been cleared of Germans. Off to our right a haystack was burning and every once in a while artillery ammunition, which had been concealed in it by the Jerries, would explode, showering burning hay around.

On the way up the mule trail on the north side we passed through a tiny village. I am sure my Jeep was the first motor vehicle ever to appear in the place. The people all came out and waved to us, greeting us with "*ciao*" and "*bene.*" They felt sure that at last they had been liberated. In a way they had, but the fighting here was not yet over. Their village lay in no man's land. Later several sharp patrol actions took place in the vicinity of that village.

It was a difficult and narrow route even for a Jeep and we were glad when we got to the CP further up the ridge. Only when we arrived did we learn that the route we took was not the one that the engineers had cleared. My Jeep was the first one into CP Forward and the mountain ridge that our Battalion had taken the day before. Everyone was glad to see us and know that a Jeep could make it. I saw Lieutenant Ware and some of the fellows from the S-2 Section, some of whom were manning OPs along the ridge.

It was only after I got there that I was requested to carry back the bodies of three of our dead. They were in white mattress covers which would show up like a searchlight as we crossed the valley under German observation. We put them crossways in the back part of the Jeep. In the meantime several walking wounded from the line companies came into the CP. It became my task to get them back to the rear as our Battalion Aid Station was back just below Sassomolare. I had an overloaded Jeep, two men with me on the front seat, two men sitting up on the hood, and one volunteer riding back with the bodies. He sat on the spare tire.

We took off on the right road this time. It was a much better road, but it was still so narrow in places that our load would catch on branches at the sides of the road. It was slow going to say the least. The road led us through a barnyard where the haystack was burning, taking the chance that no ammunition would explode as we went through. The yard contained two German 40 mm anti-aircraft guns. Two dead Jerries lay out in the bright morning sun with flies swarming about their faces. We tore through the yard and at a more leisurely pace bumped our way back to Sassomolare without a shell being fired at us. We felt mighty lucky. I took the wounded to the Aid Station and the bodies to GRO.

In the afternoon I took some replacements out to the Forward CP. I left by myself on the return trip with a flight of P-47s strafing in the area. When I was a few minutes out, I heard the planes open up with their guns when they were about a hundred feet over my head. The sound of those eight .50-caliber machine guns going off at once is a terrific racket. I thought some Jerries really must be getting hell. By myself I was more scared than usual and was thankful for no more exploding ammunition being in the now smoldering haystack and felt lucky to get back to Sassomolare without being fired upon.

Later I heard that the P-47s had made a mistake and strafed our own CP that I had just left. A few of our men were standing just outside the front door. They saw the two planes coming at the CP and dashed in the door. Inside they turned both to the right and left except one man who kept going strait ahead up the stairs. A slug came though the doorway and hit him in the leg when he was on the second step. He was the only casualty.

Mine was the last daylight Jeep trip because the Jerries started pounding our Forward CP with artillery. The order went out forbidding daylight trips. We did have a supply route we could use at night, and the Forward CP was moved to a new location because it got too hot for them. They blamed it all on my trips, and they were probably right.

7 MARCH 1945

I spent a quiet morning in the Rear CP. In the afternoon I drove Lieutenant Danoff back to the GRO. Just before dark I drove down to the Water Point for a load of water in five-gallon cans.

8 MARCH 1945

Today Sergeant Matthews was wounded seriously and Dickson received slight wounds in the same OP. They were sent back to a hospital. Lieutenant Ware asked me to check with the medics on their condition. Doc. Miller, our Battalion Surgeon, reported that Sergeant Matthews was in critical condition when he left the Aid Station in the ambulance. He had not regained consciousness. My spirits are very low tonight.

9 MARCH 1945

Today Lieutenant Ware asked me to give up my driving job and rejoin the S-2 Section because they were short handed and needed every trained man they could get. Caputo, a presently unassigned driver in the motor pool, would be given my job of driving Lieutenant Ware's Jeep and the CP supplies. I would still keep my CP map job. He said that I could keep my driving job if I wanted to. Under the circumstances I couldn't say no to his request.

So today I packed my stuff and moved forward to join the Section. It was occupying the former Battalion Forward CP, which is being vacated today as the CP because it was too "hot" a location. The CP is moving back to the village of Gualandi. When I arrived the fellows told me that this morning a mortar shell went through the roof and exploded in the room where Beck and Taylor were sleeping on a bed. They weren't scratched and the nose assembly was blown through the floor into the kitchen where two other men were sleeping.

The men of the S-2 Section are not fools. They moved out of the house into some small dugouts in the gully a hundred feet east of the house. I spent the night sleeping on a pile of hay in the barn. It was a good stone barn like all Italian barns in these parts and it seemed comparatively safe from artillery and mortar fire. One of the four cows in the barn had been hit by a piece of shrapnel that apparently came through the window. It had penetrated a lung and the poor creature wheezed as the air went in and out of the hole with every breath. The barn was not very large and the body heat from the cows made it awfully hot in there. That was the only night I slept in the barn. At the front we never see cows outside their barns.

10 MARCH 1945

At the Front on the hill called Sasso Baldino. Our good weather is still holding and it is gradually getting warmer. Italy has a nice mild climate. With little to do today I write a letter home but can say little and have no idea when I can get it mailed.

Here I find it difficult to get in the right frame of mind for writing home. I feel I am living a minute to minute existence on a hope and a prayer. It is a gnawing, bitter hope and a selfish prayer. When the shells start landing I think instinctively first of my own safety and second of my job and what is happening around me. Actually artillery and mortar fire are not as bad as the civilian envisages. It is the fear of it that is the terrible thing, and all men in varying degrees have that fear. It is a psychological problem and the way the mind meets it is to stifle the imagination, cut off the memories and thoughts of loved ones, and dwell only upon the moment.

Later in the day with heavy hearts we received notice that our Section Sergeant James A. Matthews died on the way to the hospital.

11 MARCH 1945

Our line company positions are being shelled every day about noon and shortly after five o'clock in the evening.

Since Sergeant Matthews was killed in a large well-dug-in OP by a shell hitting the roof, we have not been using regular OPs for our observation work. We observe from several different vantage points along the ridge always making sure that a foxhole is nearby, and a foxhole can seem like little shelter when the shells start falling. One feels very conspicuous on the ridge looking down and across the valley at the Germans through our 20-power telescope.

We see almost no movement on the part of the Germans. Any house they are seen near warrants going over by our artillery. Today I watched a Volkswagen go back to their field hospital with a couple of wounded. It was all decked out in Red Cross flags and was the only moving thing that I could see in scores of square miles of heavily defended territory.

It is always a relief to go back to our bivouac area a couple of hundred yards below the ridge, but to get there we have to cross an open field that is under observation from the Germans in back of us at Montese. We would surely like to get the Jerries out of Montese.

We follow the same routine day after day. We are eating C-rations and frequently go up to the house to heat our rations in the fireplace. There is a well next to the house where we get our water, and we brew coffee and synthetic lemonade. After dark C Company men come down to get water from this well in five-gallon Jerry cans and pack it back up to their area on Sasso Baldino. We have one guard on duty all through the night, but it means only an hour and a half for each man in the Section.

12 MARCH 1945

I moved to another foxhole up above the path to the house. For some reason we are always looking for a safer place to stay. If you spend very long in one hole you begin to figure out all the angles from which the hole can be hit. You sight out of the hole and speculate what a tree burst in the fork of that beech tree would do. You don't like it. Finally you see so many possibilities that you just have to move, probably going to some hole that another man vacated for the same reason. It's a hell of a life!

When some of us were in the house this afternoon, the Jerries started shelling the area trying to hit the house. We tore around the house to a strong, heavily timbered cellar in the back where nothing but a 170 could dig us out. The shells, which we figured were 88s, just barely skimmed the top of the house and burst in the woods a hundred yards beyond. They were coming from the northwest through a notch in the ridge. Apparently the elevation there just prevented the gunners from depressing low enough to hit the house but it was low enough to scare the devil out of us.

13 MARCH 1945

We are fortunate to have warm spring weather. The sun shines and the nights are fairly warm.

I watched the Jerries fire anti-aircraft at one of our artillery spotters today. The little high-wing monoplane circled down out of the bursts and flew back to our lines.

It gets tiresome to lie on my belly for hour after hour studying the face of Mt. Balgaro through the 20-power spotting scope. We know that the enemy positions are there, but they are usually impossible to find. The Germans are doing an excellent job of camouflage.

The riflemen always hated to see us Intelligence Section men come around and start using the 20-power scope. They felt that field glasses were bad enough but the scope was impossible. Some of them would even move out of our vicinity if they could because they felt that we were certain to draw enemy fire. We were careful though. We had learned our lesson the hard way. Sergeant Matthew's death was all too recent on this ridge. Death is the most compelling of teachers. C Company is averaging one casualty a day from mortar and artillery fire.

14 MARCH 1945

We had an OP over in Able Company area that we called OP West. We usually had a man spend the night there to report over the phone any artillery flashes that we could get a bearing on. This was my night. I spent the afternoon out there. Not much was happening. I watched our artillery work over the ravines back of Montese.

I spent the long evening watching and was only able to report a couple of flashes. The guns were behind a ridge and too far off to get an accurate bearing.

Our OP in this western most section was situated on a knife-like ridge that dropped off sheer on the enemy side. Our side was more sloping and on it the A Company riflemen had dug their foxholes. We had put the OP as close to the edge as possible and still have dirt to dig in. Two feet down we had struck bedrock. Out toward Montese the exposed rock tilted at about a 15-degree slope and formed a knife edge extending west from our OP. There were several hundred square yards of that great slab of exposed rock. Our hole had a roof over it and narrow vision slots. Roomy it was not. It had just enough room for one man to sit up in or to curl up on his side.

Later things seemed to quiet down and I curled up in my sleeping bag and tried to sleep. After what seemed like a long time, shells started bursting on our position. The first one hit on the rock out in front of me, the same rock slab that I was lying on, and it certainly rattled my teeth. I couldn't spot any flashes and reported it was

QUIET AFTERNOON, GUISLAND?

W.WARE 45

probably mortar fire from Montese. I curled up into as small a ball as possible and sweated out the dozen rounds that hit in the vicinity. Several hit on my rock and I was all too sure that I was the target. Fortunately no one was hit. After that the night was quiet, but I did not sleep at all well. I was a happy man when the sun came up in the morning, and with arrival of my relief I went back to our S-2 Section bivouac area.

15 MARCH 1945

It was a fine morning. When I got back to our area I heard the good news that we were being relieved. At last! We had been in the lines for what seemed like a long time. We had a long wait for nightfall. We had packed our equipment during the day and at dusk the S-2 Section hiked the short distance east to Gualandi. Our 3rd Battalion was moving in to relieve us. We oriented the new S-2 Section and waited to move out with our Headquarters Company. It was 11 P.M. before we got started. We hiked across the valley to Sassomolare, then down into the next valley and up along the road past the Montese junction for half a mile or more. There a truck convoy was waiting for us. We were a happy bunch of boys as we piled into those trucks.

We had a long ride through the night; the first twenty miles were without lights as the road was never far from the Front. The Light Line is still at the Apennine Divide several miles south of Porretta Terme just where it was when we came up to the Front in January.

16 MARCH 1945

In the early morning we arrived at the 5th Army Rest Center in Montecatini. After breakfast we went through a shower unit and got clean sets of clothes. Also I had a shave and a haircut, the latter being the first in two months. I think it had been fully two weeks since I touched a comb to my hair. Even though I had just washed it in the shower, the barber could hardly get his comb through it. I felt like a civilized man once more.

In the afternoon I went to the movies and saw *To Have and To Have Not* which I had seen once before back home. It is a good movie.

In the evening I went with some of our S-2 Section to the opera. We paid 200 lira for orchestra seats to hear *Madame Butterfly* by a traveling company from Rome. It is not my favorite opera and I have heard it before. The San Carlo Company which traveled the U.S. in the 1930s is about all I have to compare it with, and this performance was on a par with theirs. The costumes, scenery, lighting and stage management were inferior, but the music and singing was better. This company probably specializes in doing the provinces.

17 MARCH 1945

Today I went on a day-trip to Florence in an army truck with other men from my outfit. There Dickson, Taylor and I went on a Red Cross tour of Florence, also in an army truck. We visited the Pitti Palace which was constructed about 1450. We were told that there were 3,000 paintings in it, and it is now a museum. Unfortunately all the art masterpieces have been removed for safekeeping. We visited the royal chambers and went through the carriage house. We did see stored in the courtyard the huge bronze "Gates of Paradise" doors to the Baptistery that Michelangelo said were beautiful enough to be the gates to heaven. They were on their sides in crates. We could walk right up to them and see some of the panels through the crating framework.

Miss di Filippi was our guide. She had spent about fifteen years teaching Italian art in the United States so she spoke excellent English and she knew her stuff. She said that these famous doors had been stored in a railroad tunnel to protect them, but our Air Corps came along and started bombing the tunnel not knowing the doors were there. The people of Florence did not have any way to move them, but as Miss di Filippi put it, "the Germans took pity on us and moved the doors here to the Pitti Palace."

When we were going through the Palace gardens our guide stopped and asked a few question, in Italian of course, of a man trimming trees. After we had gone on she said that it made her mad when he kept using the infinitive verb form with never a proper ending. She said that the people do that in talking to American soldiers because it is easier for them to understand that way, but to talk to a native Italian that way she felt was rude.

After that we visited four churches. The first one was the Church of the Roman Soldier, in Romanesque architecture, begun about A.D. 900. It has many columns and capitals taken from old Roman temples.

Next we visited Santa Croce which contains the tombs of Galileo and Michelangelo. This church has a beautiful facade, but its architecture is thoroughly mixed.

Then we went to the Cathedral or The Duomo as it is usually known. It is Florentine Gothic in its purest form. While it looked rather gray and drab on the outside, it was magnificent inside. The Bell Tower and Baptistery in the same square are also beautiful structures. Last we saw a Renaissance church built by the Medici family. I do not remember its name but it had no decorated facade. They just never got around to putting one on. The church was plain and cold inside compared to the other churches we had seen today but it had wonderful lines.

We returned to our Rest Center in Montecatini for the night, about a two hour drive from Florence.

18 MARCH 1945

Today is Sunday. We made a second trip to Florence and decided to go on another tour. This time it was Dickson, Watzek and me. Unfortunately Miss di Filippi could not conduct the tour, probably her day off, and the substitute was not very good. We went out to Faesoli in the hills north of Florence and got a fine view of the city. There we saw some Etruscan ruins dating from the 8th century B.C. which formed part of the foundation of a Medieval church. We also saw a Roman theater in a state of almost perfect preservation, how much recent restoration I do not know. We went through a museum of Roman and Etruscan civilization and visited another church.

By the time we finished the church it was mid-afternoon and some Air Corps joker suggested that we go and see the tomb of Elizabeth Barrett Browning. That was too much for the three of us so we abandoned the tour and walked the streets of Florence on our own.

We ate dinner in a G.I. restaurant with Italian cooks and waiters where the meals cost 10 Lira, which is ten U.S. cents at the official exchange rate. The meals are rather small and the meat is Spam dressed up with a tasty sauce. I must say it was the best Spam I ever had in or out of the Army. It is customary for infantrymen to order and eat three of these meals at a sitting.

That evening we saw an Italian variety show that was much like a vaudeville show back in the U.S. Then we stopped in another theater and heard D'Artega's All-Girl Orchestra from home. They were good in looks and music.

Back at Montecatini late at night a letter from my wife brought news of the death of my brother-in-law, Franklin Shields, killed in action in the Philippines. My heart ached for Evelyn and her family, but with death so close at hand here, I did not feel it like I would in ordinary circumstances.

19 MARCH 1945

This is our last day at Montecatini. We have had a fine rest. Tomorrow we move out. We never know in advance

The S-2 Section and First Lieutenant Wilson Ware,
S-2 (Intelligence Officer), 1st Battalion,
86th Mountain Infantry at the
5th Army Rest Center,
Matecatine Terme, Italy, 19 March 1945

Standing from left to right: "Mac" Maccaluso,
Clifford Taylor, Wilson Ware, Kurt Watzek, Robert
Dickson, and Charles Beck.
Kneeling from left to right: Kurt Honberg,
Linwood Wellington and Harris Dusenbery.

Kurt Watzek had just been promoted to Section
Sergeant replacing Staff Sergeant James Matthews
who was killed in action on 8 March 1945.

where we are going. It may be to a Reserve Area or it may be back to the Lines.

Charley Beck had a picture of the S-2 Section taken. Caputo snapped it. I hope it turns out well.

20 MARCH 1945

In the morning we leave in a truck convoy for the Front. We go through Prato and the pass to Porretta Terme. Two miles north, instead of turning to the left to go up toward Gaggio Montano and Lizzano, we keep on the road north toward Vergato for several miles and then turn to the left and wind up a narrow mountain road. Our assigned space is in an orchard on a steep slope behind a farm house that is to be Battalion HQ. Many foxholes have already been dug so the first thing everybody is out after straw for a comfortable bed.

The S-2 Section and the A&P Platoon have been assigned the same area. In our section we are soon on the lookout for something better. A tunnel beneath the house is full of German ammunition, but the Commo Section has that area. We have lots of grumbling in our Section even though we are defiladed from German fire.

Our noon meal is C-rations but we are going to have B-rations here as we are now in Regimental reserve.

Things are getting settled by afternoon, and Sergeant Watzek gets us space on the second floor of the CP. One whole corner of our room has been blown out by a large caliber shell or a bomb so we have plenty of fresh air and light. Straw beds are on the floor. It is a lucky break.

The Company field kitchen is late in coming up so we don't get evening chow until dark. We are within artillery range of the enemy, but the ridge protects us from observation and all but high angle fire so we expect a quiet night.

21 MARCH 1945

We spent a quiet day in reserve without much to do. We got out our 20-power scope and watched an Italian make love to a girl in the woods across the ravine. We did not see much, but such is Army life.

We follow the news closely these days through the Communication Section radio. The Army radio station puts out five minutes of news every hour.

22 MARCH 1945

We get word today that the Battalion is going back into the lines. Someone else gets a turn to rest.

The order was for us to march up. We formed up just at dusk and marched north along the road to the Front. It was a quiet night and we made the march uneventfully in about two hours. When we arrived at our destination, a ridge just south and above Castel d'Aiano, Watzek already had our space arranged in a farm house near the CP and also near our OP. It looked like a promising set up.

23 MARCH 1945

We get oriented in our OP today. We have a fine site about twenty yards west of the CP. The OP is well dug in and strongly roofed. It appears to have been there for some time as time flows at the Front. The main drawback is the trees out in front that we have to look through. It works all right because there are no leaves yet, but we are only too aware of tree bursts. We heard that we lost men in our Regimental OP on Sasso Baldino from a tree burst. But again the trees help screen the OP from the enemy.

A Tank Destroyer sits out on the south side of our house screened by it from the enemy. The tankers from the 1st Armored Division are living with us in the east end. The Italian family is living in the west end of the house. A large shell hole in the second story wall keeps us on the first floor but it would be more comfortable and not so crowded up stairs.

24 MARCH 1945

Our good weather still continues. I am about ready to start boosting Italy as having the best climate in the world. We have hardly had a cloud in the sky for weeks now, and the people say the rainy season is just about over. I wonder what the dry season is like.

The news reports good progress being made on all fronts against the Germans, but it seems like it is taking a long time for the war to end. We know that we are not making any progress here in Italy. We read of new progress being made each day in Germany by both the Russian and the Allied armies, and we know that in a matter of days or weeks or months there will be nothing left to fight. For sure there is no need to put in years here, but the Pacific may be a different matter.

25 MARCH 1945

We heard over the radio tonight that the Rhine has been crossed in several places. Even if the news was late, we are surely glad to get it. General Montgomery is quoted as saying this is the beginning of the final round. I sure hope so, and I hope it is a quick one. We are sitting tight here with no change in activity. It looks like the War will be won on the north German plain.

We have a fireplace in our end of the farm house and we are using it to cook our 10-in-1-rations.

26 MARCH 1945

Today we have a cold East wind blowing and it feels like the coldest day in over a month. It is cloudy but not raining. Maybe we will have only a few more weeks of fighting.

Dickson was analyzing me today and he said, "Dusy is one of those timeless guys, and you can't tell whether he was born in this century or hundreds of years ago." After my visiting Florence with him for two days he had me classified as "the simple, aristocratic type."

Evelyn's letter of March 15th arrived today along with a nice little flashlight. It will indeed come in handy.

27 MARCH 1945

Boy, is it windy! This morning the wind blew over a hay stack in the yard and blew some tiles off our roof.

In writing Evelyn a letter on her birthday I had to tell her that I lost the Union Pacific calendar that she had sent me. I am afraid I left it behind when we pulled out of a bivouac area in a hurry. I last remember it hanging on that beech tree in our area west of Gaggio Montano.

Weight is always a problem with us infantrymen, and we generally leave in our wake vast quantities of personal and war equipment called *impedimenta* by Julius Caesar. When we pulled out of Vidichiatico I remember our Section left six cartons of cigarettes in a bureau drawer in the Albergo Alberto. I hope some of the hotel help found them before some contingent of G.I.s. We envy the artillery and other units that have plenty of motor transportation for carting along luxuries. I told Evelyn I have enough reading material now, including the miniature set of the works of Shakespeare, to last me for a year so I don't need any more.

Two packages and three letters arrived here at the Front tonight. One package contained a small camera, but I was taken aback by the array of lens filters that came in the other.

28 MARCH 1945

Our wind and rain is over and we are having another nice day. I guess it is a little early to celebrate the end of the War, but the Section is today consuming its bottle of carefully hoarded whiskey.

We heard from the TDs who are with us that Patton is now operating under a security blackout in central Germany. That sounds good to us. We do keep hoping.

29 MARCH 1945

Great news today! I was told that tonight I am going to Florence on a five-day pass. A five-day pass out of the lines for Easter weekend in Florence? What a break!

Later in the morning I was told that I had a phone call at the CP. The last thing I ever expected was to get a personal phone call up here at the Front. On the line was Dean Haley, a former college classmate and fellow Field Assistant in the Portland office of the Social Security Board. He was with a Chemical (4.2 Mortar) Battalion and has seen action here in Italy since Anzio. It was good to hear from him. He can't come up to see me now, but he will be in Florence on a pass right after Easter. We will try to get together there.

As soon as it got dark a truck came for us and the half dozen or so of us from the Battalion were driven back for some ten miles to a rear supply area where we spent the night on cots, quite an improvement from the Front. We were issued a new style coat, called an Eisenhower jacket, to wear to the city.

30 MARCH 1945

Today we were driven to Florence and put up in the Fifth Army Rest Center in the railroad station. The station is not being used otherwise because all the tracks into it have been destroyed by bombs. We are all congratulating ourselves on our great good luck to be here.

The War news is particularly good and we are all hoping for an immediate collapse in Germany, although it is probable that the fighting will continue for weeks. Unless a revolt starts among the people, there does not seem to be much hope for the collapse we are looking for.

31 MARCH 1945

This was a day of sightseeing in Florence. I went on a walking tour in the morning and a G.I. truck tour in the afternoon. Both were conducted by Prince Nicholas Obolensky, where he got the title, I don't know. I took a few pictures with my new camera. We duplicated part of my previous tour so I thought I was getting to know Florence pretty well.

The Prince, I don't believe, knew his stuff any better than Miss di Filippi, but he stopped at a wine shop in Faesoli and we all had a choice of vermouth or marsala drinks on his advice, but of course we paid their small cost.

Florence seems like a tourist town even in war and apparently the main business that supported this city in prewar times was the tourist trade. Great art is pervasive in this famous city, even for us to see as war rages around us.

1 APRIL 1945

As a combat infantryman back from the Lines I feel very lucky this Easter Sunday. In the morning I attend a Protestant service here at the Rest Center.

I am here in Florence with Tom Orzechowzki, a mortar sergeant from C Company, In the afternoon he and I went for a walk through the city. The people were out dressed in their Sunday best, and they were better dressed than you might think.

2 APRIL 1945

Today with Orzechowzki, I climbed to the top of the Cathedral dome. Perhaps because of its great dome, it is

usually called The Duomo. I was told it is the third largest
dome in the world. It has double walls and the dark
narrow stairs winds up between them. The dome was
constructed without scaffolding and is considered to have
been quite an engineering feat. The top of the dome is
the highest structure in Florence. It has a fine view of
the city and all its red tile roofs.

Florence has a population about the same as Portland,
Oregon, but it occupies about one tenth of the area of
Portland. The streets are very narrow and always jammed
with people. I read someplace that the apartment buildings are now only one fourth as crowded as they were
during the Middle Ages.

At 1:45 in the afternoon I located Dean Haley. We
rushed right over to the *Teatro Verdi* arriving in time for
the afternoon performance of *La Traviata.* It was very
well done. Dean thought it was a better performance than
one he had heard in Rome. Between acts we had cherry
brandies at the lobby bar. This is the only bar in Florence
that serves enlisted men other than one bar that serves
strictly rot-gut. After the opera we went there and bought
a bottle of champagne for 300 lire. Of course we knew
that it was artificially charged white wine and not very
good wine at that. Over our bottle we talked for a while
about mutual college and Social Security Board friends.

Dean brought up the subject of Emilio Pucci. At Reed
College he was ski instructor, studied political science,
and was not very well liked by the students. Dean had
known him better than I did at school as Dean lived on
campus and I didn't. I never had him in any of my classes
and my only contact with him was during a couple of his
ski lessons.

Some months ago when in Florence, Dean decided
to look him up. He asked at the Red Cross information
counter for the Pucci residence. It was just a stab in the
dark and he had no real hope of finding him or his family.

An Italian woman working at the counter spoke right up and said, "Why, yes, just go to the Palazzo Pucci. It's right here on the map," and she pointed it out to him.

Dean found it easily and visited Emelio's mother and sister. His sister is working for AMG (American Military Government), but Emelio went north with the Fascists. Not only that but he escaped into Switzerland and recently he married Edda, Mussolini's daughter and widow of Count Ciano. Boy! That's what I call sticking your neck out. The family has several estates and is one of the wealthiest in Florence. According to Dean they are typical of the Italian nobility in that they are neither pro nor anti-fascist. Their only concern is the welfare of the nobility.

Dean and I had an enjoyable afternoon and evening together. Dean has another day of leave, but at 11:00 P.M. the group from my Battalion left in an Army 6x6 truck for the north.

4 APRIL 1945

We joined the Battalion back in a rest area. They came back the day after I left for Florence, so they didn't do too badly for Easter. They are sleeping in tents and seem to have it pretty comfortable.

I drew guard duty tonight. It would be my luck just after returning from Florence, but I had no cause to gripe. The night was pleasant and uneventful, and I pulled it off even though I was short of sleep.

5 APRIL 1945

We had a Battalion parade today and General Hays awarded some medals. I guess they think we have to keep in practice for the victory parade that we are all looking for. This is our first formation marching since arriving in Italy so we are pretty rusty.

It was like other parades, a lot of standing around in the hot sun and a great feeling of relief when it was over.

We spent all morning in preparation and getting keyed up for it, but it was not nearly as bad as preparing for one back in the States. We have more perspective over here. We know what we are in the army for and it is not to march in parades. The Regimental Band was out for us, the first time I've seen them in action since arriving in Italy. I wonder what they have been doing in combat.

VI
THE BREAKTHROUGH
6 APRIL TO 19 APRIL

6 APRIL 1945

This morning I went with the Battalion advance party up to Riola. We are moving up into the lines again. We spent the afternoon getting our Battalion CP set up. Worst luck! The Regimental CP is right across the courtyard from us. Anyway we now know this is a very quiet sector, and we suspect our Regiment is to be in Division reserve.

7 APRIL 1945

The Battalion moved up today. This is a peculiar sector. In some places the German lines are more than a mile away from ours. Lieutenant Ware is thinking about setting up an OP a thousand meters in front of our lines. It sounds like a rugged deal for the S-2 Section.

We are sleeping up stairs over the CP and have plenty of straw so we are satisfied to stay right here. These appear to be the large buildings of a country estate.

While the 10th Mountain sector is unusually quiet, the papers at home report as follows: "Rome, April 7 (INS) —Troops of the British 8th Army improved their positions Saturday at the southern tip of Comacchio lagoon following a successful attack and a crossing of the Reno River northwest of San Alberto, Allied Mediterranean headquarters announced.

"The 2nd British commando brigade carried out attacks which cleared an eight-mile spit between the Adriatic and Vali Di Comacchio. Nearly 1,000 prisoners were taken.

"American 5th army troops, continuing their coastal attack, took Monte Fragolito, advanced north of the peak against scattered resistance and are now mopping up enemy pockets of opposition."

8 APRIL 1945

This is a quiet Sunday in the lines. We have a church service out on a grassy south slope in the bright morning sun. Since we are in the lines we bring our helmets and weapons with us. Somehow clutching a rifle as you listen to the "Word of God" makes you think more than usual about the message of the Gospel. This is one service I shall never forget.

In writing to Evelyn I told her that I did not comb my hair for so many weeks because I had lost my comb. I finally got one in the PX rations so I comb my hair now twice a week or better. Also at the front I make it a point to shave every other day.

I am the oldest man in the Section, the only one married, and to my knowledge the only one with a child. The fellows complain about me being difficult to argue against, but in this Section everyone starts off an argument convinced that he is all right and the other guy is all wrong.

9 APRIL 1945

We have given up the idea of putting our OP out in front of our lines. I understand higher authority frowned on the idea. Sometimes good sense comes from on high.

Now at Battalion level we are getting ready for a large scale offensive. I put in a full day working on the maps. It looks like a thrust straight ahead through the middle for us. Of course for the infantryman straight ahead is always the middle. Directly north of us stand the high cliffs of Rocca di Roffeno.

The British 8th Army has already opened their offensive on the Adriatic side of Italy.

10 APRIL 1945

Many men are going back with Yellow Jaundice. The Medics call it Hepatitis. Our Battalion will be way below strength for the "big push." Captain Nilsson, Battalion Executive Officer, has it and will go back as will Sergeant Anderson, our Operations Sergeant.

11 APRIL 1945

The *Stars and Stripes* brings word that the 92nd Division and the 442nd Combat Team have started their attack on the west coast. Our turn is scheduled for tomorrow.

Captain Neidner from Able Company has replaced Captain Nilsson as Executive Officer. Ralph Brooker has taken over as Operations Sergeant. Our section has lost several men. It means lots of work and men learning new jobs on the day before the biggest attack of our lives.

In the late afternoon word came over from Regiment that the push has been postponed for twenty-four hours. It is a great sense of relief to get even twenty-four hours of assured life. Anyway our Battalion doesn't go the first day.

12 APRIL 1945

The weather has been perfect recently. We have the most comfortable living conditions here of any place we have been at the Front. Up to now I have been busy preparing maps for the coming action, but now we are all ready and just waiting for the word to go.

War news sounds good and all the correspondents and commentators are optimistic, but here we are still fighting the war, and it is just as brutal as ever. Germany is now beyond any possibility of a comeback or even of a full scale counterattack, but she fights on.

In the afternoon word came down of another 24-hour delay. Again we breath a sigh of relief. We are all ready and waiting. It makes the days seem awfully long.

13 APRIL 1945

No letters for three days. The Communications Section heard over the radio that President Roosevelt died last night. It is certainly too bad to have occurred on the eve of victory, but many of my fellow soldiers are dying on the eve of victory.

Heavy artillery fired all evening long over in the 2nd Corps Sector. We could see the flashes in the mountains to the East. Our own artillery in the valleys behind us was very active. We have some British 5.5 units attached to our Division.

14 APRIL 1945

This morning at eight o'clock the 85th and 87th Regiments and our 2nd Battalion jumped off in a straight ahead drive to penetrate the German lines from the hills just north of Castel d'Aiano to Rocca di Roffeno. It was the toughest day of the war for the 10th Mountain Division.

Right after breakfast I went out to a vantage point taking my field glasses with me to see the action. My position was at coordinates 640242. Sergeant Watzek and others of the S-2 Section were in the vicinity. We had the 20-power spotting scope with us. Since we were in the front lines we made sure that foxholes were not far away.

From our position we could look right up the valley of the Torrente Vergatello to the village of Torre Iussi which was in German hands. Right across the valley from

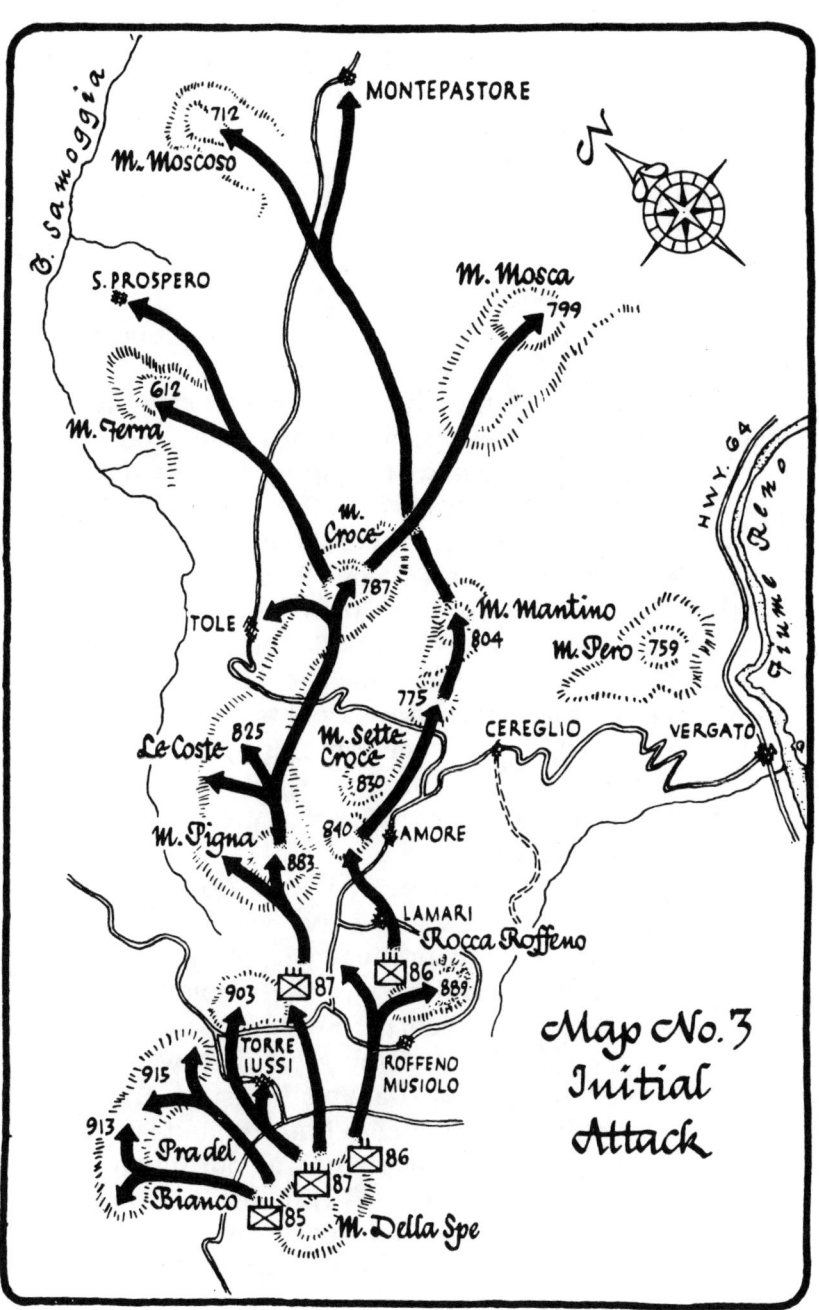

MONTEPASTORE

712
M. Moscoso

T. Samoggia

S. PROSPERO

M. Mosca
799

612
M. Ferra

M.
Croce
787

M. Mantino
804

M. Pero 759

HWY. 64

Fiume Reno

TOLE

775

Le Coste 825

M. Sette
Croce
830

CEREGLIO

VERGATO

M. Pigna

840

AMORE

883

LAMARI
Rocca Roffeno

903

⊠ 87

⊠ 86

889

TORRE
IUSSI

ROFFENO
MUSIOLO

915

913

Pra del
Bianco

⊠ 86

⊠ 87

⊠ 85

M. Della Spe

Map No. 3
Initial
Attack

us lay Rocca di Roffeno also held by the Germans. The jump-off barrage was light for a major action and from our position the attack seemed to develop slowly. We were feeling fortune's smile that morning as we were in reserve and the main break-through was being made by the 87th and the 85th Regiments.

In the late morning I spotted about a platoon of our men up on Hill 860 just to the right of Torre Iussi. The Germans were reacting strongly with intense artillery fire upon the hill. Sometimes the whole hill would be hidden by the shell bursts. When the smoke would clear away I could see our men rise up and go on. It seemed like a miracle that anyone could live through it. I wondered how many did not rise after one of those fierce barrages. It was repeated every few minutes for an hour.

In the meantime squads in open formation were crossing the fields this side, east, of Torre Iussi. They did not seem to be having much difficulty. The shellings they were getting were light and infrequent. The men would hit the ground at times for no reason apparent to us. We surmised that they were drawing some long range machine gun fire. The action made me realize what a thin line of infantry held a front and made an attack. The great burden was falling on such a few men!

During the morning Rocca di Raffeno, which was the great prominent rock across the valley from us, was under our concentrated artillery fire. From there the Germans had a wonderful view of the whole valley and could report every movement on our side. As the barrages would land the whole top of the great rock was smothered in explosions from our 105s and the British 5.5s. Also the 4.2 mortars were throwing in both HE and WP.

The action went on but there was not much more that I could see from my position until afternoon when our men could be seen working up the steep sides of Hill 866 to the left of the Rock. They occupied the hill without apparent trouble and sent on a squad to take the Rock.

Air support was light in this sector perhaps because our objectives were not good air targets or perhaps there was greater need for the planes in other sectors.

Our artillery lifted their fire on Rocca di Roffeno, and I could see the attacking squad going up the left sky-line. I watched them in suspense as they went up wondering what defense the Germans could or would put up. Our men kept right on going to the top and we could see enemy soldiers come out of their caves with hands up. Eight prisoners were all that we could count from this distance, but all we could do was speculate on how many had survived our concentrated artillery fire. We had given them TOT fire, air bursts, and everything but heavy artillery which we did not have.

This was a spectacular advance for our side, and it seemed to assure the valley on the first day of our attack. We were viewing only a small part of the Fifth Army front and about half of our divisional front. The really tough fighting was going on out of sight over beyond Castel D'Aiano but we did not know that at the time, or that over there Bob Dole as a 2nd Lieutenant platoon leader was seriously wounded. In the early evening we went back to Riola with the feeling that the action was going well. We knew that our turn was yet to come.

15 APRIL 1945

The Battalion was up early in the morning and engaged in final preparations for moving out. The order had come down that men were to carry the lightest packs, one blanket or shelter half, three C-ration cans, and two bandoleers of ammunition. We were going to be fighting and traveling fast. We did not know when our supplies would catch up with us. Thus it fell my lot to carry a heavy pack. Ralph Brooker, now Battalion Operations Sergeant and I had to carry the CP supplies. In addition to my own weapon and gear I was carrying about forty pounds of maps as we could not be sure how much ground we would cover before our vehicles caught up with us.

We were scheduled to move out at 8:00 A.M., but the starting time was delayed. We were ready to go so we sat around and waited. After a couple of hours we heard that we were waiting for the 87th to take more ground. They have not as yet taken the bivouac area that we are to go to. We were still waiting at noon and most of us ate a can of C-rations. About one o'clock the order came to get ready to move out. We lined up and waited on the road. Some 1st Armored Division tanks came along and passed us. It was hot in the sun and we were anxious to get started. We didn't know what the delay was, but we had been in the army long enough to expect delays without knowing the reason for them.

It was after two o'clock before our Headquarters Company finally began to move out of Riola. Our destination now was a forward assembly area at Locali Scuola, from which we were to jump off in a flanking attack tomorrow.

Down the winding mountain road into the valley we went. Where it began to level out and the farm fields started, we came to the mine fields. Some of them still had the German warning signs up. Obviously we were unexpected. We passed some wrecked vehicles of our combat engineers who cleared the road of mines this morning. They had put up warning signs and on the road white tapes showing us the safe path. Just east of a small village shown on our maps as Mo. Pierotto we stopped for an hour. Fox holes had been dug into the bank on the left side of the road and we took cover there. No artillery came in but we could hear it landing in other sectors. The 1st Armored Division on our right was fighting into Vergato, and the 85th Regiment off to our left was fighting for survival on the flank of Mt. Balgaro. We felt that wc were mere pawns in the vast movement of battle. How it would go and what our future was were matters over which we had no control or influence. The course of the battle now seemed to be in the hands of the gods. We accepted our circumstances and talked of other things.

Finally we went on, east to Casigno and then north over open fields on a mule path. Again we stopped and waited. Rocca di Roffeno loomed up directly to the west. After a time we went on and reached Pieno Roffeno just about dark. We kept on north past a beautiful shrine at a road junction and halted in the dark near the buildings at elevation 632. There were consultations and indecision among the officers. Our Battalion finally received orders to bivouac here for the night.

Our headquarters company went on a few hundred yards around a bend in the road and halted at an enormous demolition crater larger than the width of the road. We bitched plenty about having to bivouac here for we knew that our maps showed mines along this road, but neither did we relish going on through the mine fields in the dark .

Ralph Brooker, Operations Sergeant, and I sat down beside the road about thirty yards west of the crater. We had the heaviest packs in the company as we were carrying a big supply of maps and all the CP supplies and we were tired. The crater had a narrow lane through it that had been cleared and marked by the engineers. Lieutenant Ware went down into it, turned left, and climbed to the upper edge. The sharp explosion of a Shu mine broke the stillness and a column of light and dirt shot up in the air around him. We got to our feet but too many men were between us and the crater for us to be of any help. I sat back numbly and shivered. One man muttered, "The God damn Heinies!" Our Medics were right there and took care of him. He seemed to be unconscious when they brought him up out of the crater on a stretcher and carried him back. The order went out to keep away from the upper side of the crater and to dig in for the night in the immediate vicinity. Believe me we did plenty of probing for mines that night.

I walked down gingerly into the field below the crater, feeling every step in my stomach, to where others in the company were digging in. I put my pack down and carefully probed the area with my trench knife before digging a narrow slit trench. I got out my blanket and with distant thunder of artillery in my ears went to sleep. Our artillery had not yet moved up and now was a long way back. I could sleep only by not thinking about tomorrow.

16 APRIL 1945

It was daylight when I woke up. The morning was warm and quiet. We ate our C-rations and packed our stuff ready to move out when the word came. We heard a rumor that two men from Able Company were killed by mines during the night. Some engineers came to check on mines. From the center of the crater they studied the sides through field glasses and in an hour or so spotted three or four S-mines in the vicinity of the Shu mine that got Lieutenant Ware. If an S-mine had gone off last night it would have created havoc in our company.

Our present location was about three kilometers south of our scheduled destination for this bivouac. We were told that we were waiting for the 87th to clear out that area before we moved up. The company got under way shortly after noon. We climbed up a steep trail to the north, stopped for a while on the edge of open fields and went on. The grass was so green and the sky was so blue that I wanted to stay here forever.

P-47s were working over the town of Tole behind the hills to the north of us. After reaching the road again we came upon dozens of German prisoners coming back escorted by men of the 87th. Many of the prisoners were walking wounded as were some of their guards. The prisoners were a pitiful looking lot and one could not help but feel sorry for them. They had been through a worse hell than our men.

We went on past Lagazzuola and Ca di Bello; we skirted the hill south of Locali Scuola and halted on the mule trail north of Mt. Mantino. We dug slit trenches right beside the trail and waited until sunset. Our line companies had gone on ahead and were clearing ground to the northeast. We finally took a trail up over the ridge to the east to a road which we took heading north. The road was mined and the German warning markers were still in place. In the distance to the north we could see burning houses and off to the east a platoon from one of our line companies was advancing. We walked down the road at a fast pace as we wanted to get as far north as possible before dark.

From a distance it looked like the whole village of C. Bartolani was burning. I was well forward in our column. As we approached the village German artillery fire began landing on and near the road a hundred meters behind me. We all dived into the ditches. There was a short lull and those of us in at the head of the column made a dash for the town. It was nearly dark and after a few minutes the Germans quit firing. When the rest of the company came up, we found out that no one was hurt. Four mules carrying communications equipment were killed as they just stood still on the road during the barrage.

We got the order from Regiment to establish our Battalion Headquarters in this town for the night. Only a few buildings were burning and most of the town was now perfectly safe. We accumulated prisoners in a barn during the night. I pulled a tour of guard duty in the town square and helped handle the prisoners.

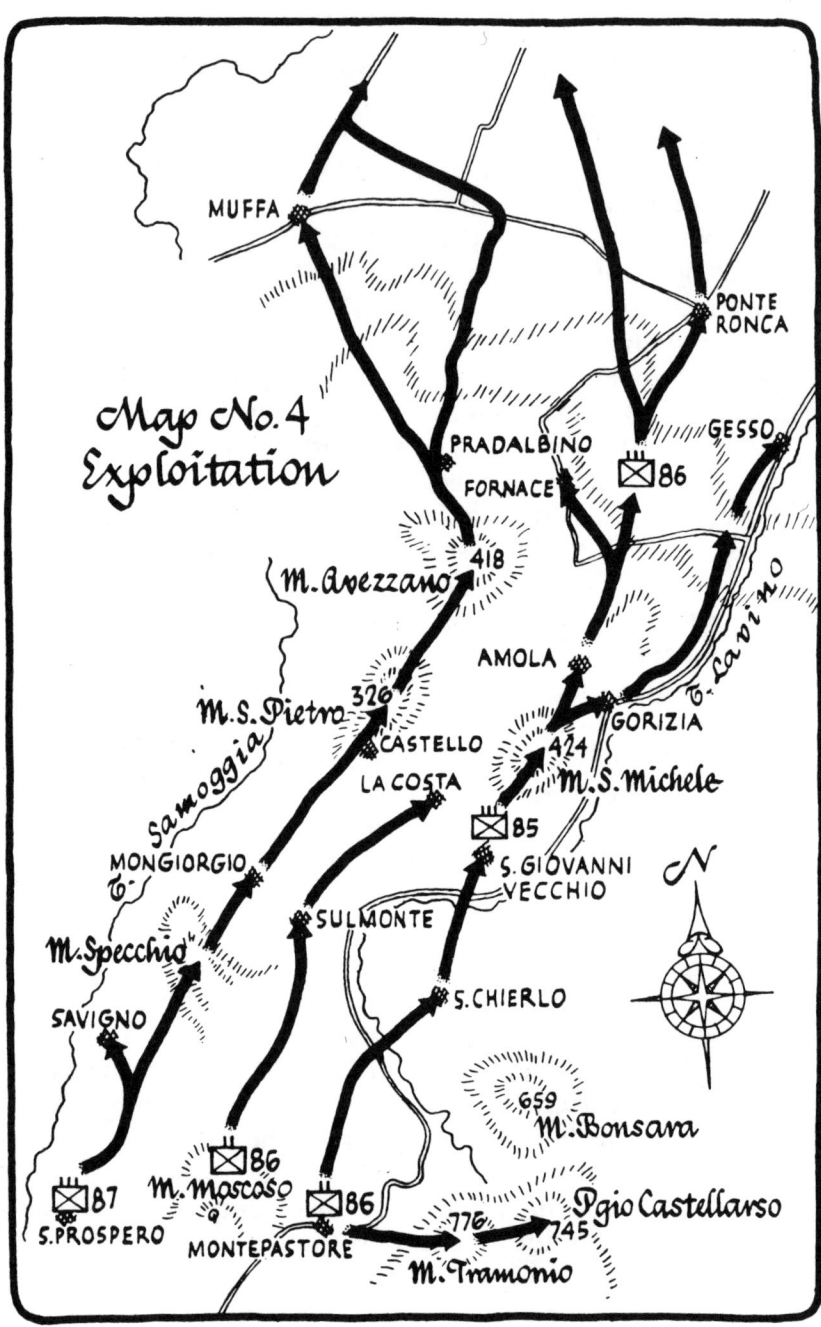

Map No. 4
Exploitation

MUFFA

PONTE RONCA

GESSO

PRADALBINO
FORNACE

⊠ 86

M. Avezzano

418

AMOLA

M. S. Pietro   326

CASTELLO   424   GORIZIA

LA COSTA   M. S. Michele

⊠ 85

MONGIORGIO   S. GIOVANNI VECCHIO

SULMONTE

M. Specchio

S. CHIERLO

SAVIGNO

659
M. Bonsara

⊠ 86

M. Moscoso   ⊠ 86   Pgio Castellarso

⊠ 87   MONTEPASTORE   776   745
S. PROSPERO   M. Tramonio

Samoggia

T. Lavino

N

17 APRIL 1945

The attack was resumed the first thing in the morning with orders to wipe out as much of the enemy defense
line as possible in a flanking attack to the northeast with
our Battalion on the right side of the Tole-Montepastore
road. Incoming artillery fire was light but fairly steady.
The Germans had a couple of self-propelled guns firing
on our village. They withdrew shortly after daylight.

We received orders to move the CP forward to C.
Costa and I went up with a small CP party along the main
road. We passed numerous enemy defense positions. We
passed two dead from our line companies and several
German dead. Many prisoners were moving to the rear
sometimes unescorted. We located C. Costa and set up
our CP in the center of the village. All roads in the vicinity
were heavily mined. The reports we were getting from
the line companies were all favorable. By noon the rest of
Headquarters Company had moved into C. Costa. In the
early afternoon one of our line companies reported that
Mt. Vignola, our main objective for the day, had been taken
and they found forty enemy dead on top. 5.5 artillery fire
from our British support had been particularly effective
there.

In the middle of the afternoon we got orders to
move up with a small party to Conti di Vignola which
will become our Battalion CP. Al Hilowitz and Ralph
Brooker were in the party. Montepastore was reported to
be still in enemy hands so we took back roads further
south, wound around hills and cut across country part of
the time. In about an hour we arrived at the village on the
slopes of Mt. Vignola and set up our CP in the big house
on the south side of the road.

Prisoners were still coming back in droves. We
searched them and sent them back. They were confused
and bewildered. Our advance had surprised many enemy
units before they had notice of the attack and our line

companies appeared at their rear. Before dusk our Battalion Commander, Major Harold Green decided that it would be too risky to send any more prisoners back in the darkness. He ordered us to hold them in the village square for the night. We posted guards and accumulated the prisoners. During the evening about fifty were brought in by the line companies. We had them sleep on the stone pavement of the square. I had to pull a shift of guard duty during the night. We were running short of men as we had sent so many men to the rear with PWs.

Late in the evening a unit from the 85th Division moved in and took over our CP. That Division was moving through the gap we had made in the enemy lines. Our line companies during the late afternoon had moved out a considerable distance from Mt. Vignola until they were ordered to halt for the night. Our objective had been taken and the enemy lines lay wide open. During the day the 1st Battalion had killed an estimated one hundred enemy and captured several hundred. They came back so fast and over different routes that no accurate count could be made, at least at Battalion level.

18 APRIL 1945

This morning we sent back our prisoners and waited for orders while other units took up the pursuit. In the late morning we got orders to move out. We were getting used to moving on short notice by now and thought nothing of it. The one worry we now had in our Battalion Headquarters was running off our maps. We didn't care much about where we were going now that the enemy lines had been cracked open. It seemed all in the days work to move on north. Sometimes it was to be a fixed objective on the map, a town or a mountain, but other times it was merely an order to get moving, other orders would come later. Often they were merely to take a certain road or compass heading across country.

We wound around the north side of Mt. Vignola on narrow roads and mule trails. No artillery fire was coming in here. All was peace and quiet. Smoke curled up from some burning buildings off to the west toward Montepastore. We finally took a short-cut down to the main road leading north from Montepastore. As we walked north along the road an occasional Jeep would pass us, but as yet the heavy stuff had not moved up. It was now just the infantry alone doing what it does best. Even though we are in reserve for today we are ahead of our artillery and other supporting units.

After going down the road for a couple of miles, and the roads are now going down heading for the Po Valley, we turned up to the ridge on our right and wandered around on numerous narrow roads. We halted for a long time waiting for our officers to find out where we are to go. We finally got word. The companies were assigned areas and we set up our CP in a country estate called Il Palazzo on the map. The main building was great for our CP. I secured a place for my bed on the floor of a second story room. It was devoid of furniture, but fortunately it had a great plenty of straw. I wondered how long the Germans had been here. Il Palazzo was populated and a group of Italian men were out on the great lawn in front of this magnificent house playing lawn bowls. The lawn was perfectly level and stretched out north from the house for a hundred yards.

At the end of the lawn the ground dropped away sharply. I walked out to it in hopes of getting a view of the Po Valley. Much country was visible but to the north lay more hills. I could see neither the Po Valley nor Bologna. Back at the CP I ate my C-ration supper and spent a peaceful evening.

Sergeant Watzek, who had been coming down with yellow jaundice (hepatitis), was sent back to a hospital. I took over his job as S-2 Section Sergeant. Now only three of us are left in the Intelligence Section, and I was the only one at the CP. Norm Wightman was with C Company and Ed Fancher, who recently joined the Section, was with B Company.

After dark I went into the Medics room as they had light and passed some time talking to them. Our Battalion is down to about half strength largely because of the many hepatitis cases. Later when orders came in from Regiment I did some work on our maps. When that was done I went up to my pitch dark room, put my blanket down on the straw, not worrying whether there were fleas or ants or other creepy-crawly things in the old straw, laid down on one half of my one blanket and pulled the other half over me. I slept well.

19 APRIL 1945

In the morning our headquarters packed up and marched down to Borgo on a main road about a mile west of Il Palazzo. There we stopped and waited. We were issued C-rations for another day and had our noon meal. We had nothing to do but lie out on the grass in the warm Italian sun and wait for the next order. It will come soon enough, but for the present we enjoy what we can.

In the early afternoon our orders come to move on. Some of our vehicles have come up and as Sergeant Brooker and I are carrying the CP supplies we get to ride in the Jeep with Lieutenant Craig, who has been made our Battalion S-2 officer. I know nothing about him and I think how much I miss Lieutenant Ware. We drove down the main road and stopped at Regimental Headquarters at Pilastrino. In half an hour we get organized and the Battalion moves on. The road is jammed with traffic. Tanks and artillery are now with us. The traffic moves slowly and halts at frequent intervals. It gets dark and we move on. Eventually we pull into Bell'Aria and set up the CP for the night.

Orders for an attack come down from Regiment and a huge overlay with checkpoints on it is included. I have a bunk picked out in a back room, but I don't get to use it. Ralph and I are up all night pasting maps together and putting on the checkpoints, battalion and company boundaries, and objectives for the attack tomorrow. Ralph and I are the two enlisted men in the Battalion who know that it is to be the Po Valley finally and to cut off Bologna from the northwest. All through the night while the CP is asleep, we work hour after hour preparing copies of the Operation Maps for the coming fateful day.

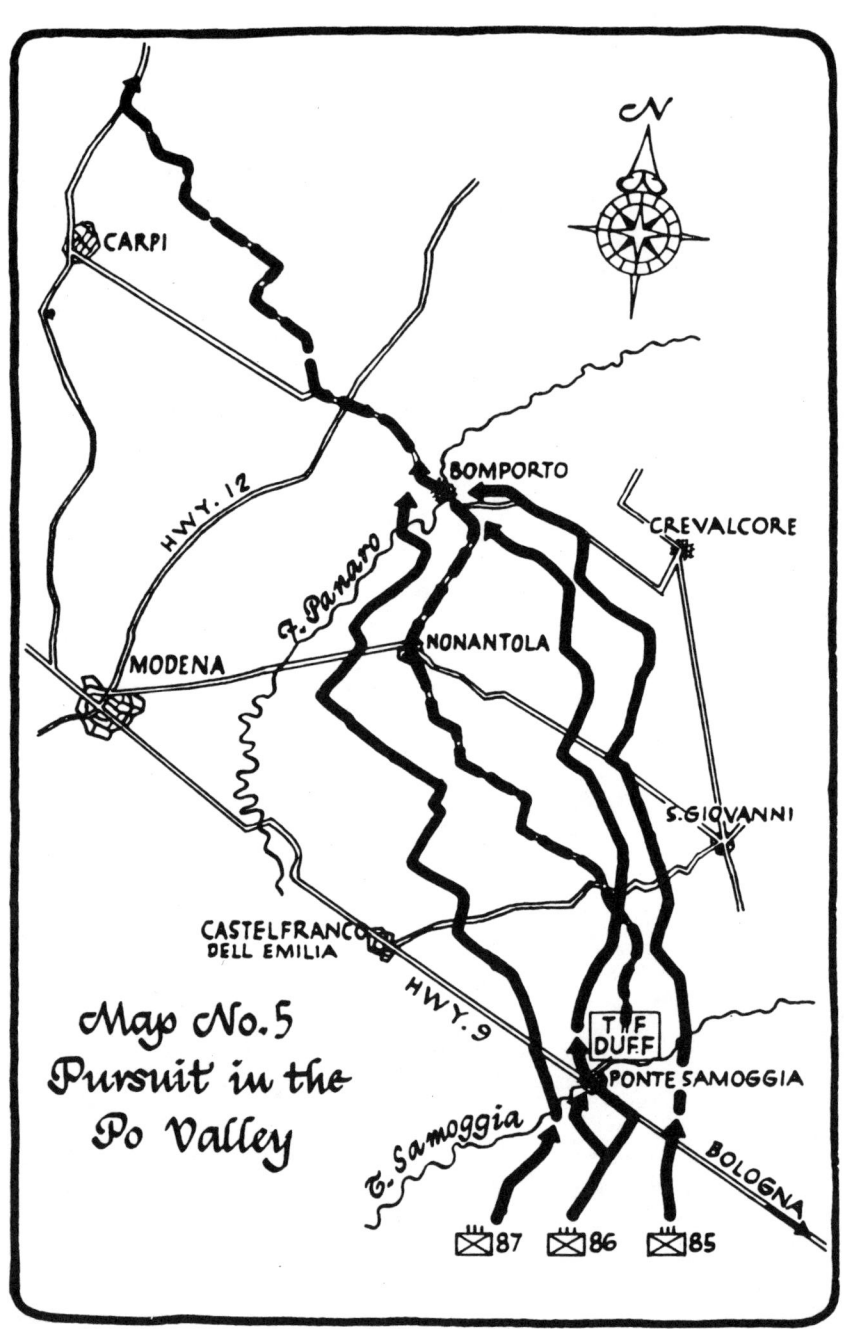

N

CARPI

HWY. 12

F. Panaro

MODENA

BOMPORTO

CREVALCORE

NONANTOLA

S. GIOVANNI

CASTELFRANCO DELL EMILIA

HWY. 9

Map No. 5
Pursuit in the
Po Valley

T. F.
DUFF

PONTE SAMOGGIA

T. Samoggia

BOLOGNA

⊠ 87   ⊠ 86   ⊠ 85

VII
THE PO VALLEY AND LAKE GARDA
20 APRIL TO 2 MAY

20 APRIL 1945

Our attack into the Po Valley was set for 8:00 A.M. from the last ridge that the 87th Infantry had occupied the evening before. We moved up most of the Battalion on foot early in the morning. It was in a valley and we were headed north.

At one crossroads, where two of our men were killed fifteen minutes before we arrived, the column halted, and we sat there for about ten minutes wondering when Jerry would throw in the next shells. Sure enough he tossed in three rounds and four of our commo men were hit. We cursed the system that stopped us at a hot spot and were greatly relieved when we moved on, leaving our wounded in the care of medics.

I was one of the lucky few to have had a Jeep ride to the point we left the vehicles in the valley. Vehicles other than tanks would not be with us during the attack. We hiked northwest through deep green wheat fields up the ridge to the Line of Departure. The line companies went up first. The plan called for our Headquarters Company during the advance to follow the line companies by about a thousand yards. I went up ahead of my Company to see the jump-off. I did not have any special mission and would not have unless the Battalion got bogged down. Perhaps not too much was expected of me as I had been up all night working on the maps in preparation for this important offensive so it was not difficult for me to persuade Lieutenant Craig that this was an intelligence mission. I knew the plan and was curious to see how it would work out. Our Battalion was on the right flank for the Division attack.

The companies were deploying just below the crest. From the top of the ridge I got my first view of the Po Valley. On my right the rising sun gleamed on the rooftops of Bologna, for so many months the goal of the Fifth Army and still firmly held by the Germans. The Po Valley stretched away to the north, flat and ever so green. Every field was bordered with precisely trimmed trees. Every bit of land was cultivated with exquisite care. What would the passage of a great army do to it?

Our thoughts were elsewhere. It gave us all a thrill to look out upon it for the first time after the long, hard months of winter warfare in the Apennines. Here we were the first troops of the Fifth Army to reach the Po Valley. To the east along the Adriatic coast the British Eighth Army had been engaged in fighting in the lower reaches of the valley for some months.

One half hour behind schedule the line companies went over the crest with scouts out and with no more apparent concern than was shown on maneuvers. Down they went at a fast walk in widely separated files with five to ten yards between men. They deployed to cross open spaces and went back to files for going through wooded areas. The enemy artillery began to fire. They pounded a village off to our left heavily. I could see the church tower ringed with bursts. The Third Battalion to our left must be getting it plenty hot. Then came our turn. I dived into a ditch and waited it out. The shells sounded close but they were landing a hundred yards away. No one was hurt. Good. Let's see how the men out front are making out.

They are still advancing with no artillery fire as yet on them.

Before long I heard the squeaking of tank tracks and roar of motors. Our supporting tanks from the 1st Armored Division are on the way down their assigned roads. It is good to know that they are with us.

They were not of much help in the mountains but down on the valley floor things may be different.

Down below the Jerries drop in several rounds on an open field that our infantry is crossing. The men go down. The firing ceases; there is a pause; the men rise up and go on at double time. Perhaps the enemy has observation on it. On the road to my right and well above that field five tanks stop and swing their guns out toward a target in the valley. I don't know what they have spotted, but they open up at rapid fire. The tanks seem to rock back from the recoil with each round fired, but they fire so rapidly it sounds like a continuous explosion. I try to pick up the target with my field glasses but am unable to find even the bursts of the shells that are landing in the haze several miles out in the valley.

I think there must be plenty of heavy stuff behind us, but it is not needed. The men keep pushing on. No small arms fire yet, and it is not until the rifle companies get out more than a thousand yards that I hear the first machine gun open up.

D Company with 81 mm mortars and .50-caliber machine guns follows out the reserve company. Soon it will be headquarters turn to go.

A colonel from Corps saw me looking through my field glasses and asked me how it was going. I told him how far out the line companies were. He asked me about the tanks. The tanks had not moved in the last ten minutes and I told him that something seemed to be holding them up on the road. He was very much disturbed by this information. I, conscious of my PFC stripe, said the infantry seems to be doing O.K. without the tanks. He went off to try to find the 1st Armored Division liaison officer.

The enemy continued to send in scattered artillery fire. It was ineffectual, but it did scare us just the same. Its only real effect was to make us want to go forward faster because none of it appeared to landing up where the line companies were. Apparently the Jerries were firing where they had observation on the hillsides. It was like this all the way through the Push. When we were in a target area and the shells start landing, we got out fast, but we got out forward.

Headquarters Company started down and I went with Lieutenant Craig. I had a heavy pack with a large supply of Po Valley maps and other headquarters essentials. I carried a Tommy Gun for protection. For a while we had quiet going. Then as we were going up a slight rise across an open field a by-passed Jerry took a pot shot at me. The bullet kicked up dust about twenty feet from me and ricocheted over my head. I did not have time to get worried because the next instant artillery shells poured in. I hit the ground and watched the stuff burst off to our left near a platoon of tanks. Artillery fire is much more frightening than rifle fire. It's the greater noise, and in many battles artillery causes the most casualties.

We hurried on to a group of houses and took shelter inside while we waited for the line companies to get further out. They were still reporting good progress. I reported the sniper fire, but we did nothing about it. Gaining ground to the north was more important than mopping up. We now got our first taste of the welcome that the people of the Po Valley were to give us. They broke out their wine stock and began giving it to us freely, but soon we had to go on.

We passed one place where a tank had a broken tread and was holding up all our tank support. The road here was very narrow. Crews were working hard to extricate the disabled tank and permit the others to go on. It looked like they would soon get the road cleared. We dearly wanted to have them with us.

As we went on we got more wine. In one place a family was standing at the gate of their home and passing out glasses of wine to the men as they walked by. Two young girls were kept busy running ahead to collect empty glasses and bring them back for refills for other soldiers.

Before noon we came to that definite break between the Apennine foothills and the floor of the Valley. We now felt that the worst part of the war was over for us. We had broken out of the mountains and had Jerry on the run. We had less fighting ahead of us than we had a right to expect, but still in the coming days the numbers of our killed and wounded would mount.

Soon we crossed a railroad track. It was the first one for me in a military operation, and it seemed like an important accomplishment. We went on north with little opposition, and the chief danger was getting too much wine to drink. The people surely let us know that we were coming as liberators, not as conquerors. To us it now seemed more like a political parade than a war. This was a type of warfare we had never imagined. So it went all that day and by evening we were well northwest of Bologna and digging in firmly astride of Highway 9. Bologna we knew was now useless to the Germans. At the time we had not yet heard that Bologna itself had fallen to other units of the Fifth Army. The end of the war in Italy was in sight. We knew it and we wanted so much to stay alive for these last few days.

21 APRIL 1945

In the morning we resumed the advance. The Battalion marched a mile to the west along Highway 9 and crossed a river at Ponte Samoggia. This bridge was being fired upon by a German battery far to the north and we crossed in rushes. We turned north down the left bank for a couple of hundred yards and waited for half an hour. Other units were crossing the bridge and shells were landing near it. We were glad that we were across, but we wanted to get further away from this prime target.

In such circumstances half an hour can seem like an eternity. Our move-out order finally came. We went over another railroad and headed north across country. We could hear the enemy artillery shells swishing directly overhead, so we knew we were headed in the right direction. We hurried on rapidly because we felt the sooner we could silence those guns the safer we would be. The valley floor was perfectly flat and intensively cultivated. We went on from one field to another in rapid succession. The fields were mostly wheat about a foot high. In about an hour we reached the battery and the gun crews surrendered to a line company without firing a shot. We kept right on going and lost little time in locating a crossing of the Canalle di S. Giovanni.

Our main object was to get north as fast as possible. We avoided towns and main roads because there was more chance of meeting Germans in such places. We were racing them to the Po River. This was action on the grand scale. We passed near Rastellino and Redu. Only rarely did we halt to wait for flanking forces to catch up. On the whole we were ignoring our flanks. We passed east of Nonantola and we stopped for the night just at dusk across the Fiume Panaro from Bomporto.

22 APRIL 1945

We marched north all day, part of the time across country and part of the time on back roads. We had no enemy resistance and it was an uneventful day. After dark on a main road we were picked up by our Battalion vehicles and enough added trucks for the whole Battalion to ride. We rode north for hours through the dark, and I slept in my seat in the S-2 Jeep.

Generally when danger comes it strikes too swiftly and events happen too rapidly for one to develop a sense of fear. Fear comes after reaction. Suddenly a ball of fire about six feet in diameter appeared before my eyes and a tremendous explosion nearly blew me out of the Jeep. I was wrapped in a blanket and in the confusion could not find either my carbine or sub-machine gun. I hit the road on the right side of the Jeep and could see and hear a German machine gun firing not twenty yards for me. I rolled down the fifteen-foot high road embankment to the ditch. I got there about two seconds after the explosion. I realized that the explosion had been from a Panzerfaust, a rocket fired weapon that resembles our Bazooka only it is about five times more powerful. It had hit the Jeep immediately in front of ours squarely on the radiator and the force of the explosion had gone into the engine. Now that Jeep was blazing up making the vicinity seem as light as day. We were lucky in that the Panzerfaust is an anti-tank and not an anti-personnel weapon. It has a shaped charge designed to penetrate tank armor. Immediately a second explosion about forty yards ahead set another Jeep blazing.

Rifle and machine gun fire made me realize that I was on the wrong side of the road, the enemy side. About four men whom I did not know were with me and the ditch we were in was not more than three inches deep, hardly any protection at all. Wheat in the field, twelve to fifteen inches high, offered us some concealment. Lieutenant Craig, Brooker and Caputo who were in the Jeep with me had disappeared apparently to the other side of the road.

We crawled back away from the fire for twenty or thirty yards and stopped while the men with weapons fired at enemy flashes. This wheat field was about fifty yards wide and Germans on the other edge were firing at the vehicles. After we started firing they realized for the first time we were there and tossed two grenades out into the field. They fell considerably short. We crawled on back for what seemed like a hundred yards and decided we would have of cross over the road even though it was in full view of the enemy. We dashed across. It seemed as light as day, but not a shot was fired at us. By now there were almost a dozen Jeeps and trucks burning.

Some D Company men broke out an 81 mm mortar and commenced firing it off-hand, i.e. without a tripod. They knew their stuff and were placing their shots fairly well. I found an M-1 rifle belonging to one of the mortar men I suppose and a few clips of ammunition. I crawled up to the road and began firing at rifle flashed. Other men got a machine gun functioning back along the convoy. When I got down to my last clip I pulled back to help protect the mortar from the rear.

What happened was that the Jerries had cut our convoy in two near the middle of Headquarters Company. The rifle companies of our Battalion were all on ahead. On our side of the block we had some men from D Company, some Headquarters men and some truck drivers to fight out the skirmish on our side of the block with limited resources. Our ammunition was running low and we weren't too happy about this fine kettle of fish. All this time the Jeeps and trucks were blazing and ammunition in one of trailers was exploding.

Next the Jerries brought up two tanks. We had one bazooka and rounds, but it misfired. We never did really get organized and we pulled back in the field waiting for reinforcements. Soon one of the German tanks pulled up onto the T road junction and started spraying the ditches and fields that we were in with machine gun fire. I can still see those colored tracers coming at me and then going overhead. We consulted and agreed that circumstances called for an attempt to save the drivable trucks at the end of the convoy and drive them back a safe distance.

Under Lieutenant Lewis' orders we dashed down parallel to the road for a couple of hundred yards. Two trucks at the end were undamaged. Drivers went up and turned them around. We piled in and sped down the road. By that time Jerry realized what was up and fired his tank gun down the road. In the dark it was blind shooting and we were soon out of range. We assumed we would come to a following unit within a mile or so, but we went back several miles before we came to a unit bivouacked for the night. There were about fifteen of us from my company, mostly communications platoon men. With few weapons and little ammunition we decided there was little point in returning until daylight.

We caught up with the company the next afternoon at the Po River. We were reported as missing in action on the morning report. One of the men from the Commo Section who was with the main body said that my being missing caused more concern in the company than anyone else. I don't know whether that is a compliment or a sign of lack of confidence. Maybe it was because I was a family man.

As it turned out the line companies on ahead proceeded a ways after the attack, stopped after finally getting word and organized a rescue mission supported by self-propelled 105s. The attack had occurred right in the middle of our Battalion communications and just about wiped out those capabilities. They returned just after we left and cleared out the Jerries in about ten minutes.

The next morning on our way to the Po we checked the area for salvageable equipment. We counted the bodies of sixteen German soldiers. We later heard that our casualties were one killed and two wounded. The Jeep that I drove for some months and now Caputo was driving was a total loss. It and the trailer looked like sieves. They had

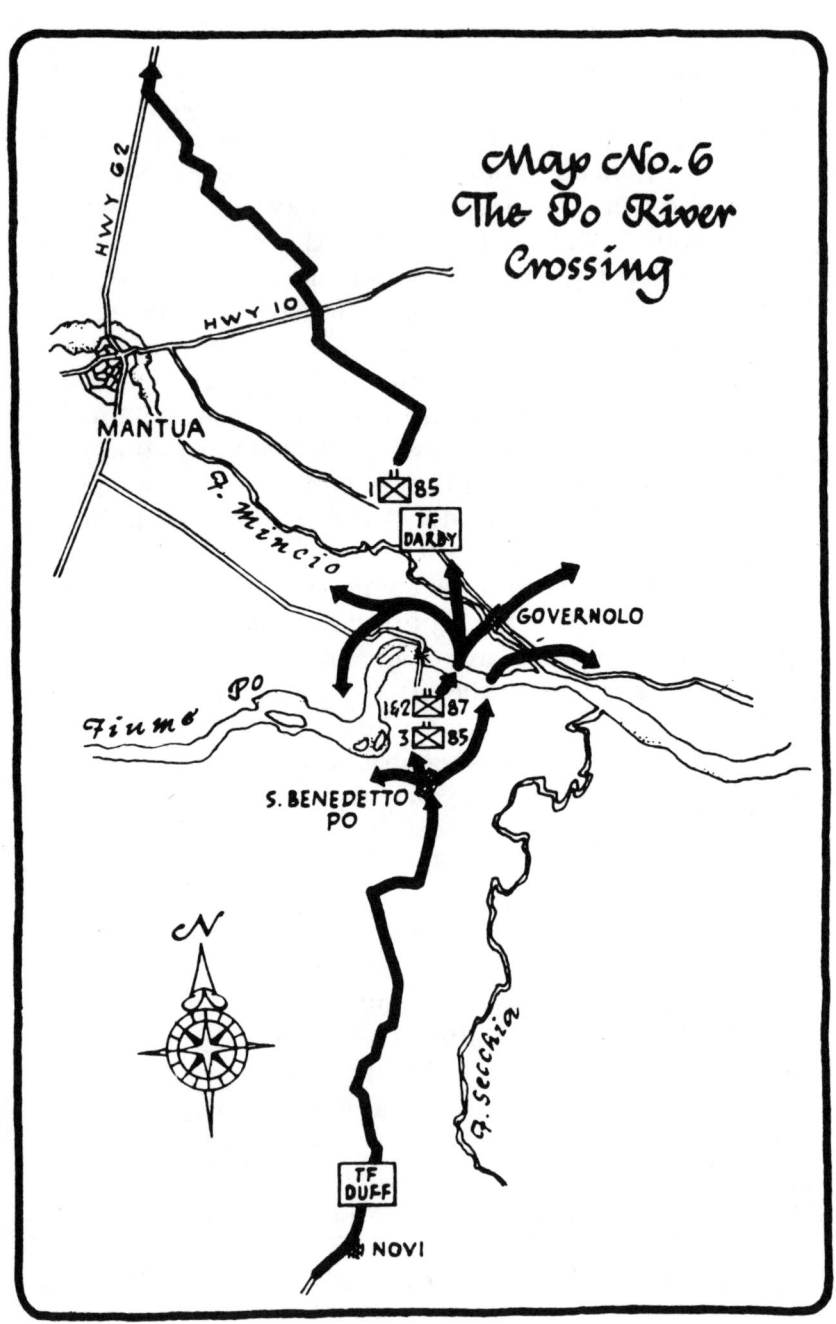

Map No. 6
The Po River
Crossing

HWY G2

HWY 10

MANTUA

R. Mincio

1 ☒ 85
TF DARBY

GOVERNOLO

1&2 ☒ 87
3 ☒ 85

Fiume Po

S. BENEDETTO
PO

N

R. Secchia

TF DUFF

NOVI

hundreds of bullet and shrapnel holes through them. My pack and all the CP supplies had many holes. Our Jeep did not catch fire unlike the one that caught the Panzerfaust and I was able to salvage most of our maps which our Battalion sorely needed. Fourteen of our Jeeps and trucks were destroyed in the action.

According to reports going around the next day, it was not an ambush, but an armored Jerry column fleeing north accidentally ran into the middle of our convoy. If I had know that I would have been a lot less worried the night before. The Jerries were alert and prepared; we were tired and taking things for granted, so they got the jump on us. That is why it was a grand fiasco. By American war standards we won because we traded equipment for dead Jerries.

23 APRIL 1945

I rejoined my company about noon at their bivouac area north of San Benedetto Po. We were located in open fields just north of a large cemetery. The men had dug their fox holes deep in easy digging. A unit of self-propelled artillery was nearby and every once in a while they would fire their 105s at enemy targets across the river.

During the afternoon the 87th Regiment crossed the Po while our 86th was in reserve. Later on our CP was set up in a house on the main road southeast of the cemetery. Ralph and I put on our packs, mine with many holes in it, and walked over to the CP. That afternoon we did not have much to do. The rest of the company also moved over. We had a comfortable place to stay. The news came through that the 87th had crossed successfully. We knew that our turn would come in the morning, but at least we now had a bridgehead but no bridge across the Po.

24 APRIL 1945

We were scheduled for an early morning crossing. We were so used to getting on the road that it took us only a few minutes to get ready and divide into 30-man "Duck" loads. We kept that formation and marched down the road to Camatta, crossed the levee, and went down onto the sands where the "Ducks" were waiting. The small willows there offered no concealment and we were somewhat apprehensive. We climbed aboard the amphibious trucks. I was in the third one with our Major Green, our Battalion Commander. The "Duck" drove down into the river and chugged across in a few minutes. There was no artillery fire coming in, no sniper fire; it was just a routine crossing like on maneuvers. The difference was the thrill to land on the north bank of the Po River.

We had reached an important objective. We were sure that the enemy was folding fast. We waited in a garden just beyond the north levee until the rest of the Battalion crossed. We got organized and marched off to the north for perhaps a mile. The orders were to wait in the area until our vehicles and some tanks could be brought across. As yet none of our artillery was on our side of the river.

Finally Battalion Headquarters was set up in a farm house on the south bank of the Mincio river, a mile and one half north of the Po. We had nothing to do but wait. In the afternoon some men took sun baths out in front of the house. We cleaned our weapons. We had no idea when we would move out, but we were ready to go on a few minutes notice.

We heard that we were waiting for the engineers to get a pontoon bridge that would support tanks across the Po. Later in the afternoon we began getting some of our trucks across.

An empty barn was attached to the west end of the farmhouse, and I bedded down there in the hay with the CP personnel.

25 APRIL 1945

In the morning Ralph and I had more overlays and maps with checkpoints and routes north to prepare. The engineers were reported to be having trouble with the bridge and still no tanks had crossed. War is mostly waiting. It always had been; it always will be. The soldier soon learns to reconcile himself to that fact. Here we wait even though we are in a race north against the Germans who are fleeing behind us and on all sides of us.

By afternoon enough trucks and Jeeps had been brought across to carry the Regiment. The order came down to get ready to proceed north toward Verona by vehicle and cut off access to the Brenner Pass route. For this purpose Task Force Darby was organized. It was composed of the 86th Regiment, attached artillery units, and tanks as soon as they get across the Po. Colonel William Darby had been recently assigned to take the place of General Duff, our wounded Assistant Division Commander.

At four o'clock in the afternoon with Colonel Darby in command we crossed the Mincio on a bridge and proceeded on by-roads east of Mantova. We went through Stradella, Chisiolo, Viallanova, Maladina, and Dosso. We reached Highway No. 62 at San Lucia. We had brief stops on the way, and the people came out and gave us bread and wine. It was a glorious ride and we were welcomed as liberators.

Our column drove north during the night keeping to the main highway but halting for long intervals. We did not know what was happening at the head of the column, but we heard no firing. Our company had no incidents during the night which we spent sleeping in our trucks or on the grassy roadsides during delays.

26 APRIL 1945

In the early morning we pulled up to the southwest side of Verona. We waited on the road beside the old city

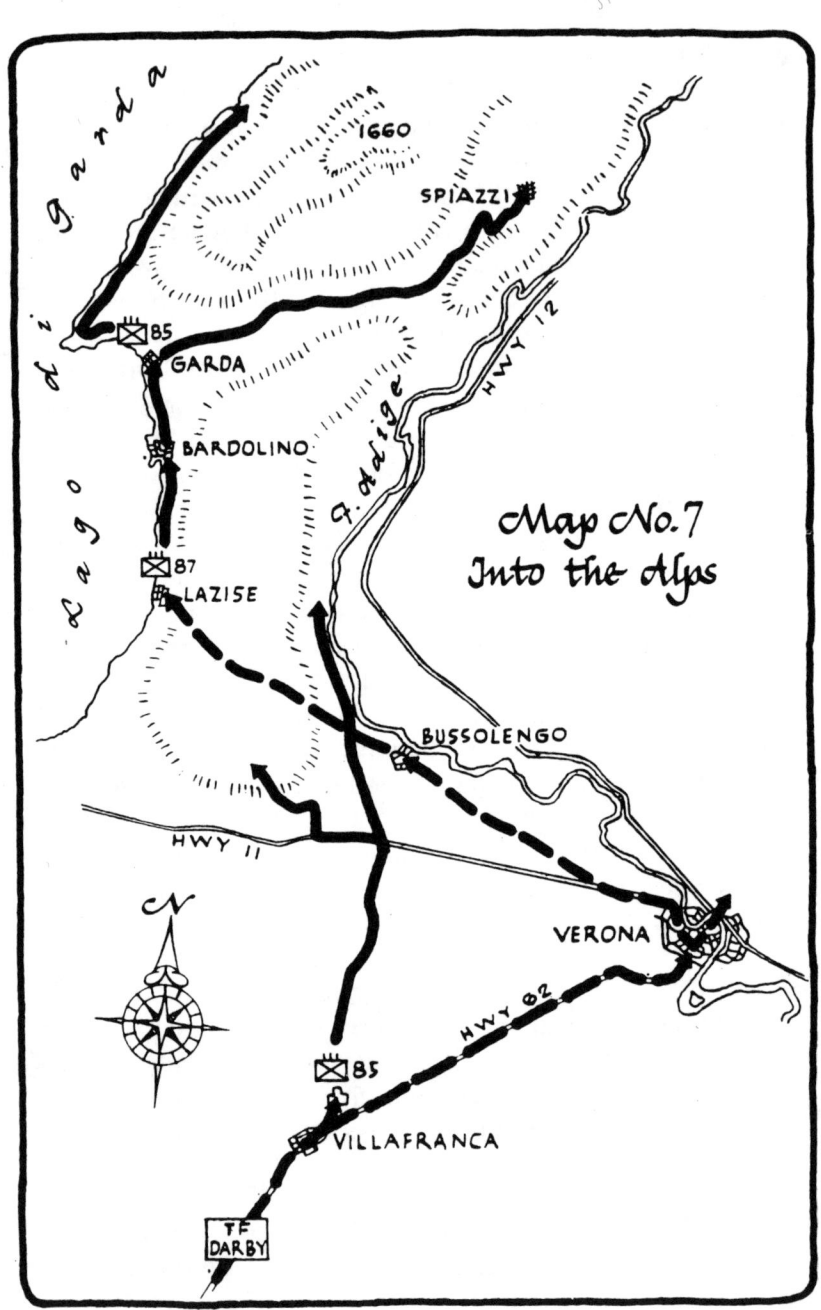

1660

SPIAZZI

85 GARDA

BARDOLINO

HWY 12

G. adige

87

LAZISE

Lago di Garda

Map No. 7
Into the Alps

BUSSOLENGO

HWY 11

N

VERONA

HWY 62

85

VILLAFRANCA

TF
DARBY

wall while some of our units were sent to reconnoiter the north side of the Adige River. We waited most of the morning and then got orders to move on to Bussolengo. We drove north skirting the railroad yards and took the road northwest toward Bussolengo. For most of the way the Adige was in sight. We could see German trucks fleeing up the highway on the other side of the river. Our P-47s were giving them a good going over with machine guns, rockets and 500-pound bombs.

We entered Bussolengo about four o'clock and got a rousing welcome from the populous. We stopped here as Division ordered and located a building for our CP. Nothing but the order had stopped us from going on. Half an hour after we arrived a rumor broke out among the Italians that the Germans had surrendered. We didn't take much stock in it. The Germans were licked anyway. We knew that and we had no official word. Besides our P-47s were still strafing the Germans on the other side of the river. We could see some of their vehicles fleeing north but out of the range of our light infantry weapons.

I was out in front of our Battalion CP shortly after sunset when General Hays drove up. He conferred with Colonel Darby on the situation and gave him a concise oral field order to block the highway and railway on the opposite side of the river. I was impressed by the efficiency with which the order was given in clear, simple and concise terms.

Colonel Darby turned to Major Harold A. Green, Battalion Commander, and ordered him to take the First Battalion across and do the job. He asked how long it would take to get the Battalion moving. Major Green said that he could start in half an hour. The Colonel said "Go to it."

It was dark when we got started. We walked down through town to the bridge, badly hit by bombs. Large holes gaped in the roadway and part of it was tipped at a sharp angle, but it was deemed safe for foot travel. We crossed over and stopped in the town of Pescantina. We were told to stop there and wait for further orders. We located an empty building and went in. It apparently had been a tavern. There were tables, benches and chairs but no wine, liquor or light. As the wait stretched out some of us got some sleep on the narrow benches and on the stone floor. About midnight the Battalion received an order to go back to Bussolengo. The highway was blocked elsewhere and our mission was not needed.

27 APRIL 1945

I slept late this morning but not as late as I would have liked to. I am still short of sleep. All is quiet around Bussolengo. Germans are no longer retreating up the east bank. No orders yet. We can see the mountainous Alps off to the north and can anticipate our next assignment. We have shut rail access to the Brenner Pass, but we expect to chase the enemy on up the Adige into the Alps.

The people had some reaction to the false peace rumor of yesterday but they still felt that at least for them the war was over. The partisans were active here this morning bringing in German prisoners. They had taken over several German vehicles and appeared to be running wild. We did not begrudge them their excitement. At last they had freedom. It was their time to celebrate and have a good time.

In the afternoon orders plus a roll of maps came down from Regiment. Ralph and I spent the afternoon pasting together 1:50,000s of the Lake Garda area entering checkpoints.

It was after dark when the Battalion pulled out in vehicles and drove northwest toward the Lake. We drove all through the night.

28 APRIL 1945

When morning came it was raining and we were riding up the east shore of Lago di Garda. The mountains rose steeply from the shore and were lost in the mists above. Soon we halted. After waiting in our vehicles for some time, we got word that this would be a long halt. I had a breakfast of C-rations. Some of us went up to a barn fifty yards above the road and I slept for a time.

About noon I went out in an advance party with Ralph and Lieutenant Craig. We located a place for our CP further on. By this time the rain had ceased and we got set to enjoy ourselves while someone else did the fighting. We could see German units retreating up the west side of the Lake. They were mostly using horse-drawn vehicles. As yet we had nothing up here to fire at them, but all kinds of stuff was coming up. We did not know what was holding us up. In an hour we received orders to get started again. By this time our artillery units were setting up their batteries in our vicinity and now our nearby tanks were firing at the enemy on the other side of the Lake. Here we had not yet received any return fire.

The Germans had blown up a couple of tunnels of the east lake shore road and a Duck battalion had been brought up to ferry the troops around the blown tunnels. We marched up the road to a point close to the beach where the Ducks were landing and awaited our turn. The Germans had 88s in operation now firing at the Ducks. The shells would throw spouts of water straight up in the air. Some of them were close to the shuttling Ducks, but I didn't see any hits. They also fired at the road and we dived for the deepest ditches. We were in a hot spot, but we had to sweat out our turn.

Our wait seemed long but it probably was not more than half an hour. When our Company's turn came, I crowded into the first Duck with the CP personnel. Crowded it was with just enough room for thirty men

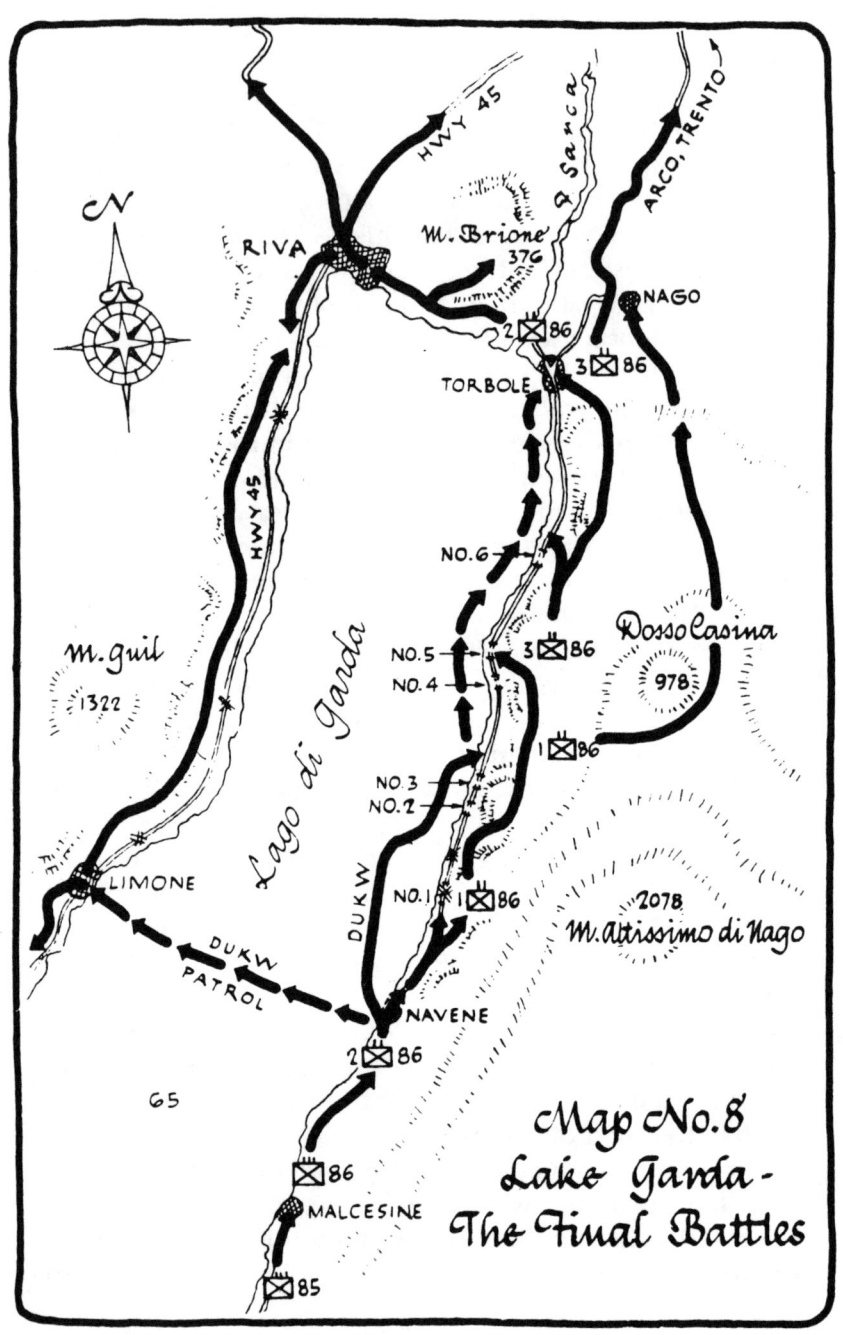

N

HWY 45

ARCO, TRENTO

& Sarca

RIVA

M. Brione
376

NAGO

2 ⊠ 86

TORBOLE

3 ⊠ 86

HWY 45

NO. 6

Dosso Casina

NO. 5

3 ⊠ 86

978

NO. 4

Lago di Garda

1 ⊠ 86

M. guil

1322

NO. 3

NO. 2

DUKW

2078

NO. 1

1 ⊠ 86

M. Altissimo di Nago

LIMONE

DUKW
PATROL

NAVENE

2 ⊠ 86

65

⊠ 86

MALCESINE

Map No. 8
Lake Garda -
The Final Battles

⊠ 85

standing up. It took about fifteen minutes to make the run with no shells being fired at us. From the lake we could see that we were getting up into the mountains and how sheer the East wall was. We landed just north of one tunnel and went inside. Before long the whole Battalion was in the tunnel. Darkness fell soon after we arrived. Flashlights were used in the CP area, an enclosed room off the main tunnel. No lights were allowed out in the tunnel. I prepared to spend the night outside but was called into the CP to make a distribution of maps to the companies. It took an hour stumbling over men in the pitch black to locate the various Company Commanders. Finally back at the CP I got a couple of hours sleep in a narrow passageway just off the CP room. The rock floor was hard but by now I was used to sleeping anywhere, The days and nights had merged into a continuous flow of time and brief snatches of sleep could be taken any time and any place.

29 APRIL 1945

Soon after sunrise, no, I should say daylight because it was many hours before the sun rose over the high east ridge, we marched off to the north on the lakeside road. The morning was bright and clear. Yesterday's rain had washed the atmosphere well, and the green fresh smell of spring was in the air.

We hiked through another tunnel to the north and on to Capo di Tempesta. From there we started climbing up a steep wash in the canyon wall. Ralph and I had our packs with the maps and CP supplies. We climbed up gaining an elevation of several hundred meters and then headed north. We halted in the vicinity of Dosso Casina about noon. Most of us had only one can of C-rations left, and some of the men ate their last can at breakfast.

We ran short of water and that mountain side was a very broken up granite. Finally after some thirsting and griping some of the men located a spring about a mile to the rear. Men went back a few at a time to get water; some of them carried as many as a dozen canteens on a pole. I went back for water late in the afternoon when it appeared the Battalion might have a long wait.

About sunset our Battalion received an order for an attack as soon as possible on the town of Nago. We advanced for a mile or so, but darkness fell before the attack could get well underway. The forward companies were ordered to halt where they were for the night. About this time the Germans in Nago and Torbole started firing at us at a great rate with machine guns and 40 mm anti-aircraft guns. They couldn't see us, but they knew where we were so they were just raking our area. Not many men were hit. With the order to halt we tried to dig foxholes, but digging was impossible in that granite.

Two guns over beyond Nago were firing at us including many red and green tracers. As the tracers would arch across the valley, they looked as if they were heading right toward us, but as they neared our side of the canyon they suddenly seemed to change direction and sped over our heads as if they were glancing off something out in the void in front of us. I suppose it was a matter of perspective. In any event for us it was a rare phenomenon, but probably something the "fly boys" see all the time. I piled up a row of rocks in hopes that such a barrier would offer some protection. With little faith in it, I went to sleep on a painfully rough and rocky bed.

30 APRIL 1945

It was daylight when I woke from my hard, rocky bed. The sky was clear and Lake Garda was a deep blue far below. It was quiet with not a shot to be heard; our world seemed to be at peace. It was a beautiful spring morning in the mountains and being peaceful we did not mind too much missing breakfast. Many in the Battalion had eaten nothing since yesterday noon.

We waited for a couple of hours for our patrols to report back from Nago. They brought back word that it had been evacuated by the enemy during the night. The dreadful news to mar an otherwise perfect day was the report that about ten men of Baker Company were killed during the night by aerial bombs. The report was that three bombs were dropped by a German plane and one of them was as direct hit on a squad from B Company closely bunched on a mule trail.

After getting word to move our HQ Company into Nago, we switch backed down the mountainside and passed the spot where what was left of the bodies lay. Blood and bits of bone and flesh and shreds of clothing lay scattered over the ground. Someone had made a partial attempt to clean up. Along the trail there was a gunny sack of arms and legs with the grisly ends sticking out. No bodies or heads were visible. We surmised that they had simply been blown to bits. This is the thing that gnaws at your heart yet in war we have been hardened. Without a tear we hurried on to get by the awful spot, silently thankful that it had not been our time to die.

We entered the little mountain village of Nago and found there a Czech labor battalion. They were happy that the war was over for them and thought it would soon be over for the Germans. They said that the Germans were definitely beaten. I moved into a clean billet with Al Hilowitz and Ralph Brook on the second floor above the CP. The Czechs, leaving a few personal articles behind them, moved out in the afternoon. They were assembled in the town square for removal to the rear.

Later in the afternoon A Company reported they killed four Germans who drove a car into town without knowing that we occupied it. Otherwise it was quiet and we waited for further orders. Where would the next push take us? We were only sure that it would be deeper into the Alps. Tonight we ate German rations. We were glad to get a change from C-rations and from nothing. A report came down from Regiment that Colonel Darby was killed in Torbole this morning.

1 MAY 1945

No sound of weapons in our area today. Some of the line companies were sent over the ridge to Rovereto on the Adige River with orders to occupy it and push north toward Trento. Battalion HQ is remaining in Nago for the time being. Our troops are bringing in many prisoners.

2 MAY 1945

We had another quiet day in our CP in Nago. At 7:25 P.M. the message that we had been waiting for so long to hear came into our CP from Regiment. I can clearly remember the wording; "Italian Theater armistice in progress. C.G. 10th Mt. Div. orders cease firing except in self-defense. All patrols are called off. There will be no firing of arms in celebration. More details to follow."

Shortly after that we heard over the radio that it was officially announced at 6:30 P.M. that the Germans in Italy had accepted unconditional surrender. The same broadcast was carrying news of Hitler's death, but it caused scarcely a ripple here.

We had no wild burst of enthusiasm when the news of surrender broke. In Nago there was no rioting or raucous celebration. The men received the new with a sort of calm elation that is difficult to describe. They knew that for the 10th Mountain Division more hard fighting lay ahead and they had lost friends and companions in the last few days. The going to this point had been rugged, and the physical and mental strain that we had undergone held our spirits down. Japan loomed large and fearsome on the other side of the world.

VIII
PEACE IN ITALY
3 MAY TO 18 MAY

3 MAY 1945

This morning General Hays assembled in the town of Torbole on Lake Garda our regiment and the British field artillery battalion attached to us. It was near the square where Col. William Darby, our Assistant Division Commander, was killed on April 30th. Our General gave a brief talk congratulating us on the campaign we had just finished. A chaplain led us in a prayer of thanksgiving for the war being over. The troops were dispersed. My company climbed back to Nago, our temporary home.

4 MAY 1945

It seems strange not to hear the guns any longer, but it is good to know the Germans are surrendering to us without holdout problems. We feel that the war is really finished here in Italy, although we still have some work to do. Mostly we are just waiting for Germany to collapse. From the news that event must not be many days off.

News of the surrender in northwest Germany came this evening. We are certainly glad to hear it. This means that the war here in Europe is just about over. I think that next week will see it though, but it may be months before I get home to my family.

Looking back on the campaign, we had rugged going until the end. Many of us did not come through. We who did are thankful and wonder why we are here and so many of our comrades are here no more.

5 MAY 1945

We are spending a quiet Sunday in the little mountain village of Nago. It is a warm clear day. I climbed up to the ruins of an old castle in the afternoon and took some snapshots of the mountains and the lake.

A flight of P-47s flew up the lake to our north end and circled around at a low level in the valley below me. It was obvious they were out for a holiday. I suppose they told their superiors that it was a training exercise. Their job of shooting up the Jerries is finished; now they can fly for the fun of it.

We are still waiting for news of the last surrender in Germany and Norway. It should come this week.

6 MAY 1945

I can imagine the happiness the news of the German surrender here in Italy brought to my wife and parents. The 10th Mountain Division spearheaded the drive all the way, and we are proud of the part we played in bringing about this victory. We lost comrades and feel deeply the cost of this victory. For this reason we have not been overjoyed by it, but we all have a feeling of relief and the lift of a burden from our minds.

Victory is merely a stage in the passage of time replacing one set of problems for the world with another set. We have paid the price for victory; we must now accept the consequences.

The news from Germany is so good that we are sure the surrender is only a few days off. Maybe sometime this week the people at home will celebrate V-E Day.

We have had rain showers the last two days, but we are fortunate to be living in houses. Today was warm and sunny but with considerable haze in the distance. I took more picture. Our duties are light. We like it here. Our only real need is for showers and clean clothes.

7 MAY 1945

Today was one to remember. For the first time in thirty-four days I had all my clothes off and took a shower, a nice hot one in a Fifth Army shower unit. Then I dressed in a completely clean set of clothes. This sets a new record for me, but I am glad it is over and with no sign of bugs. My last shower was taken in Florence on April 3rd.

8 MAY 1945

Germany surrenders! The *Stars and Stripes* came today with the headline reading, "**It's all over over here.**" From the short-wave radio broadcasts it sounds like the people in Britain are having a grand celebration. We are too far north or the mountains are too high for us to get any of the American Army stations in Italy so we don't know how the people back home are taking the news. This news caused little excitement around here among the troops.

My promotion to Staff Sergeant came through today. I have been acting as S-2 Section Sergeant since Watzek was hospitalized with hepatitis back at the beginning of the breakthrough. Of our ten man S-2 Section that came overseas Norm Wightman and I are the only ones left, so my promotion does not prove much except the terrific attrition of war.

9 MAY 1945

We are having a holiday today which merely means having no schedule. We are supposed to be celebrating the end of the war here in Europe. For us the big question now is redeployment, a new word we are hearing on every lip. We are all wondering what our status will be and whether we will have to go and fight in the Pacific.

Everyone who has been in combat would much rather stay here in the occupation troops. We can't all do that and there is a good chance that men bound for the Pacific will get furloughs home. The unthinkable is for the Division to be sent directly through the Suez Canal to a Pacific combat zone.

It is quite a let-down not to have any European war news to be interested in, and things are moving too slowly in the Pacific to arouse much interest here. It will be months before redeployment begins to affect the Pacific war in any important way.

10 MAY 1945

Today the company moved from Nago to S. Alessandra down in the valley. Kurt Honberg came back from the hospital today. He is the first of our hepatitis cases to return. Our men are doing well and will return.

11 MAY 1945

We are now quartered in a big villa at S. Alessandra about a mile northeast of Riva, which is located at the very north end of Lago di Garda, the largest lake in Italy. The elevation is about two hundred feet above sea level, but the mountains rise directly from the water to five thousand feet.

The Army announced the point system this morning, and I am afraid my discharge is a long way off. Unit censorship ended today for all mail, but base censorship continues.

I had a busy day. I spent the morning burning maps and aerial photos and in the afternoon I copied the Riva Ridge pages of our Battalion Journal into a personal notebook.

The Section received a letter from Lieutenant Ware today. He writes, "Excuse my writing. Right now I am just one big bandage and cast. Sorry to have to relate that my right leg is a peg below the knee, and my left leg has so many holes in it, it now is in a cast up to the hip. They've done some skin grafting so now I have bandages all the way up my back. And a cast on my left arm. But they say it'll all come out in the wash in time. Guess sooner or later I'll be sent home." We had heard that he had survived the mine explosion but were glad to get word directly from him.

In the evening Kurt and I went into Riva and at the waterfront got to talking with an Italian man in his fifties just back from working in Germany. All he was interested in was food. We were much impressed by the fact that he spoke Italian, English, German, French and Spanish.

12 MAY 1945

Everyone has been figuring his "points." It has become the great numbers game. It's all we talk about now. I figure I have 47 points, but I am not sure how partial months are counted. I think I can allow myself 20 months of Army service, 5 months overseas, and 12 points for my son, David. In addition to that I am entitled to two battle stars for the North Apennine Campaign and the Po Valley Campaign. Since they are worth 5 points each, my total is 47, which is far below the 85 required at this time for discharge. The First Sergeant has 105 points, but most of the men have less than 85.

This is an interesting old house we are living it. The word house doesn't do it justice. It is a country estate and perhaps small palace or castle would be more descriptive. It has a wonderful library with hundreds of old books in French, German and Italian, the great majority of which were printed in the period between 1740 and 1815. Kurt Honberg found a first edition of Schiller, and I ran across a book in French that was printed in 1646. We had fun trying to read a part from a Latin Bible printed in 1714. As the text was familiar we did not have too much difficulty. We also found a large library of handwritten music.

It looks very old, but all the portfolios were undated and we didn't know any of the pieces. We handled these old volumes carefully and put them back in their places.

Another interesting feature of this house is down in the sub-basement. It is a family burial vault in which I counted thirteen crypts. Old wreaths on the walls look like they have been hanging there for years and years. Hanging from the archways are black draperies, practically in shreds. They appear to have been hanging there for centuries. High up are some narrow ports through the four-foot thick wall to let in light, enough to only partially dissipate the gloom.

13 MAY 1945

This was Sunday. We had a morning church service on the terrace off the west wing. It was a wonderful warm summer-like day, and I could look out between two palm trees to the blue waters of Lago di Garda and the snowcapped mountains on both sides. This part of Italy is beauty beyond compare, but all the more it makes me want to get home.

I found out today that the Army will credit me with only nineteen months of service. This gives me a total of 46 points, and that's not enough. I only hope that on our way to the Pacific we get to go through the States. I hate to think of taking the Suez route, but I guess that is a possibility. The rumor is going around that we are about to make another move, but we have lots of rumors these days. I write to Evelyn by candlelight.

14 MAY 1945

Moving day again. We packed up the CP and our personal equipment and drove by Jeep south into the Po Valley.

It was a beautiful drive down the east shore of Lago di Garda.

15 MAY 1945

We have moved down to a former airfield about ten miles southwest of the Lake and about three miles northwest of Montichiari. We are bivouacked in pup tents. The weather if hot, just like Camp Swift, Texas, and we have no shade. We don't like it a bit, but all we can do is hope that it will not last long. We are still dressed in our wool uniforms.

I have just finished reading *Anything A Horse Can Do,* a book on the helicopter. We sure could have used one of those on Riva Ridge.

We hated to leave the mountains, but the ride down the east shore of the lake was beautiful. I thought about how Evelyn would have enjoyed that ride, but she would not like the little green lizards that are swarming over our bivouac area.

In the afternoon we had a Regimental parade in the hot sun, and none of us liked that either.

Tonight I went into town, Montichiari, with the men in the Section including three new replacements who just arrived. There in a restaurant we had spaghetti at 100 lira a plate and ice cream at 30 lira per dish. Later we went to a small one-ring circus. It was just a small show by U.S. circus standards, but we enjoyed it. Perhaps the *vino* helped.

16 MAY 1945

Today we were given an issue of champagne, a bottle per man. At this writing mine if half gone, but the evening is young yet. Somehow drinking warm champagne from the bottle in a pup tent doesn't seem very elegant.

Our Division captured a *Tedeschi* warehouse and drove away with seventy truck loads of champagne according to rumors going around. That sounds like at least a ten fold exaggeration to me. We are supposed to get more champagne tomorrow. I only hope they are not trying to soften us up for the news that we are going directly to the Pacific.

17 MAY 1945

No hangover from last night's champagne. A storage pond for irrigation water is near our bivouac area. We swim in it but the water is very cold. It is pumped up from about two hundred feet. The land around here appears to be rich and intensively cultivated. I have no idea what the rainfall is and how much it needs irrigation. That chore reminds me of irrigating fields of my uncle's farm in the Gallatin Valley of Montana.

18 MAY 1945

This evening some of us went on the interurban rail car to the city of Brescia. We had dinner and champagne at a sidewalk cafe. I went into an art store and saw some paintings, among them a surf scene that reminded me of Neskowin. The price was $120 at official exchange. It and the impedimenta of size deterred me from buying.

IX
THE YUGOSLAV BORDER
19 MAY TO 13 JULY

19 MAY 1945

What now! Without knowing where we are going we packed up and moved east by truck convoy. After a long day we bivouac in a field a few miles east of Udine and again are sleeping in pup tents.

20 MAY 1945

Today we went on to the Yugoslav border. After a drive through some beautiful mountain country along the Izonzo River we arrive at Bretto di Sotto and make camp. We have been alerted for trouble and our weapons are loaded. Bretto di Sopra and Bretto di Mezzo are just above us in this narrow upper Izonzo glaciated valley.

21 MAY 1945

At Bretto. We are having a cloudy day in the mountains with all the surrounding peaks shrouded, but the grasses are beautifully green and we are bivouacked in a field of clover.

News from the Pacific sounds good now. Last night's radio brought word of Japanese peace feelers and the Chinese capture of Foochow. It will surely help to have a port on the Chinese coast. Maybe the war will go so well I won't have to go to the Pacific. Evelyn's brother was killed there in the Philippines and that is enough of a sacrifice for our families.

22 MAY 1945

The radio this morning brought word that the First Army is on its way to the Pacific via the U.S. At least some troops are going before us.

Evelyn mentioned seeing the movie *None But The Lonely Heart* and my having recommended it, but I cannot recall a single scene from the picture, who was in it or what it was about. It shows how preoccupied I have been with fighting the war these last few months and what a long way I have come since Camp Swift or wherever I saw the picture.

Up at Nago a few days after the war ended Special Services gave us an outdoor movie. It was the Andrews sisters in a picture that I have forgotten the title of. It was terrible. The fact that the movie industry could and would sell such a picture to the public made me feel ashamed of being an American. I felt glad that the Italian children who seemed to be enjoying the picture could not understand the dialog and could not know how really bad the picture was. Perhaps my feelings are just a result of war, which has a sobering effect on those who fight it.

This morning I had the bad luck to sprain an ankle, my left one. I was out giving the Section a lesson in free rock climbing as we had no climbing equipment. I was giving a demonstration emphasizing safety and the necessity for testing each hand and foot hold before putting full weight on it. I knew the cliff in the place we were climbing was soft in spots and tricky. I was not careful enough in testing a foothold and it gave way beneath my weight. I dropped about eight feet and landed upright on a ledge. I had my balance all during the fall and landed perfectly, I thought. I went on with the class and it was not until a couple of hours later that the ankle started to swell up and ache. From the Medics I got an elastic support bandage. My right knee has also been troubling me some for the last few days. It took me through our few months of combat but the first morning I tried to do setting up exercises I strained something in it, and it has bothered me ever since, being too much for setting up exercises and some mornings too much for close order drill. I hate to think of missing out on some real rock climbing.

Speaking of my knee being shot (in slang usage) reminds me a joke that happened to some Jerry prisoners last winter. Lieutenant Ware finished his questioning of them, turned to the guard and said "Shoot them back to Regiment." One of the Jerries, horrified, stepped forward and begged, "No, no. Don't shoot." Lieutenant Ware, by the way, was always shooting things and people to various places.

I am working through my third roll of film. I don't know when I can send them home. I am hoping censorship will be lifted on films soon, so I can send them home direct.

If I had a choice I would rather occupy than go and fight some more, but the choice won't be mine.

23 MAY 1945

Unit censorship is off again and I can once more tell Evelyn where I am, but she has probably read it in the newspapers. We are up in the mountain knot where the borders of Italy, Austria and Yugoslavia join. The mountains remind me of the Beartooths in Montana. The grass is wonderfully green and the scenery beautiful. We had a hard mountain shower yesterday afternoon and more showers today, but I still like the mountains. We are living in pup tents so the rain is annoying.

My ankle is better today. The Medics say it was not a serious strain and I can resume normal activities in a couple of days.

I saw Jack Coppock for a few minutes this morning. He is just back to C Company from a bout with jaundice. He lost a lot of weight and is not too happy about being back, but then he never did like any place in the Army. He said Jack Oates is now a buck sergeant with the job of Communications Sergeant for C Company.

In a letter to Evelyn I wrote as follows: I imagine you have read in *Time* magazine about Colonel Darby. He founded and commanded the Rangers while they were in existence. Just before or perhaps during our final drive he was named Assistant Division Commander. After we crossed the Po he commanded a unit known as Task Force Darby, which consisted of our regiment, an attached artillery battalion, a tank destroyer battalion and other smaller attached units. In the final days of the war our division had the toughest fighting in Italy driving up the east shore of Lago di Garda. Colonel Darby was killed by an 88 shell in the town of Torbole at the northern end of the Lake. It was only a day or two before the surrender in Italy. He was made brigadier general posthumously. We all thought he was a good soldier and we will miss him.

For our job here the 10th Mountain Division has been attached to the British Eighth Army. The 2nd New Zealand Division is on our right. We are maintaining a defensive line from Austria to the Adriatic. News concerning the temporary border settlement at the Morgan Line is satisfactory, so we don't mind being over here. I guess we are on some type of international police mission.

We maintain road blocks and do some minor patrolling. I have not heard of any use of weapons and things are really very quiet.

24 MAY 1945

We had rain and more rain last night and today. When the clouds finally cleared off, the peaks revealed new-fallen snow. These mountains I believe are called the Julian Alps. We are bivouacked right beside an Austrian military cemetery from the last war. The iron crosses all bear dates in 1916 and 1917. There must have been some difficult fighting in these mountains, and I am glad we did not have to fight in them.

We all figure that the longer we stay in Europe the better off we are. We hope this political affair of the Italy-Yugoslav border keeps us here for several months. We don't relish the prospect of fighting in the Pacific. We can forego an early furlough home.

My ankle is much better today. My fall resulted in only a slight strain. I hope it doesn't rain tonight as I am Sergeant of the Guard.

25 MAY 1945

Late mail last night brought in Evelyn's letter of May 12th. I miss her and wish that she could share some of our experiences and places now that peace is here. The days pass slowly, slower than in combat.

We have had clouds today but no rain. Our schedule is still mostly rock climbing and athletics at which I can't participate but my ankle is much better.

The people here are mostly Slavs and among the minorities more Austrians than Italians. The native language is Slovenian, but the adults speak Italian. I have tried out my Italian on several children. They do not understand me and I do not think that it is my Italian that is at fault.

26 MAY 1945

A typical day in the mountains with clouds and showers. My ankle is just about back to normal. In the evening we had an outdoor movie, *Bathing Beauty* with Esther Williams. The legs were nice in Technicolor.

27 MAY 1945

I just found out that I had forgotten all about Mother's Day. It reminds me that during the push we lost all track of dates and days of the week. It was just a never ending succession of days with all our thoughts on the enemy.

There is no church service today, and we are just spending a quiet Sunday holding down the Yugoslav border.

28 MAY 1945

Another day spent waiting for redeployment. It did not rain today and we had fried chicken for supper.

29 MAY 1945

Another slow day with little to do. I wrote Evelyn a long letter describing our ambush in the Po Valley.

30 MAY 1945

We are still holding down the border and all is quiet. We speculate about when and where our next move will be. It is cloudy to the east over Yugoslavia tonight.

31 MAY 1945

Evelyn's letter of May 21st arrived today and she certainly sounds enthusiastic about my points. I am glad that she is glad, but my tenure is pretty uncertain.

Sergeant Watzek and Charley Beck came back to the Section from the hospital today. Watzek has seniority over me for the job of Intelligence NCO. I understand the Company has ninety days to transfer me to a new job of equivalent rank or to "break" me. So many factors enter into the picture, like the total strength of Company noncoms, theater policy on over strength and such, that it is really impossible to say what my future will be.

I drew for the first time my Staff Sergeant's pay, $86.02. I put $50 of it into my Soldier's Deposit Account which pays 4% interest. I have $200 in that account now. My pay as a PFC was $34 a month.

I wrote Evelyn that there is no point in thinking of me as being indispensable to my unit. No one in the infantry is indispensable; we are every one of us expendable. That is the way the infantry has to be organized.

1 JUNE 1945

Saturday. Good news. Tomorrow I am going to Venice on a one-day leave. I went to bed before dark because we have an early start.

2 JUNE 1945

I got up at 3:30 A.M. Several truck loads of us left at 4:30 for Venice. It was a long ride in Army 2-and-a-halfs, and we arrived there about 10 A.M. I got a haircut and a shave and took a gondola ride in the morning. I went on a tour in the afternoon and saw the Doge's Palace and St. Marks Cathedral. They have just started putting back the famous paintings, so from an artistic standpoint the tour was not so profitable. Venice is the most congested city I have ever seen, and you have to go by water if you travel any distance. I admire the way the gondoliers handle their boats. I took a few pictures. I had one picture taken by a street vendor, but I look like a sad sack in it. There is much fine glass work here. Evelyn would have had a field day. The city is full of British soldiers and sailors.

We left about 8:30 in the evening. On the way one truck broke a fan belt and had to be towed so we did not get back to camp until 4:30 in the morning. I can assure you that a twenty-five hour day is too long.

3 JUNE 1945

After sleeping all morning I had to get up in time for early noon chow. We then fell out in battalion formation for Field Marshal Alexander. He came about 1:30 shook hands with the officers, and gave the Battalion a talk in the best British diplomatic style. He said that the position of a front line infantryman was one of honor. He would have been extraordinarily proud to have been an enlisted man in the 10th Mountain Division; as it was he was pretty proud to have us in his command. He reported that General Marshall was sorry for the Italian Theater when he asked for the divisions to invade southern France, but General Marshall said he would make it up by sending his best division to Italy—the 10th Mountain. Alexander all but said that we more than any other division are responsible for the early defeat of Germany. This speech would create more dissension in other 5th Army ranks if it were to appear in *Yank*.

Later in the afternoon some of us rode over the pass to Cave di Predil, our Regimental Headquarters, to see a USO show. The girls from home look good.

As I write my evening letter home I am drinking a bottle of champagne, Henriot, Reims, 1933. It is good stuff, more of the seventy (?) truck loads we captured from the Jerries. We have had two bottles apiece so far. Also I have a bottle of cognac. Jimmy Durkin doesn't like it, so he gave it to me.

4 JUNE 1945

Our S-2 Section took a trip today, road reconnaissance we called it, north into Austria and visited Villach and Spittal. This section of Austria is under British occupation and some of the fellows bought pistols from the British troops. The mountains are not as rugged in this part of Austria as they are back at Bretto, but they have much more timber. The trees run very small in our area, Bretto, southeast of Tarvisio.

The sight that interested the boys the most was at a swimming pool, women in two piece suits. They were cut much closer than they are at home. Some British soldiers told about seeing Russian army women take off their clothes and swim in the nude, not being at all concerned about the presence of men. Immediately we asked how to get there. It didn't work out.

When we got back to our camp at Bretto di Sotto about 4 P.M. I was told that my name had been put in for a seven day pass to Rome and that I would fly there. That certainly would have been a good deal. Later I found out the plans were changed and we will go by truck which takes two days each way so I will only have three days in Rome. But that is still something.

My getting this trip to Rome was just a lucky break. I do not at all deserve it since I had the pass to Florence and some of the men have not had any passes at all yet. Battalion called up the companies in the middle of the afternoon saying they had to have the names of three men by 4 P.M. to go to Rome. That didn't give much time for checking and our first sergeant was gone so the company clerk submitted the names of men he thought deserved it, the ones who went through all the Po Valley Campaign. I did not feel that I was in any particularly select group.

It was perhaps just my luck that I was on the trip to Austria at the time. I am afraid this will be my last pass in this Theater.

5 JUNE 1945

Today was the first leg of an over 500-mile trip to Rome in Army two-and-a-halfs (2 & 1/2 ton trucks). We went through Udine, Ferrara, Bologna, and on via Highway 65 to Florence where we spent the night at the Fifth Army Rest Center in the railway station.

Coming into Florence from the north reminds me of the approach to Portland via Barbur Blvd. Florence has more trees and parks that most cities and it is a pretty sight to come upon it from the hills just at sunset. We had a late dinner with no time to see much of the city.

6 JUNE 1945

Today we went on to Rome via Siena. On one stretch south of Siena for about thirty miles we traveled through an area, almost a desert, that looked like parts of Eastern Oregon. The countryside was eroded and thinly populated. We arrived in Rome about 4 P.M..

We are staying at the Army Rest Center in Mussolini's former athletic center on the north bank of the Tiber River. It is a swanky place with numerous marble statues on the grounds. What got me is the statue of a nude skier. Also in one of the buildings is a big bronze head of Mussolini sticking out of a tiger's mouth. This artistic atrocity is about six feet high.

In the evening Sgt. Nick Peretti and I saw a movie and then went to the Summer Festival, where D'Artega and his All-Girl orchestra was playing. According to the program there was dancing with "beautiful Roman girls," but the REBs had them all sewed up. I wrote to Evelyn that in case she doesn't know that stands for rear echelon bastard.

We are particularly bitter tonight because we learned that there is no clothing exchange here in Rome and we have to wear our dusty wool uniforms. I notice that the REBs learn to speak Italian faster then the fighting men. They get a better opportunity to practice on civilians.

7 JUNE 1945

I had quite a day with morning and afternoon tours to the Forum, the Coliseum, the Catacombs, the Basilica of St. Paul, Hadrian's Tomb, and other places I can't think of at the moment. We also expected to take the Vatican tour, but Nick and I were about two minutes late for the bus. We will go another time.

8 JUNE 1945

I wrote a letter home sitting at a comfortable table in the Rest Center. Some time ago Evelyn mentioned yellow jaundice and asked whether we had shots for it. The correct name for the disease the fellows got is Hepatitis, which means inflammation of the liver. Jaundice is just a symptom of it. The doctors know practically nothing about the disease. The best cure they have is bed rest and a high protein diet. They don't know what causes it and how it is transmitted.

C Company had over eighty cases and for the first time the doctors got on track of something. They found that all the men who got it had been drinking water from a particular well on our front line near Sasso Baldino. They sent samples of the water back to the U.S. for analysis, and they got volunteers from a hospital to drink the water to see if they would get the disease. I never heard how many came down with it. Some research medics cleaned out the well and found lots of trash in it including dead and decaying rats. The water tasted perfectly all right. I know because I drank it for nearly two weeks when I was up there.

Our Halizone tablets, used for water purification, had no effect apparently in preventing the disease. A certain number of men like myself are probably naturally immune to the disease. Anyway the investigation continues. The Army is particularly interested because the cure requires up to two months in the hospital. I haven't heard of any deaths yet, but I guess there were some. Men who got hold of liquor early after getting Hepatitis have been sent home with permanently impaired livers. All this information is from other G.I.s in the Battalion.

Tonight at 5:30 Nick and I are going to the Royal Opera House to hear *IL Trovatore*. We are paying 310 lira per seat. At official exchange that is $3.10.

9 JUNE 1945

This was a busy day for me with no time to write home. I visited the Capitaline Museum, an exhibit of Italian art at the Palazzo Venezia, the Pantheon, and the Borghese Gallery. It was an all day trip taken on my own. I saw a lot of great art, too much to remember I am afraid. In the evening I went to a ballet at the Royal Opera House with Al Hilowitz and Nick Peretti. What energy we had in those days!

10 JUNE 1945

In the afternoon I took a bus with Al Hilowitz to Lido di Roma for a swim in the Mediterranean. The water was warm and the sky was blue. It was a perfect day for my first swim in that sea.

One thing I don't like here is the commercialization of everything. The sightseer is always being pestered by men offering their services as guides. Personally I don't like going through a museum with a guide. If he knows only Italian all he can do is point out features that are obvious anyway. He sets the pace and hurries you through so he can get to the next customer. I had one for about five minutes but got rid of him and went back over it all at my own pace. If a picture interests me I stop and look at it for some time, otherwise, I give it a glance and pass on. I want to see all of Rome in my week here.

We soldiers are always being pestered on the streets by hawkers, men and boys wanting to buy cigarettes or candy, shoe shine boys, pimps who offer "room with signorina" or in G.I. slang "shack job." Then there are dirty ragged children who run up and hold out a piece of cardboard with a message in English something like this:

"Daddy was killed in the war. We are starving. Go to (address). Mama will give you what you want, soldier." Some of them are just plain begging notes. There are many variations on this theme.

Thousands of streetwalkers are out after business at all hours, but particularly in the evening you see them in every block arguing with soldiers over the price of their services.

Before the ballet yesterday we went into a bar across the street from the Opera House. Five or six girls were in the bar pursuing their trade. Most of the soldiers were English and the girls were working them. One soldier said that they wanted 1,300 lira for an hour and 3,000 lira for all night. This was early in the evening, about five o'clock, so the price was high. The price goes down during the course of the evening as the better looking girls make their hauls and the less desirable ones see their chances slipping away. It is a vivid illustration of a fundamental law of economics.

Undoubtedly it is the war that makes the situation so bad here in Rome. Many of the girls have lost their families and friends and have no other way to make a living. In addition to local girls and girls from the provinces many have come from France and some from Spain.

I saw an estimate of the present population of Germany being 36 million women and 24 million men. There will be many lonely women in Germany. I suppose that some of them would ordinarily drift into prostitution, but when the soldiers leave there will be relatively few men in the age brackets that support prostitution. Besides there will probably be so many amateurs in the game that there will be no price for the professionals. Lack of opportunity for marriage will reduce the sex standards of women.

It is a problem caused by war and I can see no solution for the present generation. The solution for the future is to see that there are no more wars, but admittedly chances for this are remote.

I feel sorry in many ways for the girls in the profession. They all have such a lonely look about them. They may get sexual satisfaction and temporary companionship out of it, but I suspect that they are in the business in order to eat. Most of them are out for what they can get in the way of money and food, and stealing is as good a way as any.

It seems to me that a large percentage of the unmarried soldiers patronize the girls and a considerable percentage, 25 to 50%, of the married men patronize them occasionally. In the infantry opportunities for such activities are not nearly as great as they are for the guys in rear areas.

11 JUNE 1945

This afternoon I went on the Vatican Tour. We saw the museums, the Sistine Chapel and St. Peters. The museums had some wonderful pieces of sculpture such as the Laocoon Group, Apollo Belvedere, and the Torso of Hercules. I was impressed with some beautiful modern paintings the best I have seen anywhere. The Chapel has its walls and ceiling completely covered with Michelangelo paintings. The human figures are wonderful; they look almost real. St. Peters for me was just another church, larger than others and more elaborately decorated. Its proportions are good so it does not look especially large to the viewer.

When I was in the Pantheon I felt that I was in an immense building, but it is just the size in diameter of the dome of St. Peters of which the dome is just a small part. As I walked out on the portico of St. Peter's and looked out over the great oval, I wondered why it was called a square.

It was just six months ago yesterday that I left Hampton Roads on the SS *Argentina* with 5,000 men including all of the 86th Mountain Infantry. I really think we have a good chance of getting home for a furlough before going on to fight in the Pacific. Some of the men talk about going through the Suez Canal and around that way, but we shudder at the thought.

Early in the evening I went with Nick Peretti down to the Forum and the Capitaline Hill. We poked our noses into all sorts of old Roman ruins and I told him about old Rome. We two were the only people in the entire Roman Forum. I was able to read a couple of Latin inscriptions for him. He said I was better than any of the Italian guides he had.

It is too bad that the Church in the Middle Ages destroyed so much of old Rome. They took the marble from practically all the old public buildings. All the marble facing was stripped from the Coliseum, and they used the structure as a stone quarry for several centuries. Two thirds of the material for St. Peters came from ancient Roman buildings. Only in the 19th Century did the Church change its ideas and begin preserving what was left of the ancient monuments.

We went to the opera again tonight to hear *Carmen*. It was great and the most elaborate production of opera I have ever seen. All the staging and scenery has been far superior to anything I have seen before. They must have many skilled artists to paint such back drops and sets.

12 JUNE 1945

We did more resting and less sightseeing today, our last day in Rome. We are sorry to leave this historical city.

13 JUNE 1945

Our trucks drove up from Rome via the coastal route to Livorno and then inland up the Arno Valley to Florence, where we are spending the night at the Rest Center.

I saw something new today, men and women threshing grain on a brick floor with flails. I did not know that it was still done that way in Italy. Also I have seen people cutting grain with hand sickles and tying it into sheaves by hand. The more progressive farmers use a team of oxen to pull a binder. I saw as many women as men working in the fields.

I got weighed today, 70.5 kilograms.

14 JUNE 1945

We got back to Bretto di Sotto this evening after a long, hard ride. There have been a few changes since I left. Sergeant Newman, our First Sergeant, had 106 points. He left the company with the expectation of flying home. Other high point men are expected to follow.

15 JUNE 1945

This morning Lieutenant Craig, our Battalion S-2, left for home. We seem to be getting personnel changes every day. With our losing so many key people I can see that we will need more training for the Pacific.

In the afternoon four of us from the S-2 Section were sent up to Bausizza in a little hanging valley to the southeast of Bretto. There is no road into this valley. On a narrow, steep mountain trail we encountered two peddlers who were packing in pots and pans and other hardware. They trade their stock for goat cheese, which they also have to pack out on their backs. We agreed that this was making a living the hard way.

About four days ago a woman was murdered here and yesterday one of our engineers calling on a girl-friend was shot at. He has quit calling. We are being sent up there to 'investigate' and give some protection from rumored German SS troops and Chetniks in the area. These are good mountains to hide out in.

We were welcomed into the valley with open arms. By way of celebration they killed a kid, and for supper in the evening we had delicious roast kid.

We took turns standing armed guard during the night.

16 JUNE 1945

The night was very quiet and nothing happened. About ten families live here on a strictly pastoral economy. The woman we stayed with is very proud of her stove which was carried into the valley by four men.

In the afternoon we had to say our reluctant farewells and leave these kind people to their unknown dangers. We were called back to Bretto because this valley is on the Yugoslav side of the Morgan line agreed upon at Trieste.

17 JUNE 1945

Our camp routine goes on in just the same old way. We have not had as much rain this week as in the first three weeks here.

We have a new man in the S-2 Section, Werner Von Trapp. It sounds like he pronounces it Verner and the "a" in Trapp is an Italian "a." He transferred from our 3rd Battalion to be near his older brother Rupert, who is in our Battalion Medics. The Von Trapps went to the U.S. shortly after Hitler came to power in Austria. Last week they went to Salzburg to find out what condition their old family home was in. I guess it is quite an estate and they found out that Himmler had taken it over for his own residence and had completely redecorated it. When they got there they found an AMG (American Military Government) sign on the gate that read "Keep Out. Property of Rupert Von Trapp." In retelling the story Rupert said that the AMG

Colonel in Salzburg was most surprised when he went up and announced that he was Rupert Von Trapp.

Perhaps it was Rupert's American uniform and sergeant's stripes that surprised him most. The property was in good condition. It shows that AMG was on the ball. I don't know how they discovered that it was the Von Trapp property.

Another afternoon shower has started. Such is life. If it stops we will have an outdoor movie tonight.

18 JUNE 1945

I went to the Medics to see about my knee and Doc Miller is sending me back to a hospital for a check-up. We had a long wait for the ambulance at the collecting company (I believe it was B). I wondered if it was like this in combat.

19 JUNE 1945

I am at the 56th Evacuation Hospital to have my knee looked at. They took X-rays this morning. All the doctor said was that I had a loose knee. He felt sure the X-rays would show nothing very wrong with it.

The hospital is located in tents out on the hot plains near Udine. I envy the patients going around in cool pajamas, but I am still wearing my wool ODs.

Life here is not too bad because there are plenty of books in the Red Cross tent and movies in the evening. I have been reading Brogan's *The American Character* and find it interesting. It is a book attempting to explain us to the British, but it is also good reading for Americans.

In my ward is a British soldier who was seriously injured by a German mine, so the war is not over for everybody. Last week a British engineer about five miles south of our bivouac area at Bretto di Sotto was killed by a booby trap on a ladder leading to a German fortified position. You can be sure we don't do too much "monkeying around" in places that the Germans have occupied. The residuals of war are still close at hand.

20 JUNE 1945

Hospital life is soft. Nothing to do but lie around and read all day and go to the movie in the evening.

21 JUNE 1945

I saw the doctor this morning and he said the X-rays showed a slight arthritic roughening of the bone that was probably caused by my knee injuries. He said that he would send me to a reclassification board if I wanted to go, but he was doubtful they would reclassify me and they certainly would not send me back to the U.S. for it. The continued use of my knee will not do it any harm. He thought it was best for me to go back to my outfit and get along with it as best as I could. He did not give me any hope of my knee getting better, but he did not think it would get worse. Actually it is weaker and bothers me more now than it did last summer. Anyway I can ask for reclassification at any time.

I talked to a 91st Division man who claimed that the 10th is slated to stay in Italy until December. I will be going back to our outfit tomorrow. I figured if I was reclassified I would probably be sent to AMG and would be over here in Europe for another year. Here the nurses, who are mostly southern gals, refer to men from the 10th as "mountain boys."

22 JUNE 1945

I came back to our outfit today. It is cloudy and much cooler up here in the mountains. Ralph Brooker said I was a fool to come back. Maybe so, but I did not want to ask for reclassification without knowing more about it and what I could get out of it. Major Small seemed to think it might be best to wait until I get back to the States and then ask for reclassification. He said if I get reclassified over here I might have to stay longer than if I remained with the outfit.

23 JUNE 1945

Early to bed. Tomorrow we are going to Austria in the S-2 Jeep for sightseeing and to see our Division ski meet on Grossglockner. We start at 4:00 A.M.

24 JUNE 1945

On the trip up into Austria we saw some fine mountain scenery and traveled about one hundred thirty miles from Bretto. Our mountain destination is Grossglockner. It is the highest mountain in Austria and it has an enormous glacier on the east side running down into the valley. I took some pictures from the vicinity of the Franz Josef Haus, but it was cloudy over the mountain. The snow depth was adequate for the ski meet but I did not waste time watching it. Lieutenant Lewis, Sergeant Watzek and I went for a climb to see more of this beautiful mountain area.

This region is the eastern end of the Austrian Tyrol and is located about half way between Villach and Innsbruck. We are at an elevation of 2,300 meters, well above timberline and up where there is plenty of snow on the north and west slopes. It is really majestic mountain scenery.

I picked two blossoms of Edelweiss, a rare alpine flower that is the symbol of the German mountain troops. This was on our climb well up above the Franz Joseph Haus. We rode back to Bretto after a long day.

25 JUNE 1945

I took a short climb up the valley wall back of our bivouac area today. It is nice up here in the mountains even though it is raining some nearly every afternoon. I had no trouble with my knee.

26 JUNE 1945

Another routine day in camp. Tomorrow is my turn for a day in Trieste. We always look forward to these trips as they break up the monotony of camp routine. Fortunately it is not nearly as far as Venice.

27 JUNE 1945

Today I had my truck ride into Trieste. I had a good time but did not see much of the city. It was a rainy day and five of us from the S-2 Section went down to the waterfront. Two British cruisers were anchored out in the harbor. We asked a coxswain of a boat if we could come aboard. He said to hop in and he took us out to the light cruiser, Ajax. You will perhaps remember that this was one of the three British ships that fought the German pocket battleship *Graf Spee* off Argentina. We were shown through a main turret and the bridge and had tea at four o'clock with the sailors. We liked the men and had a good time. We had tea with milk in it and bread with lobster piest as they pronounced paste.

Trieste seemed quiet but it is full of New Zealand troops as their division is holding the south half of the Morgan Line including Trieste.

The rumor has it that we are now classified as occupation troops. I do not know what there is to it, but it surely means that we are not to be the first troops sent home from Italy. On the other hand it may simply mean that things have settled down here along this border and the Theater Command has decided that we can be on a lower state of military alert.

28 JUNE 1945

Many of our men are acquiring pistols these days. Some of them are making special trips to Austria to get them. Most are purchased for cigarettes from British and Yugoslav troops.

29 JUNE 1945

I went out in a party from our Battalion CP today to try to find an area for a rifle range, but we didn't have much luck. The valley is too narrow and too dangerous for the civilians to shoot up or down it.

30 JUNE 1945

I was paid $96.10 today and put $75.00 into Soldier's Deposits. There is not much here in Italy that is worth spending money on at our exchange rates.

The paison line is an institution that is typical of every mess that we have had in Italy. At every meal the people from far and wide come with pans and buckets. First they collect the leftovers from the soldiers, coffee and everything. Then they line up and the cooks hand out to them all the food that is left over from the meal. I would guess that the leftovers from a company kitchen provide enough food for thirty or forty people. Those who come are of both sexes and all ages from three to seventy. Children generally manage to get the most.

The Priest here in Bretto says that since our Battalion moved into this valley the people are living better, at least eating better, than they ever have before. While they are Slovenians, they do not want to see Tito's men come in here and us leave. Their troops would live off the land. The Germans took most of their livestock and the people would be close to starvation if it were not for the U.S. Army and its abundance that is a never-ending source of amazement to the people here.

1 JULY 1945

A newspaper story appeared stating that we are slated for occupation duties. If true, it means that we will be over here for a long time. We have been talking it over among ourselves. To me the most logical explanation is that we are again being put in strategic reserve. The Army

did not commit us to combat here in Italy until the
end of the war was in sight. The same may hold true for
the Pacific.

Since we are a specialized division, the Army will
commit us under two conditions: (1) circumstances arise
in combat where there is a pressing need for our specialty,
or (2) the war has progressed so far that the Army can
clearly see that our specialty will not be needed. This is
pure speculation on my part. Some people would probably classify this as wishful thinking, because the last thing
we want to do is go fight another war in the Pacific.

2 JULY 1945

Today we had a hard, cold rain. The weather was
really raw and it felt cold enough to snow.

3 JULY 1945

This morning started out clear, but the clouds are
forming again. The top of Mt. Mangart is white and the
other peaks around us also have new snow on their upper
slopes.

More rain is falling this afternoon. This is the wettest
summer climate that I have seen. It is so wet that the farmers cannot dry hay on the ground but have to put it up on
and around spiked poles in order to dry it. This is also
done in Austria.

I have started reading Beard's *Republic*. So far away
from home I find it an especially interesting book.

4 JULY 1945

What a day! I had it tough beginning at 6:00 P.M. I
was Sergeant of the Guard beginning at that time and a
Battalion party was held in the evening. For refreshment
we had a 150-gallon hogshead full of a combination of
vermouth and cognac. It tasted good and was very potent
stuff. As I was on duty the one taste was all I got. We had

many drunks and for some hours we were worried about maintaining order.

At the height of the rowdiness we called out a double shift of guards to patrol the party but nothing serious developed. We had a few fights and scores of drunks to get back to their bivouac areas but that was about all, no rapes or murders. In fact we had only one man in the guard house, and we ran him in for picking a fight with an officer. No charges were made and we turned him loose in the morning. After all it was a big celebration. I did not get to sleep until after 2:00 A.M.

5 JULY 1945

I was glad to be relieved of guard duty this afternoon and I am looking forward to hitting the sack early tonight.

6 JULY 1945

I took it easy today and all I did was prepare an orientation lecture on the Pacific campaign. We get some good display maps of the Pacific War and keep up fairly well with what is happening there by reading the *Stars and Stripes*, *Newsweek* and *Time*. Both news magazines now have editions printed in Europe. We would just as soon leave the fighting in the Pacific to others.

7 JULY 1945

This morning I gave the company an orientation lecture. I G-2ed the Pacific campaign, pointing out the significance of the conquests of Okinawa, the Philippines, and the invasion of Borneo. The generals, correspondents and everyone seem to be optimistic about the situation there. Japan is helpless and it is doubtful if she can mount more that a local attack anywhere.

This evening I had two drinks of vodka mixed with grapefruit juice. It makes a good drink at least good by our low standards. Straight it is about like grappa, which looks like and probably is almost straight alcohol.

8 JULY 1945

Today I received a package from home with a can of fudge and three cans of seafood.

9 JULY 1945

We made a climb up the east wall of the canyon. It was raining most of the time so we weren't too enthusiastic.

10 JULY 1945

I gave Sergeant Brown $24 for a pistol. It is a Smith & Wesson .38-cal. revolver with a six inch barrel. With the canvas holster I guess that it was a British army issue. It is an excellent hand gun with a velvety trigger squeeze.

11 JULY 1945

The latest rumor is that we are scheduled to leave in November. The information is supposed to be based upon a Paris edition of the *Stars and Stripes* which listed all the divisions in Europe and when they would sail for home. I do not know why that paper would have this information and not the Mediterranean edition. I personally feel that if we do not leave until then, we may well miss out on the Pacific war. Oh, how nice to be home on furlough for Christmas! A guy can dream, can't he?

12 JULY 1945

We are getting a Unit School under way and it is supposed to start tomorrow. I have decided to attend a class in sketching.

13 JULY 1945

Our Unit School is gradually getting under way. This afternoon I attended the class in sketching. The instructor said that he was going to teach graphic draftsmanship. We started out drawing boxes, cans, tables, etc. trying to get the proper perspective. I think we made some progress. This class will be for three hours four times a week.

This evening we heard that unit censorship started again. Something's up. Could it be a trip home? My one day sketching class now reminds me of my two or three day class in the Japanese language just before we left Camp Swift naturally for Italy.

X
HOMEWARD BOUND
14 JULY TO 26 JULY

14 JULY 1945

We spent the day getting ready to leave, packing, tearing down shelters, filling in latrines, and many other jobs needed to leave our area in a half way decent condition. It's too bad after only one day in our new school, but such is Army life. Much speculation about where we are going makes its rounds. We are to leave early tomorrow morning.

15 JULY 1945

The men of the 1st Battalion of the 86th Mountain Infantry give Mt. Mangart a last look as it has become our pin-up mountain for these many weeks that we have been stationed on this troubled border. We climb into trucks with our duffel bags and are off down the valley and out of the mountains into the plain of Udine.

At Udine we board a freight train and head west. The rumor is that we are going home. I think I would rather ride in a freight car, a bumpy, rickety Belgium car, than ride in a truck. At least we can move around more in the freight car. We spend the night on the train.

16 JULY 1945

This morning we are rolling south through the Po Valley. We cross the River on the only railroad bridge yet in operation on the entire length of the River. An hour or two later we arrive at Bologna and spend an hour in the railroad yards before going on. We see much damage from bombing in the vicinity of the yards.

We are bound for Florence. The trip south from Bologna is through Second Corps territory where intense fighting took place all through the winter. The country-side certainly shows it. This section seems much dryer than the mountains we fought in and was not as highly developed. We have an American diesel locomotive to pull us through the tunnel which I have heard is fourteen miles long. I don't know if that is right or not, but it took us fifty minutes to get through. It is down hill on the other side into Florence and we arrive about six o'clock. We have a hike of about a mile through the city to our quarters. This is it! The Florence Redeployment Center, and it is within short walking distance of the center of town. We have large tents, cots and a mess hall.

17 JULY 1945

I got a pass into Florence tonight. I wandered around and took five pictures, two of the great facade of Santa Croce which I much admired. I went to the leather shop nearby for a picture frame, but the shop was closed for the evening. I wanted it for mounting the two Edelweiss flowers I had picked near Grosglockner. This I thought would be a nice souvenir to take home for Evelyn. I went on to the Ponte Vecchio to shop there, but I could not find anything that appealed to me. Silver is very scarce. All the shops have a lot of junk jewelry made out of antimony.

I sold my old Elgin watch, which no longer ran, in a watchmaker's shop for $25. Not bad, considering the $10 I paid for it many years ago.

By eight o'clock my feet were getting tired so I went to a movie, *Something for the Boys*. It was not very good.

After I got back to the Center I was told that we will only be here in Florence for one more week.

18 JULY 1945

I got stuck with guard duty tonight.

19 JULY 1945

Guard duty kept me busy because the orders and posts were changed three times. I will be glad when this day is over.

The time is passing ever so slowly now that coming home seems so near. Every day seems like what used to be a week. Already I feel that I have been in Florence for weeks.

20 JULY 1945

I mailed a package home containing some maps I had accumulated since the end of the war. I was worried about getting it through censorship, but I got it mailed without a hitch.

In the evening I went into town and heard a musical called *The London Revue.* It was straight from London for the entertainment of British troops. There are as many of them here as Americans. I missed some of the English jokes. The dances and songs were good and I enjoyed it. In some ways it was like high-class American vaudeville.

21 JULY 1945

I spent this afternoon with Dean Haley, my old friend from college and Social Security Board days, who has been over here for a year longer than my stint in Italy. He has 87 points and is on his way home for a discharge. We saw the movie *A Tree Grows in Brooklyn* and enjoyed it. We stopped in at the leather shop and I bought a picture frame. I think I got a good one, but they have sold practically all their fine leather goods and now most of their stock consists of cheaper items obviously made for the soldier trade.

22 JULY 1945

This afternoon I went with Dean Haley to an exhibit of French art in the Pitti Palace. It had paintings from the 17th Century down to the Impressionists.

23 JULY 1945

Today I was told that I have been awarded the Bronze Star for meritorious service in the Po Valley Campaign. Any points I get are welcomed. This gives me 51 by my count.

This afternoon I went to an exhibition of modern Italian art. I saw some excellent pieces and if I had a hundred dollars I might have bought something. The teenage girl who showed Ed Fancher and me around was very excited because her older brother had come home this morning. He had been a prisoner of the Nazis and had been gone for over three years. She said he is six feet tall and weighed only 48 kilograms when the Americans came to his prison camp. Her name is Anna Marconi and she is not related to the radio Marconi. She said her brother had a long black beard, and when he took a bath the water was simply black. She is interested in studying Latin, Greek and Sanskrit. She added considerably to our enjoyment of the exhibit. You can see she speaks English very well. I preferred this to the exhibit I saw yesterday.

24 JULY 1945

We are doing what Bill Mauldin calls "Sweatin' it out." It is very hot today and time passes slowly, especially on a day like this without much to do.

25 JULY 1945

Today I wrote home my last letter from Italy. I do not know for sure when we are sailing but all indications are that it will be soon. We have been turning in supplies, packing, having inspections and handling all the other little details that seem to be preparatory for departure.

26 JULY 1945

This is the day we have been waiting for. We board a train for Livorno with the same old box cars. We ride west through the beautiful Italian countryside of the Arno valley. We are happy because we are going home, but it is only for a 30-day furlough, then more training and on to the Pacific war still raging around Okinawa. Our spirits are happy but our minds caution us that we would be much better off if we could remain here in Italy until the Pacific war is over. We pass through Pisa and go on to the port at Livorno. The trip has taken about four hours.

We see our ship, the *Westbrook Victory* tied up to the dock. We line up outside our boxcars and march with our heavy duffel bags out to the ship, lining up in single file before the gang plank. We file aboard. As I came up to it, the pretty WAC calling off the names, sings out with "Dusenbery." I answer with "Harris," and thus depart from Italian soil. It takes several hours to load the ship. The *Westbrook Victory* gets under way in mid-afternoon, steers an irregular course through the wrecks in the harbor and through the narrow gap in the row of ships that the Germans sank to close the harbor. We enter the Mediterranean Sea.

In the late afternoon I secure a seat on a capstan at the fantail and watch Italy slowly sink down below the horizon. I resolve that I will come back to Italy some day. Tomorrow I'll find a place up in the bow eagerly awaiting my arrival home. The days are too long when all one can do is wait.

PART II
THE RIVA RIDGE OPERATION

INTRODUCTION

The Riva Ridge Operation was the first offensive action of the 10th Mountain Division. In one sense it was a side show being merely preliminary to the main action which was to take Mt. Belvedere, Mt. Gorgelesco, and Mt. Della Torraccia. Riva Ridge being first is only a minor reason for it being famous in the lore of the 10th Mountain Division. The main reason was that it was a spectacular and precipitous mountain ridge that required the use of mountaineering skills.

The *Report on the Mancinello-Campiano Ridge Operation of The 1st Battalion, 86th Mountain Infantry* dated 12 June 1945 is the most complete and accurate account that I have seen. It was signed by Lt. Col. Henry J. Hampton and I am sure written by him. He was the Battalion Commander for the operation and was most intimately involved in the planning and execution of it.

The history of the name Riva Ridge is interesting. When we Americans arrived upon the scene, the Italians had no particular name for the whole ridge. They had names for summits along it like Spigolino, Mancinello, Serrasiccia, Cappel Buso, and Pizzo di Campiano. In planning for the operation the section of the Ridge that was of most interest extended from Mt. Mancianello to Pizzo di Campiano so that became a working designation. Later someone noticed an insignificant peak just north of

Mancinello shown on the maps as M. Riva; ah, ha, a name we ignorant Americans could pronounce. Even before our action to take it we were calling it all Riva Ridge.

This report is well-typed and has few typing errors. In order to retain the military flavor of the report I have included it almost as written. The few minor changes that I have made are italicized and a few explanatory comments are also italicized.

On June 29, 1979 William W. Boddington mailed me a photocopy of this report along with some other materials. Bill was a great friend and highly respected member of the National Association of the 10th Mountain Division. He maintained a life long interest in the 10th Mountain Division Foundation and in all aspects of the Association. He died in 1996. We all miss him.

I served all my military career in the 1st Battalion, 86th Mountain Infantry from Recruit School and C Company at Camp Hale to Headquarters Company at Camp Swift and in Italy. All during my military experience with Lieutenant Colonel Hampton I felt I was serving under an exceptional commander. Unfortunately he was seriously wounded by a mortar round in the fight for Sassomolare on March 4th. He was evacuated not to be seen again by the 1st Battalion. Later he returned as 86th Regimental Executive Officer.

Lieutenant Colonel Hampton's report on what generally came to be called the Riva Ridge Operation must have been written after the Division moved to the Yugoslav border. Regimental Headquarters was established at Cave del Pradil and was there on the date of the document, June 12, 1945.

From then on it was all down hill for the 10th and within a few months the Division was deactivated and most of its men discharged. Lieutenant Colonel Hampton remained with the Army to see duty in Korea and there to find death in the valiant service of his country.

On May 2, 1945 upon the German surrender in Italy, Headquarters of the 1st Battalion, 86th Mountain Infantry was in the village of Nago on the heights a few miles northeast of Lake Garda. After a few days the Battalion was moved to San Alessandra a short distance north of Lake Garda. Our Headquarters Company was located in a grand villa. We were still carrying several hundred pounds of maps, aerial photos and records and all were declared surplus. One morning I was assigned the task of burning them.

We had hauled them down out of the mountains and across the Po Valley. We had rescued them from our Jeep trailer destroyed in an ambush south of the Po River. We brought them through the fighting up the east shore of Lake Garda. Now that the War was over they had suddenly become so much useless *impedimenta.*

I had our Jeep trailer backed up into an open area behind the villa so the material would be handy. I started a fire with some of the maps and spent the whole morning feeding into it hundreds of maps and Signal Corps ground and aerial photographs. I looked at many of them before confining them to the flames and some I just did not have the heart to burn. I set aside several dozen photos and maps with the intent of taking them home and saving for posterity, which I was able to do.

Many years later I donated these maps and photographs to the 10th Mountain Division Resource Center of the Denver Public Library where Barbara Walton is doing an excellent job of preserving the records and making them available for research on history of the Division.

In the afternoon I learned that our Battalion Journal was going to be turned in to Regiment and from there who knew into what entrails of the Army. I seized the opportunity to copy in a small notebook the entries covering the actual Riva Ridge Operation from the time we established the CP at Farne on February 18, 1945 to the time our relief was completed on February 22nd. I have included them in Part II of this book. I knew them well. I had been in the Battalion CP at Farne during the Riva Ridge action, much of the time keeping this message log.

The 1st Battalion Journal is essentially a log of telephone and radio messages received and sent at Battalion Headquarters. I am sure I copied every entry and the text itself with so many minor entries speaks for a complete copy. The reader may see gaps that he wished had been filled. I believe them to be messages failed to be received or recorded at the time.

I have included a picture of Riva Ridge, a definition of terms used in the log and an outline map that gives the location of the villages and the mountains, showing spatial relations drawn on a grid of kilometer squares. Of course it does not show contours and how precipitous Riva Ridge is on the east side. The elevations are shown in meters. Lieutenant Colonel Hampton's report gives an excellent description of the terrain.

Riva Ridge from near Vidiciatico   2-21-45   sc 282200

This picture shows Riva Ridge three days after the 1st Battalion captured it and on their last day on the Ridge. From the terrain shown I believe the picture was taken from the vicinity of Plinardo. Most of Mt. Serrasiccia appears on the right side of the picture with the summit just off the upper corner. Mt. Mancinello is in the center and Le Piagge is on the left side. The Jeep is probably the Signal Corps photograher's vehicle. It looks strange to me because it has a top. All the time I was driving a Jeep at the front, the top was stored someplace back at the Motor Pool and the windshield was folded down and covered. This picture shows the snow conditions at the time and how rugged a military objective Riva Ridge was.

This wartime Signal Corps photograph was supplied to me by the 10th Mountain Division Resource Center, Western History Department, Denver Public Library.

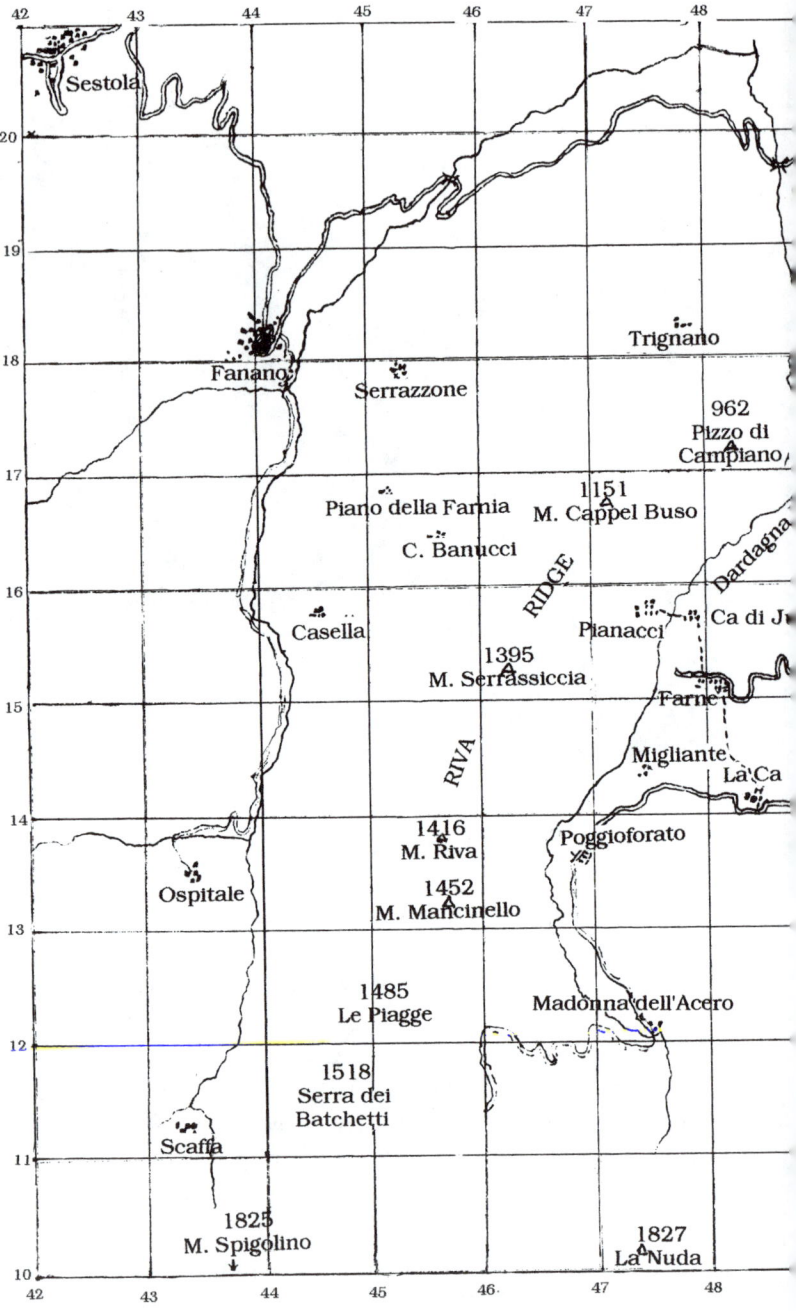

Map of the Riva Ridge–Mt. Belvedere Region

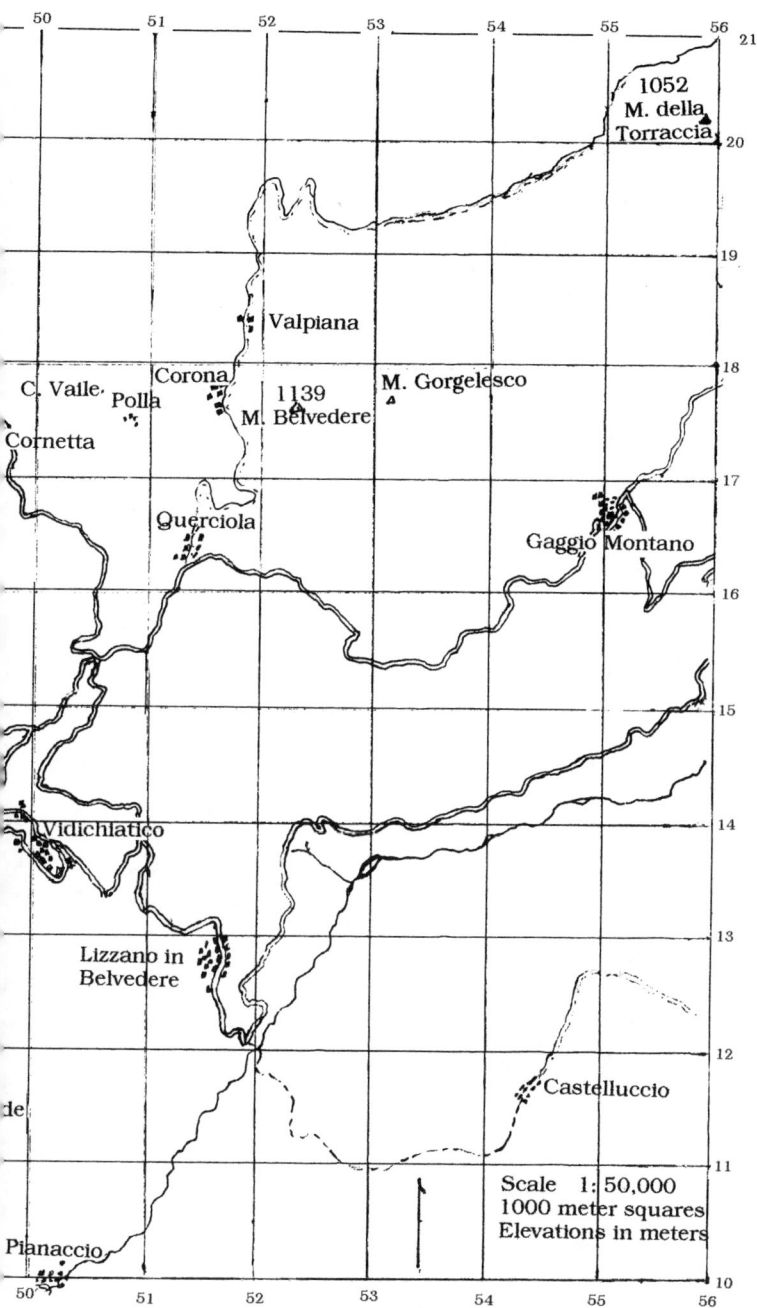

I drew this map in about 1950 based on my wartime
maps to go with a typewritten copy of my Italian Diary
and Battalion Journal of the Riva Ridge Operation. I
have replaced the original hand printed names with
computer printed names.

THE RIVA RIDGE OPERATION
REPORT OF LT. COL. HENRY J. HAMPTON

HEADQUARTERS
86TH MOUNTAIN INFANTRY
APO # 345, U. S. ARMY

12 June 1945

REPORT ON THE MANCINELLO–CAMPIANO RIDGE
OPERATION OF THE 1st BATTALION,
86th MOUNTAIN INFANTRY

The 86th Mountain Infantry Regiment was the first of the 10th Mountain Division to arrive in Italy. It debarked at Naples on 23 December 1944. On 25 December 1944 the 1st Battalion, with attached Service and Headquarter Companies, was moving north to Pisa by rail, with the remainder of the Regiment to follow by water in seven or eight days. Because of the Serchio Valley "scare" at this time, the remainder of the Regiment left for Leghorn by water on 26 December 1944. All units were concentrated in the Pisa Staging Area where motor transportation was issued and "show down" inspections held.

By 30 December 1944, the Serchio Valley had quieted down and the Regiment was moving to Quercianella, seven miles south of Leghorn for training and firing of weapons. On 6 January 1945, the 86th Mountain Infantry came under control of Task Force 45 and prepared to move into the line in the Apennines, relieving various "ack-ack" battalions. *The* 86th Mountain Infantry relieved the 900th AA Battalion in the Belvedere area on the night of 8th-9th January. At this time there was from four to five feet of snow on the ground in this location. The relief was made at night after an all day motor movement from Querc*i*anella to three miles east of Poretta Terme. The men were heavily laden with winter equipment, packs varying from 45 to 55 pounds. Four blankets had been issued to each man, as no sleeping bags were available. Two were made up in a roll and dropped at the detrucking point to be picked up later when transportation became available. "B" Company marched 18 miles this night over icy roads, as the trucks which brought them were not equipped with chains, so they detrucked at Poretta Terme. "A" Company, who had farthest to go, dropped their packs or they never would have made it. The relief was completed the morning of 9th of January, without incident, and before daylight.

The Battalion defended an area of 11,800 yards of very rugged and precipitous terrain, especially in the west, where there was in all sense of the term an open flank with some 25 miles of mountains between our left and the next unit on the left. On the right was the B.E.F. *(Brazilian Expeditionary Force)*. The "Krauts" held all the high ground, and one felt like he was in the bottom of a bowl with the enemy sitting on two-thirds of the rim looking down upon you. There was about as much concealment as a gold fish would have in a bowl. The Battalion CP was set up in the town of Vidiciatico.

Due to the lack of over-snow equipment not as much patrolling could be accomplished as was desired. Finally, upon the arrival of some skis and snowshoes,

3 to 5 patrols per day were sent out. This proved to be excellent training for the men being their first time in the line, and tended to make them combat wise in later offensive operations.

To the west of the town of Vidiciatico and running generally southwest was a very precipitous and rugged escarpment called the Mancinello–Campiano Ridge. This chain of summits rose from the very steep canyon of the Dardagna River to various heights. Rising abruptly from the fortified town of Rocca Corneta, it extended to M. Spigolino, a distance of about seven miles. The summits from north to south were Pizzo di Campiano (3175 ft.), M. Cappel Buso (3800 ft.), M. Serrasiccia (4600 ft.), M. Riva (4672 ft.), M Mancinello (4800 ft.), Cingio del Buro 4628 ft.), Le Piagge (4900 ft.), Serra dei Barchetti (4350 ft.), Cingio Sermidiano (5400 ft.), and M. Spigolino (6030 ft.). The elevation of the Dardagna canyon varied from 1600 feet at the north end to some 2500 feet at the south end.

There were no sharp breaks or passes. On the east side it is generally very steep, broken, with cliffs, steep ravines and shoulders. The west side is by comparison very mild, ranging from broken and steep through rolling to nearly a plateau west of M. Riva. The watershed on the east side is abrupt, characterized by fast flowing waterfalls. They empty into a stream which flows parallel to the base of the ridge, whose banks range from steep to a gorge. One of the important factors to be considered was the gradient of the east side of the escarpment which would have to be scaled to take this ridge held by the enemy. At the shortest place, the average gradient to M. Cappel Buso is about 40 degrees. (The average gradient of the Hornli ridge of the Hira Herborn is 45 degrees). The average gradient to M. Serrasiccia was 30 degrees. *(From my knowledge of the terrain I believe that the above gradients to Cappel Buso and Serrasiccia are reversed.)*

Of course the Kraut held all this high ground. At the time of the 1st Battalion's arrival no great activity was noted upon the ridge except for a few known OPs from which he directed artillery and mortar fire when he saw any daylight movement in or around the town of Vidiciatico. At first movement was restricted to a minimum. As the days went on traffic during the day was allowed to increase, so if and when an operation was started against Belvedere an increase in volume of movement would not unnecessarily alarm the Kraut. The amount of enemy mortar and artillery fire was surprisingly small.

In planning for the Belvedere operation it was decided that the Campiano–Mancinello Ridge (sometimes called Riva Ridge from M. Riva) would have to be taken prior to an attack against Belvedere because of the importance of its observation. Once this ridge was taken our own field artillery observers could direct artillery fire on the Kraut positions which ran along the line Rocca Corneta–Polla–Corona, Belvedere. If the ridge was not taken then the Kraut could direct artillery on the backs of our troops attacking Belvedere. After a reconnaissance by the Division Commander, Major General George P. Hays, the 86th Mountain Infantry was given the mission of taking the Campiano–Mancinella Ridge prior to any attack that would be launched against Belvedere, with the 1st Battalion, 86th Mountain Infantry making the main effort against the Pizzo di Campiano–M. Cappel Buso–M. Serrasiccia–M. Mancinello terrain features. The Mancinello–Campiano Ridge was considered the second most important terrain feature in the area, and M. Belvedere the most critical. This ridge provided excellent observation of the west portion of the area, especially on Belvedere itself. From here observation could be had in most of the area behind the Belvedere–Della Torraccia Ridge. If heavy resistance was met in the taking of this (*apparently referring to Riva*) ridge, it was considered advisable to delay the main attack until superior observation could be attained.

Prior to the arrival of the 1st Battalion, 86th Mountain Infantry, to the Belvedere area, no patrolling had been accomplished against the Mancinello–Campiano Ridge. On the 15th of January 1945, a patrol was sent to Campiano with the following mission: 1. Report, locate strength of enemy on Campiano. 2. Secure enemy prisoners. This patrol consisted of five expert mountaineers as the trail was covered with snow and ice, and in places was rugge*d* and very precipitous. This patrol was led by Sergeant Casperson of Company "B". Skis were used, but *before* the top was reached they were cached and the patrol free climbed up a cliff to the top. As they neared the top, a dog barked, and a Kraut came out of the trees, looked about, did not see the patrol crouched against the side of a rocky ledge, so then he returned. As Sergeant Casperson and his men continued forward up the ledge, the dog barked again. Three Krauts came out, one armed with a slung carbine, the other two unarmed. They moved over towards the ledge where they observed the patrol in column along the ledge. Sergeant Casperson and Sergeant Froelicker raised their Tommy guns and Casperson in English said, "Hands up." The Krauts were both surprised and dazed, whereupon the one with the carbine attempted to unsling the weapon. At the first movement both Casperson and Froelicker let go with a burst from their Tommy guns. The Krauts dropped, a machine gun opened fire, and the patrol rapidly retraced their footsteps down the ledge with bullets splattering all over the mountain. From then on, there was increased activity on the ridge. There was continual improving and digging of old and new positions. Result of this patrol was that we had one trail over which a small force of well-trained mountain men could advance. More trails were needed if the ridge was to be taken. This trail was designated #1. It took this patrol 4 ¹/₂ hours from Ca di Julio to reach the point where they met the Krauts. This point was just short of the top of Pizzo di Campiano. Men were without packs and carried only rifles and ammunition. Trail was impossible for mules. Width of trail varied from one to two feet, and fixed ropes would be needed on the last pitch to the top for men. A bridge crossed the Dardagna near Ca di Julio, was of stone and five feet wide. It was felt a platoon of men physically conditioned and trained in the mountains could climb this trail and take the summit of Pizzo di Campiano.

Trails were difficult to find because of the snow conditions. As the snow began to settle and with aid of partisans, a trail was pointed out which went from Farne–Pianacci–Ca di Julio up to M. Cappel Buso. This trail, we were told, could be used by mules when the snow melted. Lt. George R. Schiemier was sent out at night to locate and reconnoiter the trail. A patrol of eight men went out on skis. The trail was found, and the patrol went just short of the top of Cappel Buso, where a Kraut patrol was heard approaching, so *our* patrol returned. The trail was good, but impassable to mules because of the snow. This trail was designated #2. Without packs it would take 3 ¹/₂ to 4 hours hard work to reach the summit of M. Cappel Buso from Ca di Julio. If packed well or snow melted, mules could use it, and even pass in two directions. This trail was considered good and two days of man use would pack the snow sufficiently to permit the passage of mules. Ordinary troops could pass over it either day or night. No fixed ropes at any point would be needed. Main drawback is that the trail is completely exposed to hostile small arms fire for its entire length from the right, left and front. Possibility of advancing in a broad front was not feasible.

All men and officers hoped that the snow would melt before we had to take the ridge as it would facilitate the movement a great deal. On the 28th–29th of January, the 86th Mountain Infantry was relieved by the 85th and 87th Mountain Infantry. The Regiment was concentrated in the vicinity of Lucca for training. The 1st Battalion and a reinforced company from the 2nd Battalion were to take the ridge. Regiment was also in IV Corps Reserve. The attack was planned for sometime in February. A detachment under the 1st Battalion S-2, Lt. Wilson Ware, was left at La Ca with three officers and twenty-one enlisted men to carry on the patrolling and reconnaissance of trails and trail conditions. This detachment found two more trails. One to M. Serrasiccia, which was very rugged and would require some fixed ropes to get over several rock ledges. Lt. McGowan pioneered and found this trail. One night his patrol reached the top and found Kraut positions and wire. The positions were not occupied as we later found the Krauts spent the night in their dugouts to the rear of the ridge. This trail was designated #3. It was *a* rugged and very steep trail, but it gave us a direct route to the top of M. Serrasiccia, a summit that was necessary to hold. It started from the vicinity of Miglianti and Casa Tonelli, went down into a deep gorge, crossed the Dardagna and then ended at two deserted houses about 1500 feet below the summit. From there up it was a series of rocky ledges, cliffs and ravines. This trail would have to be used initially for supply and evacuation by hand pack only until lateral supply lines and trails could be developed from the mule trail head at M. Cappel Buso. The climbing of this trail by "C" Company, reinforced, was a physical accomplishment to be admired, and showed what men could accomplish when trained in the mountains. The upper reaches of the trail were exposed to small arms fire all the way to the top. Six fixed ropes would be required to facilitate the movement of troops over the rocky ledges and two small cliffs. Lt. McGowan, who was killed the night of 20 February 1945, while leading a patrol, is to be commended on selecting a trail which brought this company to the summit without a casualty. It was also necessary to construct a very crude foot bridge across the Dardagna on the night of the attack. A pioneer squad from the Battalion A & P Platoon was attached to this force for that purpose.

Lt. Gordon Anderson of Company "A" found another trail south along the Dardagna then up a very steep talus slope on to the top. Lt. Anderson had reconnoitered for trails for his company for a long period, attempting to find a suitable route to M. Mancinello. Eventually a trail was found by Lt. Anderson's patrol from Poggioforato south across the Dardagna, then up a canyon to the top of the ridge by way of M. Cingio del Bure. The company would have to advance down the ridge and take M. Mancinello from the south. This trail was designated #4. The trail up from the canyon bottom was protected by small trees from small arms fire from the flanks, but not from the front above. The Krauts were looking down our throats on this one too. A pioneer squad was attached to this force also to build a bridge over the Dardagna the night of the attack.

By 12 February 1945 the snow was no longer an obstacle on any of the trails, as it had either melted or was so packed down that it would hold the weight of a man without requiring skis or snowshoes.

As a result of this continual reconnaissance the following plan was evolved, to assault the ridge in five columns, using five different trails. Company "F", reinforced, had found a trail from Madonna del Acero up to the high ground south of M. Mancinello called Le Piagge. Once they had arrived on top, they were to protect the left flank of the 1st Battalion. When the ridge was secured by the 1st Battalion they ("F" Company) would rejoin their

Battalion as Division Reserve, and the 1st Battalion would be responsible for its own left flank protection. The trails were numbered from right to left with #1 going to Pizzo di Campiano, #2 to M. Cappel Buso, #3 to M. Serrasiccia, #4 to M. Mancinello, and #5 to Le Piagge.

At Lucca the companies were organized into forces. Each company was to select an assault platoon of its best mountain men. This platoon was to be preceded by a trail party of 3 to 4 men, who selected the trail and could fix ropes at the required places.

1. Only trails #1 and #3 would require fixed ropes. The trail parties were equipped with ropes, pitons, and piton hammers. It was decided that a piton hammer could be muffled by wrapping it in cloth. This was tried and proved satisfactory. *It* was also decided to take the chance in putting in the fixed ropes as it would facilitate the ascent and prevent any accidents from men falling.

2. It was originally planned that the assault platoons should be hand picked men from the Battalion. About 70% of the men in the Battalion had been trained at Camp Hale in the Rocky Mountains. As a result it was decided that there would be no hand picking of assault platoons, but each company commander would designate a platoon from his company as the assault platoon. This was done, and it increased the morale and spirit of the men as they all considered themselves mountaineers, even though they had not all trained in the mountains. When near the top, the trail party would allow the assault platoon to pass through it and assault the ridge. Each assault platoon had an A-6 machine gun and at least six Tommy guns. After their two weeks training at Lucca, especially in a quarry, we found the 30% not trained at Camp Hale were fairly good in movement over rough terrain as they were young and desired to be as good as the rest of the mountaineers. Of course if

we had had to use skis and snowshoes, it would have been a different story. Skiers and snowshoers are not trained in two weeks.

The following is a breakdown of the various forces:

Force A–Trail #1, Objective, Pizzo di Campiano
- 1   Platoon Company A (2 A-6 MGs)
- 2   Litter Squads
- 1   Forward Observer and party.

Force B–Trail #2, Objective, M. Cappel Buso
- 1   Company, Company "B"
- 1   MG Platoon, 1st Platoon, Company "D", equipped with LMGs
- 2   Sections 81mm Mortar, 1st and 2nd Sections, 3rd Platoon Company "D" equipped with 1 long barrel and 1 short barrel 81mm mortar
- 2   Litter Squads
- 1   Forward Observer and party

Force C–Trail #3
- 1   Company, Company "C"
- 1   MG Platoon, 2nd Platoon, Company "D", equipped with LMGs
- 1   Section 81mm Mortar, 3rd Section, Company "D", equipped with two short barrel 81mm mortars
- 3   Litter Squads
- 1   Pioneer Squad
- 1   Forward Observer and party

Force D–Trail #4
1   Company less 1 Platoon, Company "A"
2   Litter Squads
1   Pioneer Squad
1   Forward Observer and party

Force E–Trail #5
1   Company, Company "F"
1   MG Platoon, 1st Platoon, Company "H"
1   81 mm Mortar Section
2   Litter Squads

The above forces worked together for about two weeks at Lucca. The roughest terrain in the area was utilized and all loads packed as would be required in the operation. The men were given further training and practice in moving along rock ledges and walls fully equipped. Also while at Lucca a sand table of the Mancinello-Campiano Ridge was constructed to scale by use of map and up-to-date aerial photos. A continual flow of photos were available which proved very valuable. The plan was made into an order and the order was issued orally seven days prior to the operation which was tentatively set for the 19th-20th of February. A room was set aside in which were placed the sand table, maps and aerial photos, and all reports that were sent down by courier from the detachment at La Ca under Lt. Ware, who was continually patrolling and checking trails and trail conditions. Company commanders of the 1st Battalion used this room for the orienting and the issuing of their orders to all the men in their companies and attached units. As a result each individual man and officer had a thorough and comprehensive knowledge of the operation, and what his job would be. The sand table and aerial photos proved very valuable, and was partly responsible for the later success of the operation.

The following intelligence was available to the Regiment. The 7th Company, 1044th Panzer Grenadier Regiment, 232nd Division, with possible elements from the 14th AT Company held a triangle bounded by Pizzo di Campiano, M. Spigolino and Fanano, with approximately 170 men. Two mountain battalions had been reported in Sestola on the 14th of February by Italian partisans. The strength on the ridge at any one time was estimated to be 40–50 men. They manned well dug-in positions, covering all possible routes of approach. Positions were mutually supporting, good fields of fire mostly plunging, and excellent observation. As the only approaches to the ridge were along narrow trails a well placed machine gun could prevent the advance of the columns up any of these routes that had been selected. To make the attack a success concentration of troops must be accomplished with secrecy in close proximity of an enemy with excellent observation. Also, surprise must be complete and it was decided to attack during the night, the 1st Battalion making the main effort, using four columns and four trails.

The Battalion order was very minute and prepared to the last detail. The following maps were used: Italy, 1:25000 97 I SE Gaggio Montano, 97 I SW *Fanano,* 97 II NW Cutigliano, 97 II NE Lizzano in Belvedere. All platoon leaders had the maps in their possession. As the battalion had to detruck near Poretta Terme it was decided to march to the foot of the Mancinello-Campiano Ridge, and stay under cover in the houses of the villages of Ca di Julio, Pianacci, Farne, Migliante *and* Poggio Forato. "F" Company, reinforced, would move into Madonna del Acero ahead of the 1st Battalion. All men were required to remain within the houses with guards posted inside at all windows and doors. This allowed the men to rest one whole day after the march of 14 miles from the

DP *(Departure Point)* on Castelluccio Ridge to the areas of departure *(for the attack)*. Also, it gave them time for a final review of the plan of attack. The 1st Battalion left Lucca on the morning of 17 February by motor, and arrived at the DP at dark. Once the Castelluccio Ridge was crossed during daylight all movement was under observation from M. Belvedere, hence the night march.

On 15 February the Battalion Commander flew over the ridge for a final *re*connaissance for any new movement and a last terrain study. As a result of this flight, the following plan was worked out. To the west of M. Cappel Buso was a ridge extending from M. Serrasiccia which we called Ridge X. This, as seen from the air and by photographs, was important as it controlled M. Cappel Buso which along with Pizzo di Campiano must be held at all costs to deprive the Kraut of observation of the approaches to M. Belvedere. From Campiano and Buso our artillery observers could also place observed fire on the rear of Belvedere and M. della Torraccia as well as the whole Kraut line from Rocca Corneta, Polla, and Corona. Ridge X was also a good route of approach for counterattack against M. Serrasiccia. A plan of attack was worked out whereby Force "D" (Company "A" less one platoon) would leave one platoon on M. Mancinello and would relieve Company "C" and attachments on M. Serrasiccia; Company "C" would then occupy and defend Ridge X. If Ridge X was held by the Krauts, an attack would be launched on order of the Regimental Commander through the 1st Battalion Commander by this company the next day.

A very complete and detailed written field order was drawn up along with an overlay. This was distributed four days before the Battalion moved out, so all had enough time to study it. The complete order follows with overlay.

As this was this unit's first entry into offensive combat involving a difficult, specialized operation, all instructions were very complete and detailed.

The units arrived at the areas of departure on the night of February 17th–18th. The motor movement worked very smoothly. To cut down on the weight, the men had to carry an extra 48 rounds of ammunition, giving them 96 rounds, was issued at Vidiciatico as the troops moved through as well as extra "K"-rations. *(I believe this awkward sentence means that the men picked up 48 more rounds and extra "K"-rations as they marched through Vidichiatico).* Organic vehicles had preceded the troops so that mortars and machine guns and extra ammo had to be hand carried only from $^1/_2$ to $^1/_4$ of a mile. All vehicles were returned to the rear under Battalion control prior to dark. *(Possibly it should read daylight but there was considerable vehicle traffic under enemy observation during the day in this area.)* This was considered tactically sound as our front was covered by a battalion of infantry.

On the night of 16–17 February, 110 wire had been laid by a small advance wire party from the Battalion CP at Farne to all areas of departure. This wire was laid in the snow and concealed. The plan was that each column would have a wire team of five men with 130 wire. They would follow the column up, and report to battalion on the hour the approximate location of the column. This worked very well. Under no circumstances would radio be used, except in emergency on contact *(with the enemy)*. It was planned that if any column met resistance, and could not advance during the night, at daybreak they would call for artillery and supporting fire and attack. The supporting fire consisted of the following: three battalions FA in direct support of the 86th Mt. Inf. for period 18–19 February, seven .50-caliber MGs firing direct fire on Campiano and Buso in vicinity of La Ca and Plinardo. Battalion AT guns (75 Pac How) direct fire from vicinity of La Ca, 1 platoon medium tanks, in position for direct fire on Campiano, Buso and Serrasiccia, one platoon chemical mortars. These were all in position the night of 18th–19th February, and were subject to fire on call from the 1st Battalion Commander. No registration fires were desired by the *Battalion Commander*, so as to not to jeopardize the element of surprise that was needed to make the attack a success. A complete fire plan was worked out between the 1st Battalion Commander and Lt. Col. Pearson, commanding officer of the 605th FA Bn, our combat team artillery. This plan was a series of numbered concentrations covering the whole ridge at key terrain features. Each unit commander had a forward observer and party with wire and radio, and was familiar with this fire plan. As soon as the ridge was taken, registration of defensive fires would begin.

Communications with the direct fire weapons were by wire from the battalion CP. Fortunately the direct fire weapons were not needed in the initial attack. Only the .50-caliber MGs were used at a later period. The chemical mortar platoon was provided with a #300 radio and put on the same channel with the companies. Numerous times their fire was directed by the company commander with his #300. This was an expedient and though satisfactory at the time was not practical. These mortars assisted in stopping counterattacks and were used on houses for harassing purposes.

The mission of the battalion was three-fold:

1. Take Mancinello-Campiano Ridge and occupy, organize and defend its key terrain features.

2. Protect the left flank of the 10th Mountain Division in its attack on M. Belvedere.

3. Support by fire and aid by observation the left regiment (87th Mt. Inf.) in its attack against M. Belvedere.

To accomplish part 3 of the mission it was decided to move up on to the ridge four .50-caliber MGs and one 75mm pack howitzer. The purpose being to emplace those guns in the vicinity of Campiano or M. Cappel Buso and fire direct fire on the known Kraut line which extended from Rocca Corneta, a very strongly defended natural terrain feature, through the fortified towns of Polla and Corona. The forward observers could direct fire from these two terrain features very efficiently in support of the attack. Of course the first problem was to secure the ridge, then hold it against counterattack which we knew would come. After that, the guns could be brought up. The .50-caliber MGs were not such a problem, but the 75mm Pack Howitzer gave us a little concern.

The attack hopped off at dark, 1930, the night of 18th–19th February. Attached to the battalion was a porter platoon of 30 men from Service Company, 86th Mountain Infantry, following Company "B" up trail #2. Four .50-caliber MGs on packboards, mortar ammo, and .50-caliber ammo was carried by the platoon. These guns were principally for direct fire on the Rocca Corneta and Polla Ridge in support of the attack of the 87th Mountain Infantry. A MG Platoon from "D" Company was organized to fire these guns. It was contemplated to use mules from Alpini pack companies on trail #2 which was to be the MSR *(main supply route)* of the battalion. This was the only route over which a mule would be able to go. Also attached was the 256th QM Pack Company under Capt. Fred Burke. These men packed with packboards up trail #3 and supplied "A" and "C" companies with water and ammo. this route was impassable for mules. Company "Z" *(Typing error. It should be "A")* over trail #4 packed all basic loads of ammo and rations on their men. It was planned to supply them over trail #3 and eventually laterally by mule up trail #2.

The battalion was over strengthened eighty men. Thirty of these men were given to "D" Company to be organized into a pack platoon for *this* heavy weapons company. Fifteen men to "B" Company, fifteen men to "C" Company and twenty men to "A" Company, to be used as packers. All company headquarters including cooks were used as packers and did an excellent job in packing rations, water and ammunition to their respective organization. All supplies and ammo could only be hand packed or on trail #2, mule packed.

Evacuation was planned over trail #2 and #3. All would be hand packed with plasma stations on each trail. This was actually used and not one casualty was lost. Company "D", of the 10th Mountain Engineer Battalion completed a tramway to M. Cappel Buso on the 2nd day after the ridge was taken. *(It terminated on a shoulder above the steepest part of the trail and more than half-way to the summit.)* This tramway proved invaluable for supply and evacuation and was built in excellent time under very difficult conditions. This company was in direct support of the 1st Battalion, 86th Mountain Infantry. It was necessary for them to pioneer a road of one and one half miles in order to get their equipment in to build the tramway.

The attack proceeded according to plan. Only one contact with the enemy was made and that was "B" Company on trail #2. As the assault platoon reached the top of M. Cappel Buso the Krauts opened up with machine guns and machine pistols; taking advantage of lessons learned previously not to return fire at night, the leading echelon continued to move forward and the Krauts pulled out. Not a shot was fired *(by our men)*. All columns reached their objectives without a casualty. The Krauts had pulled back in their dugouts for the night, not leaving a man in position. The ultimate had been gained, surprise was complete, and an important difficult, rugged terrain feature had been taken without a casualty.

At 0117, 19 February 1945, "B" Company's assault platoon was on top of M. Cappel Buso. The remainder of the company was 500 yards down the trail. At 0250 all of "B" Company was in position on Buso and digging in. The enemy machine gun and machine pistols had withdrawn to Ridge X and were still firing intermittently. No fire returned. At 0258, 19 February, "A" Company was in position and digging in with no contact and no Krauts. At 0407 the company commanders of "A" and "F" Companies had established command liaison and contact boundaries were fixed. At 0305 "C" Company was all on top and digging in. Patrol out in front made no contact. All this time fog and clouds had been closing in. Force "A", on trail #1, to Pizzo di Campiano had not reported in. This was a very difficult trail and anxiety was felt for this column. At 0545 Force "A" reported in by wire. Just before daylight all units were on top.

Force "A", under Lt. Loose of Company "A", had a very difficult time. This trail was very dangerous as well as steep and long. Early in the evening a heavy fog had closed in. The wire party with the forward observer from the artillery had become lost, and were not found until the next day. The platoon was split but by daylight had all arrived on their objective. The artillery radio refused to function, so the infantry SCR 300 was used to direct artillery fire. This platoon moved in and took over the Kraut positions which were beautifully prepared and had overhead cover. The Krauts had retired to their house for the night, so at daybreak Lt. Loose took a patrol, went to the house where he captured three and killed four. A brief-case of German documents was captured along with an 81mm mortar, 165 rounds ammo, 20-power scope, machine guns, and food and supplies.

During the early morning a very heavy fog had settled over the whole Mancinello-Campiano Ridge. This was an extreme advantage to us as it concealed our movements on the ridge, and allowed more time for digging in and preparation of positions. Prior to daylight all units had closed in on the ridge and were preparing and organizing their positions. Patrols were sent to the flanks and front, but no enemy had been contacted. Radio silence was lifted at 0600 on the 19th of February.

At 1100 the fog began to lift, and artillery and mortar fires were registered. The first fire mission was fired by Company "A" at 1106 on some Krauts in the vicinity of houses at Sega. By 1200 "C" Company's patrol had contacted "B" Company on M. Cappel Buso, and a "B" Company patrol had contacted "A" force on Campiano. "A" Company on M. Mancinello had engaged an enemy patrol of 12 men who were allowed to advance to about 200 yards of machine guns. Six were killed and six surrendered. They were very much surprised that American troops were on the ridge. At 1300 an enemy force of 40 men was observed by "C" Company advancing toward M. Serrasiccia and "C" Company's positions. The Krauts observing a few of our men waved at them. Our men returned the wave and waited for the Krauts to come into close range. Fire was opened at 200 yards, and the Kraut column disintegrated; at 1355 the remainder of the Krauts launched a counterattack which was beaten back by MG, rifle, artillery and mortar fire. What was left withdrew into a draw. At 1530 forty more Krauts attempted to attack "C" Company from the direction of Ridge X. Driven back by artillery, mortar and MG fire, they disappeared into the woods on Ridge X.

On the morning of the 19th of February at 0300 two squads of mules arrived from an Italian Alpini Pack Company. They had marched 20 miles so were allowed to rest until 1000 at Farne. One pack howitzer had been brought to Farne by *Weasel and* was packed on sleds (*this howitzer can be broken down into several loads*), and an attempt was made to pull them up trail #2. The Italian mules were considered too small to pack the tube. The complete AT platoon of the 1st Battalion was given the mission of getting this pack howitzer into position on the ridge. The sleds were not practical and finally the pack howitzer was placed on mules. The mule packing the tube made it up to the top of Buso where the gun was emplaced to fire at 1650. The mule died a few hours later.

The four .50-caliber MGs had been placed at the trail head of trail #2 where they were picked up at 1925 by Lt. Bouderes and the pack platoon from Company "D." The wire between Pizzo di Campiano and "B" Company was out. As Lt. Bouderes was advancing along a knife ridge to Campiano, a Kraut MG opened up wounding the Lt. and four men. It was learned that Krauts had infiltrated in the darkness and were between "B" Company on M. Cappel Buso and Lt. Loose's platoon on Campiano. They had cut out the wire. The .50-cal. were then emplaced on M. Cappel Buso where they still could fire on Rocca Corneta, but at a greater range.

During the night of 19th and 20th February, Lt. Loose's platoon was counterattacked, the first attack coming at 1820. At the time the FO called for artillery on his own position. Verified and mission fired. Thanks to the excellent Kraut positions we suffered no casualties. This position was the hot spot, and the Kraut fought hard for it. Throughout they attempted to surround the position, but *were* driven off by artillery directed over the platoon's SCR 300 and by grenades. Attempts to contact this platoon during the night failed as the Krauts had a strong position covering a knife ridge which had to be crossed in single file by any relieving force. By noon the next day, Lt. Loose's platoon was relieved (*I believe the writer meant reinforced*) by a platoon from "B" Company. They (*Lt. Loose's platoon*) had nine casualties which had to be hand carried to the Battalion Aid Station at Ca di Julio. Six men killed. As a result of the night's action, 26 enemy dead were counted around this position. From 19 February until the 1st Battalion was relieved by the 10th Mt. Division AT Battalion on 23 February the Pizzo Di Campiano summit was subject to six counterattacks. The last *was* on the early morning of 21 February when 70 men attacked from two sides and were driven off with heavy losses. The .50-caliber MGs at Plinardo had great sport picking off the ambitious Krauts attempting to work up the northeast slope of Campiano. Division attacked Belvedere—11 P.M.—19 February.

At 1310, 20 February, the plan for taking Ridge X was put into effect as enemy troops were observed moving into the woods. Company "C" attacked, supported by artillery fire, 81mm mortar fire from "B" Company in M. Cappel Buso area as well as .50-caliber MG fire from Buso. Ridge X was taken and the secondary part of the operation worked according to plan. At 1145, 20 February, "F" Company was ordered down from the ridge and the 1st Battalion was responsible for its left flank. A platoon was left at M. Mancinello to accomplish this. Small patrols of Krauts were still wandering around this area seemingly very much confused.

At 2000 on 20 February, "E" Company was relieved from positions at Castello and Sussadello who had been protecting the right flank of the 1st Battalion. As M. Belvedere-Corona, Polla had been taken there was no need for this company. 2nd Battalion was regrouped for Division Reserve. During the afternoon of 20 February the 75 pack howitzer and two .50-caliber MGs fired on Rocca Corneta and the garrison eventually surrendered to elements of "E" Company.

Counterattacks of diminishing strength continued along the ridge throughout the 20th, 21st, and 22nd of February. *They* were of patrol size of 10 men to company size of 70 to 80 men. At no time did they get into our positions. On several instances the Red Cross flag was used by the Krauts in an attempt to get into our positions, but this met with failure. Small groups of 3 and 4 were often taken under mortar and artillery fire which, when they were caught on open slopes, was very effective.

The installation of the tramway, built by Company "D" of the 10th Mt. Engineers Battalion, was of great assistance in supply and evacuation. The hand packing of the 256th QM Company and the evacuation of the wounded down trail #3 was excellent. The Service Company porter platoon found themselves packing up ammo and supplies, and wounded and dead down. The Company Headquarters men also were of great assistance, and all packers worked themselves to a point of exhaustion, some making three trips in a 24-hour period. By 21 February, 10 ³/₄ tons of ammunition alone had been packed on to the ridge and there was never a shortage of ammo, rations, or water. The small Italian mule did yeoman service though the Battalion Commander found it necessary to supervise their work by four or five of his own mule men with some Italian speaking American NCOs along to keep them moving.

On 23 February the 1st Battalion, 86th Mt. Infantry was relieved by the 10th Mt. AT Battalion. The objective had been taken without a casualty, but the following counterattacks took the following toll of 17 killed, 38 wounded and 3 missing. None of the wounded were lost due to the use of plasma, although in some instances it took from 6 to 12 hours to pack a casualty down *(from the ridge)*. When the tram was operating this was cut to 4 hours and sometimes 2.

From prisoner interrogation the following was learned: The 7th Company of the 1044th Regiment of the 232nd Fusiliers held the ridge. This company was to be relieved by two companies of the 4th Mt. Battalion on the 19th of February. A 3rd Company of this Mt. Battalion was in Sestola. This probably was the 75 men that the

P-47s strafed on the road to Fanano. The 7th Company lost heavily in the fighting on the 19th–20th February. "F" Company, 86th Mt. Inf. had annihilated a column of 30 Krauts with machine guns, so it can be assumed that the 4th Mt. Battalion ceased to exist as a fighting organization. At no time did they expect an attack on the ridge, and it came as a complete surprise as they felt it too rugged an obstacle for a very large unit to take.

The success of this operation which was the prelude to the Belvedere operation and the final breakthrough to the Po and to the Alps can be accredited to the following:

1. 70% of the personnel had been mountain trained in the American Rockies. They had no fear of rugged, precipitous and difficult terrain.

2. Early and complete reconnaissance of the objective for routes of approach by officers and men who knew the mountains.

3. A complicated plan made easy by detailed orders, use of sand table, aerial photos, and complete orientation of the plans to every man and officer in the battalion by use of sand table and aerial photo.

4. Aerial reconnaissance by the Commanders of terrain that could not be observed by ground reconnaissance.

5. A period of practice over terrain near as compatible to the terrain you are to operate over.

6. Night movement both in the approach and attack phase.

7. Physical condition and stamina which was the most difficult obstacle to overcome initially.

8. High morale and esprit de corps of the men who knew they were a specialized mountain outfit, and when given an object will do their utmost to surmount it to justify their specialized training.

/s/ Henry J. Hampton
/t/ HENRY J. HAMPTON
Lt. Col., 86 Mt. Inf.

BATTALION JOURNAL
1ST BATTALION, 86TH MOUNTAIN INFANTRY
RIVA RIDGE OPERATION 18 FEB. TO 22 FEB. 1945

DEFINITION OF TERMS

Remount 86th Mountain Infantry Regiment

Remount 1 Adjutant

" 2 Intelligence Officer

" 3 Operations Officer

" 4 Supply Officer

" 5 Executive Officer

" 6 Commander

(The same numbers apply to corresponding officers in battalions and other echelons.)

Remount Red	1st Battalion, 86th Mountain Infantry
Remount White	2nd Battalion, "
Remount Blue	3rd Battalion, "
Retread Red	1st Battalion, 87th Mountain Infantry
Retread White	2nd Battalion, "

Able   A Company, 1st Battalion, 86th Mountain Infantry

Baker   B   "   "   "

Charlie C   "   "   "

Dog   D   "   "   "(Heavy Weapons)

Easy   E   "   2nd Battalion   "

Fox   F   "   "   "

CO Commanding Officer

CP Command Post, the headquarters of any unit

OP Observation Post, a place used by artillery forward observers, intelligence sections and officers for observing enemy positions and movements

FO Forward Observer, a lieutenant usually in artillery who goes with advanced infantry units to direct fire on enemy installations and counter attacks.

LD Line of Departure, an arbitrary line selected in the planning of an attack to be crossed at a set time, coordinating the action

HE High Explosive, a type of grenade, mortar or artillery shell

WP White Phosphorous, usually a 4.2 mortar shell that burns the enemy out of uncovered positions and makes large quantities of smoke. WP can also mean water point.

499140   A map coordinate. Read to the right at the top or bottom of the map to 49.9 and then on the side to the coordinate line 14.0. The intersection gives a precise location. On large scale maps it was carried out another place and would be written for example as 49961402.

A6 Machine Gun   A light machine gun mounted on a bipod and carried at times by regular infantry rifle squads

Able Forward   The forward CP of A Company where the company commander is usually located. It is the tactical CP.

Able Rear   The rear CP of A Company in charge of the executive officer or other subordinate officer. It is the logistical CP. In many situations, particularly static, these are combined.

Artillery Liaison Officer   He is in battalion headquarters and higher echelons to coordinate the Forward Observers and oversee his artillery unit's support of the infantry.

AT Platoon   AT stands for Anti-Tank. In battalion headquarters companies, a unit peculiar to the 10th Mountain Division. It used light 37 and 75 mm guns and was not equipped for anti-tank work.

Battalion Aid Station   A platoon of Medics headed by the Battalion Surgeon which sets up close behind the lines and sometimes right in them to take care of the wounded.

Burp Gun   A German machine pistol with folding stock that fires .30-caliber pistol ammunition at a very high rate of fire.

Channel 16   Wavelength channel for radio communications. It is changed occasionally to hinder enemy interception.

Clark Gable 6   Commanding Officer, A Company, 84th Chemical Battalion

Collecting Company   Provides litter bearers and ambulances to carry casualties from the battle field to Battalion Aid Stations and to hospitals.

Fire Fight   A small arms engagement with enemy units such as squads, platoons and occasionally a whole company.

Ridge X   An unnamed plateau-like extension from the main ridge north of the C Company area on M. Serrasiccia.

Searchlights   Batteries of huge searchlights were located about ten miles behind the lines and pointed out over the front to light up the forward slopes of the mountains. It was easier for our troops to observe with the lights than it was for the enemy to look against them. These were common in all fronts in Italy. Two sent their beams over Riva Ridge for this action.

SOI   Standard Operating Instructions, issued by the Signal Corps to achieve security in the use of radios at the front.

Time   Time in the army was kept on a 24 hour clock.

Weasels   Light full-tracked vehicles built by Studebaker for carrying loads up to 1000 pounds and pulling sleds over snow and swamps. They had wide tracks and put less pressure per square inch on the snow than a man's footsteps.

Zebra Sugar Nine   Radio code signal for the A Company platoon on our right flank on Pizzo di Campiano.

BATTALION JOURNAL

18 Feb. 45

Time (24 Hour clock)

1525 CP established at Farne.

1830 Remount White 2 called to give their means of identification.

1831 Observation Post parties left CP.

1922 OP parties reported in from Charlie and Baker Companies.

1935 Baker and Charlie moved out on time.

1950 Remount 5 called and is now at 499140.

2000 Negative report to Remount.

2030 Negative report to Remount.

2100 Negative report to Remount.

2130 Negative report to Remount.

2140 Baker Company reported assault platoon was at 47551650.

2147 Charlie Company reported they were at 468147.

2200 Negative report to Remount.

2209 Communications established with Able Company.

2219 Negative report from Remount White.

2220 Suspected light signals reported from house at 481150.

2225 Raiding patrol assigned to investigate.

2230 Negative report to Remount.

2235 Negative report from Able Company.

2300 Negative report to Remount.

2301 Able Company crossed bridge (467130) successfully. Time undetermined.

2310 First Platoon Baker Company reported at 473168.

2315 Negative report by patrol investigating the light signals.

2320 Able Company wireman at rear of the column reports being one third of the way up.

2324 Negative report from Remount White.

2329 Battalion Aid Station established at Ca Di Julio.

2330 Negative report to Remount.

2345 Able Company reported rear of their column at 468147 at 2330.

19 FEB. 45

0001 Negative report to Remount.

0025 Charlie Company reported rear of their column at 469150 at 0010.

0029 Baker Company reported assault platoon on top, 2nd Platoon approaching the top (471169).

0030 Negative report to Remount.

0034 Able Company reported front of column over top of the ridge (454131).

0042 Able Company assault platoon on top and advancing toward their objective. Able 6 requests we inform Fox Company that they are in Fox Company vicinity.

0051 Fox Company has been notified of Able's position.

0055 Able Company on top one mile south of objective. Negative report on small arms fire.

0100 Negative report to Remount.

0115 Remount OP reports action on Buso.

0117 Baker Company assault platoon on top. Rest of the company is 500 yards from summit. Report an enemy machine gun is in action.

0120 Baker Company reports all quiet. Action was probably an enemy patrol. Main body advances another 100 yards.

0130 Negative report to Remount.

0133 Baker Company reports a total of 2 1/2 platoons on top of Buso. No casualties. Enemy machine gun is still active.

0135 Charlie Company reports main party is 135 yards from the top and they think the assault platoon is on top.

0156 Forward Observer with Baker Company reported 150 yards from the top. Company is still moving.

0158 Baker Company reports all quiet. No casualties. All are up except mortars which will remain in defilade. Enemy machine gun fire has stopped.

0200 Negative report to Remount.

0222 Baker Company called for one litter squad. One casualty. (Intercepted radio report within Company)

0230 Negative report to Remount.

0239 Able Company on top. Assault platoon moving toward objective laying wire as they go. They have had no enemy fire all evening.

0250 Forward Observer Baker Company is in position. The Company is digging in.

0258 Able Company less one platoon in position digging in.

0300 Negative report to Remount.

0301 Charlie Company reports from phone at rear of the company that the head of column is almost on top.

0320 Baker Company in position digging.

0330 Negative report to Remount.

0337 Fox Company contacted Able Company.

0340 Remount OP reports a few rounds of rifle fire in the Buso area.

0343 Charlie wire team report in from rear of column all is quiet, and they think assault team is on top.

0345 Explosions heard on ridge exact location undetermined. Reported to be on Buso.

0348 Anti-tank platoon ordered to be ready to move in 15 minutes.

0349 Three large explosions heard in the vicinity of Rocca Cornetta. Liaison officer reported that is was not our artillery.

0400 Negative report to Remount.

0407 Commanding officers of Able and Fox Companies have met and personally established a boundary.

0408 Anti-tank platoon waiting arrival of two weasels from Remount.

0412 Charlie wire team is behind the company and has not yet reached the top. They report having enough wire.

0416 All artillery up to Corps checked and report no fire on Rocca Cornetta.

0426 Guide will be sent from Aid Station for two litter squads from the Collecting Company.

0430 No new information from Charlie Company. Negative report to Remount.

0431 Negative report from Able Company.

0440 Able Company changing phone. Will be out eight minutes.

0445 Tanks are moving into position to give support if needed. One platoon. Will be ready to fire in 15 minutes.

0456 Remount OP reports no activity heard from Charlie sector. OP has no visibility.

0459 Engineer lieutenant reports can put road through slide in about three hours of daylight work. They are having trouble working bulldozers in the dark and they tend to bog down in the muck.

0500 Negative report to Remount.

0503 Able Company reports all is well. The squad sent out to reconnoiter known enemy dugouts had not yet returned. Fog is settling in.

0515 Charlie Company reports all on top. Dugout squad is out half an hour. A few stragglers have not arrived. The Company is organized and digging in.

0520 Able Company is informed that Charlie Company is on their objective.

0530 Radio message from Zebra Sugar 9 (with right flank platoon) Objective reached. Enemy still present.

0535 This message reported to Remount.

0540 Charlie Company reports by radio all in position; very foggy.

0548 Dog Company men leaving Baker at 0300 saw no litter bearers on the way down and they think casualty report is false. This is reported to Remount 3.

0610 Anti-tank platoon left with guns on Weasels 15 minutes ago.

0619 Baker Company reports over the artillery wire that one casualty is on the way down.

0626 Wire from Able Rear to Able Forward is out.

0627 Baker Company reports enemy burp gun at approximately 469170.

0707 Communications between Able Rear and Forward re-established.

0810 OP Serrasiccia reported in position.

0815 Charlie Company wants to send patrols to Able and Baker.

0835 Able and Baker notified of Charlie patrols.

0845 Charlie Company notified that it can send the patrols.

0850 Remount OP reports rifle and machine gun fire south of Able Company.

0855 Two bursts automatic fire undetermined distance south of Able Company objective.

0857 OP Cappel Buso reported in and were oriented.

0904 Charlie Company reported one round of artillery landed south of them.

0915 Charlie Company reports hearing one round go overhead from direction of Fanano.

0917 Radio message from Baker Company; Phone out of order, short of wire; no action since 0130; visibility low; OP established.

0940 Guide left Remount CP for Tocalino to guide 10 mules to Plinardo.

1013 Wire party left the Battalion CP in an attempt to establish communication with Baker and Charlie Companies.

1023 The Right Flank Platoon called for a fire mission. Request 303, infantry assembly area. Request White Phosphorous. Will adjust. Correction on fire mission 809.

1035 Mission on the way. Could not observe. Error in original fire mission. Request mission 378.

1040 Guide reported in at Tocalino. He is prepared to start for Plinardo.

1041 Charlie Company reported everything quiet.

1045 Able Company reported in. Reported did not request fire mission. Visibility 500 yards at best. Intermittent clouds.

1055 Mission 378 on the way.

1056 Baker 6 checked in.

1058 Remount OP reports enemy personnel moving southeast in back of Rocca Cornetta, 497175.

1105 OP Serrasiccia observed truck moving west over the bridge at 457146 at 1018. Bridge at 487197 is intact.

1106 Fire mission 378 fire for effect. Cease fire. End of mission. Call it mission A. 50% on the target, personnel in houses.

1115 Fire mission. Request concentration #384.

1120 3 Kraut prisoners at Battalion CP.

1125 Charlie Company contact patrol reported in at Baker Company.

1130 Able Company reported elements engaged a 6 man enemy patrol at 453135; fire fight still going on.

1145 Report on prisoners taken by Right Flank Platoon. Captured 3 Krauts, one wounded, and evacuated them to Regiment. Our platoon killed four Krauts, captured one 80 mm mortar with 165 rounds of ammunition for it, a large amount of food and supplies, and one 20-power telescope. Prisoners believe that there are still enemy in the area.

1200 Contact has been established between Baker Company and the Right Flank Platoon.

1208 Charlie Company patrol to Ridge X is on position and digging in. Coordinates to follow.

1210 Charlie Company reports firing on left flank. Able Company reports firing on one Kraut caught in open field. Patrol to Ridge X has not yet reported.

1220 OP Serrasiccia established at 1100 at 45911595.

1235 Charlie Company patrol to Ridge X reported to have a strength of 15 men. Position is now 465162.

1250 4.2 Chemical mortars registering in defensive fire for Baker Company.

1305 A Quartermaster Pack Lieutenant will report in to Battalion CP at 1500 about packing ammunition and supplies up to Able Company.

1310 Able Company reports the capture of 6 prisoners.

1325 Able reports two more prisoners of war taken.

1355 An estimated 40 Germans are attacking Charlie Company from 451161. Three prisoners have been taken.

1410 Artillery fire reported by Charlie to be 200 yards over and 100 yards right.

1415 Enemy reported to have moved to 457152.

1420 Enemy is withdrawing. Charlie Company is firing their 60 mm mortars at them.

1421 Forward Observer is moving to a better position for adjusting fire by radio.

1430   Charlie Company reports 40 counterattacking Germans have surrendered and are now covered.

1438   Krauts dropped into firing position and fire fight was resumed after they came over a ridge with their hands up.

1509   One round of enemy artillery or mortar fire landed 35 yards east of the Battalion CP.

1510   Charlie Company reports enemy is withdrawing. Called off 4.2 fire.

1512   Baker Company line out as of 1508.

1514   Right Flank Platoon receiving fire from direction of Trignano.

1515   Prisoner of War Report from Regiment. Prisoners say their company strength is 120, only 80 of whom are fighting men. They are from the 7th Company, 1044 Panzer Grenadier Regiment. This outfit held the ridge Campiano through Spigolino. Our attack was a complete surprise to them.

1520   Pizzo di Campiano received 5 rounds of mortar fire.

1530   Charlie Company report on enemy attack of 40 men. The enemy was first seen at 454158, advanced 200 yards up the ridge on a 90 degree azimuth, received Charlie Company fire and then withdrew to the vicinity of 455155 and on down the draw and out of sight. Patrol of one squad plus an officer are following the enemy.

1555   Artillery will place harassing fire on these points until 1800: Rocca Cornetta, Piano della Farnia, Serrazzone, and two places on the road junction in the vicinity of 455194.

1559 Right Flank Platoon reports 3 enemy dead and 4 PWs. 3 PWs are coming down; the fourth PW died on the way down and was buried by the other PWs.

1600 Charlie Company contact patrol never reached Able Company. Reason: met enemy and captured 3 prisoners.

1650 The 75mm howitzer is in position. It can fire on the Rock (Rocca Cornetta).

1700 Remount Red 6 will return to the Battalion CP around 1900.

1715 OP Serrasiccia reports small arms fire in the vicinity of Pizzo di Campiano.

1730 Able Company reports 3 PWs on the way down. These are the 3 reported at 1559.

1731 Position of the 75 mm howitzer recorded at 1650 is 457166.

1800 German passwords received from Division and given out to the companies: 19 Feb., *Diwan Perser*; 20 Feb., *Case palme*; 21 Feb. *Adria meer;* 22 Feb. *Arrak wein.*

1820 Charlie patrol has returned.

1821 Our artillery is falling in the vicinity of Pizzo di Campiano. Counterattack reported by Forward Observer. No reports over our communications.

1825 OP Serrasiccia sent in a negative report.

1826 Red 6 reported that he was sniped at from the north while coming down the ridge from Buso.

1833 Baker Company reports over the radio that all their phones to Battalion CP are out.

1835 Baker told to try the phone from OP Cappel Buso.

1845 Remount ordered use of Channel 16 on radios beginning at 0600 and gave the SOI call sign for the 87th.

1910 Wire communications OK to Able and Charlie Companies: out to Baker.

1925 Baker 6 on OP line is given Channel 16 message to relay to the Right Flank Platoon, but the wire is out between Cappel Buso and Pizzo di Campiano. A lieutenant and two men are wounded, with the .50-caliber machine guns half way down to Campiano. He reports all quiet on Buso.

1935 The Aid Station reports that a body from the Right Flank Platoon is in a building one-third of the way down from Campiano.

1945 Remount reports that Easy Company has one platoon at Plinardo, one at Sussadello, and one at Ca di Julio to protect our right flank and communications.

2000 Remount reported that a PW from the 234 Fusilier Battalion said that 22 men under Captain Maas came into Sesstola today.

2100 Negative report to Remount.

2110 Right Flank Platoon called for artillery concentration A.

2115 Right Flank Platoon call for the assistance of one platoon.

2125 Baker Company is sending 8 men plus one .50-caliber machine gun. 3 more are on the way.

2145 Right Flank Platoon reports that they are cut off and surrounded by about a 40 man enemy patrol.

2150 Eight to ten men on the way from Baker Company.

2158 Baker is sending 16 men instead of 8.

2215 Right Flank Platoon is still adjusting artillery fire.

2217 Able and Charlie Companies are alerted and oriented on the situation.

2220 Remount asked for and given all available information on the reported loss of three .50-caliber machine guns.

2227 Artillery mission is completed.

2231 A messenger from Able platoon on right flank to Baker Company reported through and saw no Krauts on the way. Able is sending out men to get the machine guns.

2245 Red 2 and two radio operators are on the way to the top of Buso in compliance with Remount order.

2252 The searchlights are turned off in accordance with Red 6 request.

2315 Red 2 and party checked in by radio.

2340 Man from Dog Company reported to the CP. He told of knocking out an enemy machine gun at 477173 and he located our .50-caliber guns on the map.

2345 Remount is sending one 75 mm howitzer to Plinardo to be ready to fire on Rocca Cornetta in the morning.

2350 Lieutenant Hallett's platoon from Baker Company will be sent down to support Lieutentant Loose's platoon on Pizzo di Campiano.

20 Feb. 45

0012 Negative report from Charlie Company.

0020 Two .50-caliber machine guns and 1200 rounds are now at Baker CP.

0030 On the attack on Mt. Belvedere the 1st Battalion, 87th Mtn. Inf. is 800 yards over the L.D. (Line of Departure).

0040 Charlie Company patrol is in. No prisoners and no casualties.

0101 Negative report from Able Company. Fog is coming in.

0105 Red 2 (Lieutenant Ware) and party are on top.

0125 Lieutenant Ware checked in. Situation unchanged since platoon from Baker Company left to support Lieutenant Loose.

0245 Everything quiet in Charlie Company area. They can hear automatic fire in the Campiano area.

0415 Two machine pistols fired in Charlie area. Visibility is good. The men have been alerted. The fire is from the right side of Ridge X. Artillery is not needed.

0440 Charlie Company reports white parachute flare over their area. They shot it out. Dog 6 is checking the area for machine gun emplacements.

0505 Charlie Company reports fire fight against 2 machine pistols.

0510 Remount reports Rebate Blue took objective C at 0410. Remount Blue took their objective at 0350. Retread Red took objective B on an unconfirmed report.

0525 Red 2 reports hearing the sound of a motor convoy in the direction of Mr. Belvedere.

0528 Charlie Company called for 3 volleys of artillery on the right flank of Ridge X (455156).

0545 Concentration fired.

0547 Retread White 3 called for observed fire from our howitzer on Buso on the draw 100 meters north of C. Valle (502179).

0615 No communications yet through to the Anti-tank platoon.

0617 The artillery is putting in orders for the Retread mission.

0625 This mission is out of their sector and they cannot fire it.

0632 Radio communications with the Right Flank Platoon is reestablished.

0635 They request artillery mission 858.

0640 Baker Company cannot yet see Florio.

0641 Right Flank Platoon is under intense fire and cannot stick heads up to observe.

0646 They report the urgent need for help.

0700 Baker Company is sending an A6 machine gun and 10 men to aid the Right Flank Platoon.

0705 Red 2 reports mortar rounds falling in Charlie Company area.

0710 Our artillery is still firing the mission for the Right Flank Platoon.

0711 Charlie reports 12 Krauts with one machine pistol at 459158 and one machine gun at 462158.

0715 The artillery mission for the Right Flank Platoon is completed. The last volley will be #861.

0725 Baker CP reports machine gun fire on it from due west. The gun is too close for their mortars to get.

0730 Several 50 mm mortar rounds landed on Baker CP. One casualty is reported.

0733 The Right Flank Platoon radios in a message that they are running short of food, ammunition and men.

0735 Red 6 requested Remount for air support on the approaches north of Campiano.

0755 Radio message from OP Serrasiccia reports that the enemy have occupied the main ridge at 46491589.

0800 No communications with the Right Flank Platoon for the last ten minutes.

0807 Communications established with that platoon.

0808 Charlie Rear reported that one of their squads has probably been lost on Ridge X. Two squads have been sent out to investigate.

0810 Support from Baker Company to the Right Flank Platoon is involved in a fire fight on the way. It will get to the Able platoon as soon as possible.

0815 Charlie Company requests a patrol to Ridge X from Baker Company.

0818 Charlie Company was told by Red 6 that they would have to take care of themselves.

0819 On orders from Remount, Able Company was alerted to occupy positions of Fox Company which was being pulled off the Ridge for other operations.

0825 Able Company reported that they will be ready to occupy Fox Company positions in half to three-fourths of an hour.

0835 Lieutenant Colonel Hampton issued an attack order to Able and Charlie Companies.

0855 Wire communications with our anti-tank platoon have been established.

0900 Dog 6 requests more ammunition for his guns.

0930 OP Serraciccia reports seeing no enemy traffic on the roads through Fanano and Sesstola and no enemy activity in the valley. Enemy are still reported on Ridge X.

0931 Enemy appeared on main ridge at 467163. 15 Krauts came north along the ridge, shouted "friend," flew the Red Cross flag while coming down at 469166, and then took up attack positions. They dropped down the draw to Ridge X and withdrew south to the main draw. They went to the flank at 468165. We fired mortars and probably got several. Finally the enemy withdrew to a grove of pine on Ridge X. We confirmed 8 enemy dead. This report was from Red 2.

0932 The 4.2s are firing for Charlie Company.

0940 Dog Company ammunition is on the way up as of 0920.

0950 Able Company is ready to move in accordance with the Battalion Commander's attack order.

0951 Checked communications with Right Flank Platoon.

0955 Charlie Company requests slow fire of 4.2s on Ridge X.

0956 Baker Company reports an artillery time burst over their rear CP.

0958 Red 2 reports seeing no enemy on main ridge between Baker and Charlie Companies.

1000 Baker Company reports being unable to help Charlie with riflemen but can send mortar fire.

1001 Charlie asks for mortar fire at 465159.

1004 4.2 mission is completed.

1006 The artillery is firing a mission on Campiano.

1008 The artillery is also firing a mission on Ridge X.

1021 Baker Company has no new information.

1025 Our 75s and .50-caliber machine guns are now firing from Plinardo.

1050 Red 6 contacted Lieutenant Loose by radio. Their total casualties are 1 killed and 4 wounded.

1050 Contacted Red 2 by wire. He reported all quiet.

1055 Remount 6 has been at the Battalion CP since 1045.

1101 Grenades and machine gun ammunition left Farne for Baker Company.

1112 80 rounds of H.E. light, 81 mm mortar left Battalion on mules for Baker Company.

1130 From Charlie commanding officer by radio. "Unable to take Ridge X with one platoon. Request permission to attack with two abreast."

1131 Permission granted for Charlie Company to attack as desired.

1132 OP Serrasiccia reported a small group of men moving on foot and bicycles toward Fanano at 1120. 14 men with full packs and a machine gun crossed Ridge X at 46121710.

1135 14 men with Red Cross flags walking along trail into San Bonnucci with one wounded prisoner.

1145 Able Company has relieved Fox Company and Fox is coming down

1150 Encoded message from Right Flank Platoon confirming the report of 1050. "Since 1200 19 Feb. 45 our casualties, 1 killed, 5 wounded (3 of them evacuated). Killed 20 enemy. Situation tense. Need everything. 1105."

1220 Charlie Company checked in and reported ready to jump off with two platoons against Ridge X. Asked for 81 mm mortar fire at 1300. Baker said they could give 60 mm mortar fire. Charlie asked for 60 and 81 mm mortar ammunition.

1230 Right Flank Platoon reported direct artillery fire on their position from az. 140 degrees.

1239 The Right Flank Platoon reports about six Germans moving up toward Buso.

1250 Remount reported that they were withdrawing Easy Company from our right flank below the Ridge and gave orders for the Battalion to form a reserve.

1310   Charlie Company started their attack and asked Baker Company to lift their mortar fire.

1315   Remount 1 called up to confirm the report of Lieutenant McGowan's death with a Charlie Company patrol.

1320   Charlie Company reported that they are on their objective and reorganizing.

1325   Red 2 reports 75 men with packs going toward Fanano from Sesstola.

1345   The wire to Baker Forward is out.

1400   Charlie Forward reported that Krauts moved into new position under a Red Cross flag to the left of their area.

1405   Able Rear asked for 35 rounds of 60 mm mortar ammunition, 3 "536" radios, and rations for 100 men.

1410   Charlie Company radios that the knob on Ridge X at 465160 has been captured with several prisoners. The fighting is continuing.

1412   Red 6 called through Baker Company to have Red 3 alerted to relieve him at his present position on the Ridge.

1420   The line to Baker Rear is through. Lieutenant Hallett's platoon has made contact with the Right Flank Platoon.

1425   Remount is notified that this contact has been made.

1430   The Able wire is back in. Report on situation is given them.

1435 A strafing mission on the 75 men going to
Fanano has been requested.

1515 Two .50-caliber machine guns are at Plinardo
available for our use. The Battalion is ordered to
garrison Ca di Julio and Plinardo.

1522 Request moving the 4.2 mortars (6) from La Ca
to Ca di Julio. Remount line went out.

1530 Clark Gable 6 said he would comply.

1535 Charlie Company radio reported that at 1536
four P-47s bombed and strafed Piano della
Farnia damaging and setting fire to three houses.

1610 Red 6 wants wire laid laterally from Charlie to
Baker Companies.

1652 Report from Lieutenant Loose by radio signed
1610. Support arrived with ammunition.
Evacuated 6 wounded. Two killed since taking
objective. No enemy advance since 0800. Have
received enemy mortar and artillery during the
day. Have killed 26 Krauts and taken 3 prisoners.

1700 Radio from Charlie Company reports that
Charlie now has communications with Able
Company.

1715 Messages from OP Buso. Gun flash at 492199.
12 men crossing bridge at 457196 heading due
east at 1500 hours. 9 men in extended order and
in same direction coming from Fanano. 9 man
patrol leaving house at 468194 heading south
east at 1630 hours. Enemy OP spotted at 413194.

1730 Lieutenant Colonel Hampton and Lieutenant
Ware with party returned to the Battalion CP.

1745 Report from Baker Company. 6 Krauts surrendered to a wire party.

1750 Charlie Company asked for and was granted permission to go off the air tonight.

1820 Charlie Company now reports their position as 465158.

2000 Easy Company has been relieved.

2015 Guards checked through the Battalion CP with 7 prisoners from Baker Company. The PWs were tagged and sent on to Regiment.

2130 Baker Company requests water.

2200 The artillery is placing harassing fire on a house at 468194.

2300 Baker Company 1st Sergeant called and said Red 4 had authorized the release of 25 men to the Regimental Surgeon.

2325 Casualty report from Charlie Company: 3 men and 1 officer killed. 7 men wounded.

2342 Baker Company reported that they received a burst of machine pistol fire from an unknown position at 1130 and also sniper shots from an unknown position at 1140. *(Possibly P.M. times.)*

21 Feb. 45

0010 Remount 2 called in results of prisoner interrogation. They were from the 232nd Fusiliers. They reported Captain Maas was at Ospitale with an undetermined number of troops. The enemy is planning a counterattack from the direction of Scaffa and southwest of it. The 232nd was considered a good outfit by the Germans. The

2nd Company of the 4th Mountain Battalion was coming to relieve the 7th Company of the 232nd. The 2nd Company suffered heavily in killed and wounded yesterday. The 4th Company was supposed to join the 2nd Company. The prisoners did not know where the 4th Company is now.

0220 Red 3 reported that a 6 man enemy patrol was spotted in the Baker Company area. Machine gun and 60 mm mortar fire forced their withdrawal.

0332 Red 3 reported that artillery rounds were landing on Campiano.

0333 Our artillery say they are firing—will determine the mission.

0340 Call put through to Ca di Julio to alert that flank platoon for a possible dawn attack.

0345 The artillery is firing Concentration #861 which is west of Scaffa.

0400 Able Company reports all is quiet. They can see some lights in the vicinity of Scaffa. Charlie and Baker Companies report all quiet.

0425 It is reported to Remount 3 that all is quiet from Riva to Ca di Julio and Campiano.

0610 The artillery, mission number unknown, is being fired for the observer on Campiano.

0625 The Concentration is reported to be #868.

0705 Able Company report they are moving their Rear CP to Charlie Rear.

0720 A shell hit in Farne from an azimuth of 328 degrees. No casualties and no damage.

0800 Remount called to alert all companies for a move sometime today. Leave behind one officer per company and one noncom per platoon.

0845 1st Platoon, Company A, 84th Chemical Battalion is now located at 477122,

1025 Two enemy soldiers are in a dugout east and north of the house at 44781936 (Nome Croce). Also a position has been seen 10 yards in front of the southwest corner of the house. Both positions are larger then normal machine gun emplacements. They are covering the road and appear to be anti-tank positions. Reported by OP Buso.

1130 One round of artillery landed 100 yards from the Battalion CP. It came from an azimuth of 200 mils.

1135 81 mm mortars fired on an enemy OP at 47121932. 8 Krauts are on the run.

1140 Approximately 35 Germans in extended order are advancing along the highway toward the bridge at 457196. The Forward Observer can see. They were moving east at 1120 hours.

1145 Remount reports that the left flank of the 87th Inf. is at 49171680.

1203 Refer to the 1140 message. 7 more Germans are moving along the road at the same coordinates. Also there is a horse-drawn vehicle, possibly an artillery caisson.

1215 21 Krauts moved into the house at 454194.

1250 Two rounds of enemy artillery landed in the vicinity of our Battalion CP in the same area and from the same azimuth as the shell that landed at 1130. This was reported to our artillery.

1302 One more round landed in the vicinity of our CP.

1320 An 8 man enemy patrol heading from Cappel Buso toward Piano della Farnia entered the house at 45211680. A machine gun is in a second floor window. Reported by OP Serrasiccia.

1325 Baker Company reported they had 8 casualties from a high velocity shell. Patrol from Buso to Campiano has started.

1430 An enemy gun was seen at 47081990. This was reported to the artillery.

1450 A radio message from Lieutenant Loose confirmed the arrival of his relief on Campiano.

1530 During the period from 1200 20 Feb. to 1200 21 Feb. the Campiano platoon evacuated 6 casualties (4 wounded and 2 dead). Received enemy artillery and mortar fire. Had a counterattack at 0740. Killed 3 more Germans. Total German killed is 29. Report by radio from Lieutenant Loose.

1620 Report from OP Buso. Possible demolition set by 5 men under the bridge at 457196. The artillery position at 470199 was hit by our P-47s. 7 men moved from the bombed area into houses at 47182009.

1647 Artillery adjusted on houses at 47182009. 16 Krauts took off to the north. One house is burning.

1730 OP Buso reports that 25 men with automatic weapons moved into houses at 454195. Impossible for artillery. Request air attack.

1735 OP Buso reports 6 men on the road from Sesstola to Fanano. They have one machine gun with them. They were seen crossing the bridge at 457196.

1745 Able Battery, 10th Mountain Antitank Battalion, which is relieving us and organized as infantry for the job, left Farne for their position on the Ridge.

1755 Remount 2 sent in this report. The enemy 1st Battalion, 741st Regiment, 114th Division has counterattacked at Valpiano. Their 2nd and 3rd Battalions are some 7 miles to the rear. The 1043 Regiment has been noted at 555193.

1815 Charlie Company reported that 40 to 50 men moved into Piano della Farnia (451169) about two hours ago. They could not get the message through until now.

2015 We are leaving in place for the night one platoon on Mt. Mancinello, Charlie Company on Ridge X, one Baker Company platoon on Buso plus one section of heavy machine guns and one section of 81 mm mortars, and one Baker platoon on Campiano. These units will come down after daylight tomorrow. The remainder are coming down tonight to the base of the Ridge. No relief has been made yet.

2130 The artillery liaison reports that Charlie Battery, 605 Field Artillery is maintaining its Forward Observers on Serrasiccia, Buso and Campiano.

2300 Lieutenant Loose on Campiano reports that his relief is in position and that he is starting down with his platoon.

2305 Relief on Buso is being made. Relief to Ridge X is on the way from Serrasiccia.

2325 The artillery liaison officer reports that Campiano is receiving enemy artillery fire.

2330 The artillery report that they are firing counter battery.

2331 Report that relief group had passed through Mancinello.

22 Feb. 45

0035 The arrival of the relief troops at Ridge X is reported.

0045 The relief arrived at Serrasiccia and is being oriented.

0105 All relief troops are in position.

0125 Gun flashes on road between Sesstola and Fanano were seen. A gun at 471201 is firing at Mt. Belvedere.

0705 The relief has been completed and command of the sector has been relinquished by 1st Battalion, 86th Mountain Infantry.

APPENDIX A

A TIMELINE OF THE 10TH MOUNTAIN DIVISION

1938   Charles Minot Dole was important in the founding of the National Ski Patrol. Later Dole made it responsible for recruiting experienced skiers, mountaineers and outdoors men for the 10th Mountain Division.

May 1940   Minot Dole, Chairman of the National Ski Patrol System (NSPS) and Roger Langley, President of the National Ski Association, associated as the Volunteer National Winter Defense Committee, offer Secretary of War Harold Stimson the NSPS network to recruit skiers for mountain warfare.

June 1940   Dole meets with the II Corps commander in New York.

July 1940   Dole and NSPS Treasurer John Morgan write Army Chief of Staff General George Marshall and President Roosevelt urging the establishment of mountain troops.

Sept. 1940   Dole and Morgan meet with General Marshall and learn that some divisions will get cold weather training in the coming winter.

Dec. 1940   A 3rd Division Ski Patrol is formed at Ft. Lewis, Washington. Men from the 15th Regiment train at Mt. Rainier under Lt. John Woodward.

Feb. 1941   1,000 men from the 26th Infantry Regiment of the 1st Division have ski training in rotation at Lake Placid, NY. The 44 Division Ski Patrol from Fort Dix trains at Old Forge, New York.

Mar. 1941   The 41st Division Ski Patrol train at Mt. Rainier and on a two week ski trip in the Olympics.

22 Oct 41   General Marshall authorizes the activation of the 1st Battalion of the 87th Mountain Infantry Regiment.

15 Nov 41   1st Battalion (Reinforced) 87th Mountain Infantry Regiment is activated at Ft. Lewis, Washington.

13 Feb 42   The companies of the 1st Battalion in rotation begin training for two months each at Paradise Lodge, Mt. Rainier.

Apr. 1942   The Army decides to activate a full mountain division and begins construction of Camp Hale at Pando, Colo. over 9,200 feet elevation near Tennessee Pass.

01 Jun 42   Activation of the 87th Regiment is completed.

Aug. 1942   The Mountain Training Center is set up at Camp Carson, Colorado as command for the incoming units of pack artillery and other units for the future mountain division.

Fall, 1942   The 87th Infantry goes from Ft. Lewis to Jolon, California for maneuvers and additional training.

16 Nov 42   The Mountain Training Center units move to Camp Hale.

26 Nov 42   The 1st Battalion, 86th Mountain Infantry is activated.

06 Dec 42   The 87th moves to Camp Hale.

20 Dec 42   The 86th Mountain Infantry Regiment is activated.

29 Dec 42   The NSPS is asked to supply within three months 2,000 men for Camp Hale.

Feb. 1943   Battalion-size war games on Homestake Mt. near Camp Hale fail due to lack of training and a subzero blizzard.

15 May 43   The 85th Mountain Infantry Regiment is activated.

11 Jun 43   The 87th Regiment departs for Ft. Ord, California, and at the end of the month leaves San Francisco for Adak.

19 Jul 43   The Mountain Training Center is deactivated and the 10th Infantry Division (Light) is activated at Camp Hale.

15 Aug 43   The 87th Regiment lands on Kiska with a large task force only to find the Japanese had evacuated it.

19 Dec 43   The 87th returns to Ft. Lewis and then goes on to Colorado.

Feb. 1944   The 99th Battalion, composed of native Norwegians, arrives to train at Camp Hale,

possibly as a deception against the Germans.
They are there only a short time.

24 Mar 44   The 10th Light Division starts its
infamous "D Series."

14 Apr 44   "D Series" ends.

Apr. 1944   General George Marshall tells Minot Dole
that he does not want to commit the 10th with
out a specific mission.

22 Jun 44   The Division starts the transfer to Camp
Swift, Texas.

26 Jul 44   The first *Blizzard* issue is published at
Camp Swift.

07 Nov 44   The Division is renamed the 10th Mountain
Division.

17 Nov 44   The 10th Division's Assistant Commander
Robison Duff arrives in Naples to plan for the
Division arrival in Italy.

23 Nov 44   General George P. Hays takes command of
the Division.

28 Nov 44   The 86th Regiment clears Camp Swift for
embarkation.

11 Dec 44   The 86th sails from Hampton Roads on
the *Argentina*.

20-21 Dec.   The 85th and 87th leave Camp Swift for
Patrick Henry.

22 Dec 44   The USS *Argentina* anchors in the Naples,
Italy harbor.

23 Dec 44   The 86th is trucked to a staging area at
Bagnoli, a suburb just northwest of Naples.

25 Dec 44   The 1st Battalion of the 86th in the afternoon leaves for the north by train.

26 Dec 44   The rest of the Regiment leaves Naples on the *Sestriere* for Livorno and a staging area northwest of Pisa.

04 Jan 45   The 85th and 87th Regiments depart from Hampton Roads on the USS *West Point*.

06 Jan 45   The rest of the Division depart on the USAT *Meigs*. The 86th has its first casualties of 8 killed and many wounded when S-mines are accidentally set off in the practice clearing of a German mine field in a staging area near Quercianella.

08 Jan 45   The 86th enters the front lines in the north Apennines as the major element of Task Force 45.

13 Jan 45   The 85th and 87th Regiments arrive at Naples.

15 Jan 45   An 86th patrol finds the first trail up Riva Ridge and retreats under fire.

18 Jan 45   The rest of the Division on the USAT *Meigs* arrives at Naples.

19 Jan 45   The 87th opens a new bivouac area at Villa Colli.

20 Jan 45   Some elements of the 85th enter the front lines.

28 Jan 45   Battalions of the 85th and 87th relieve the 86th in front line positions.

15 Feb 45   Colonel Clarence Tomlinson, 86th commander, takes an aerial reconnaissance flight over Riva Ridge.

18 Feb 45   The night attack on Riva Ridge by 1st Battalion and F Company of the 86th starts at 7:30 P.M.

19 Feb 45   The attack on Mt. Belvedere, Mt. Gorgolesco and Mt. della Torraccia by the 87th and 85 Regiments, and the 3rd Battalion of the 86th starts. This is also a night attack. The action continues to Feb. 24th, when Mt. della Torraccia is taken.

26 Feb 45   Division Headquarters is established at Campo Tizzoro and takes over from Task Force 45.

03 Mar 45   Attack begins at 7:00 A.M. by elements of all three regiments with objectives Mt. Grande d'Aiano, Mt. della Spe and the town of Castel d'Aiano. It is completed on Mar. 5th.

12 Apr 45   The planned date for our major breakthrough.

14 Apr 45   The attack begins in mid-morning by the 85th and 87th Regiments and the 2nd Battalion of the 86th. The 10th Mountain Division is the 5th Army spearhead and this is the Division's worst day of the war for casualties.

17 Apr 45   The breakthrough of the German defense line is completed.

20 Apr 45   The three Regiments with the 87th on the left, the 86th in the center and the 85th on the right drive out of the hills into the flat Po Valley and cut Highway 9.

21 Apr 45   Task Force Duff consisting of the 2nd Battalion of the 86th Regiment and associated tank and engineer units reach and secure the Bomporto bridge.

22 Apr 45   Task Force Duff reaches the Po River.

23 Apr 45   The 87th Regiment led by its 1st Battalion cross the Po River in assault boats and DUWKs. By evening of the 24th all three Regiments are across and a treadway bridge and a pontoon bridge are under construction.

26 Apr 45   Task Force Darby consisting of the 86th Regiment, and associated tank, artillery, engineering and medical units reach Verona in the morning and go on to Bussolengo. The 87th replaces the 86th and goes on to Lake Garda.

27 Apr 45   The 87th in the lead advances up the east side of Lake Garda meeting little resistance except at Borgo.

28 Apr 45   The Division, rotating regiments in the lead, fights up the east shore of Lake Garda through and past tunnels, encountering numerous enemy delaying actions.

29 Apr 45   During the day the 86th fights up the east shore. The 87th advances along the high mountain ridge east of the Lake. The 1st Battalion takes Spiazzi before this mountain route is canceled. Elements of the 85th crosses the Lake in DUWKs and take Gargnano and other towns on the west shore. By the end of the day the 3rd Battalion of the 86th has reached Torbole at the northeast corner of the Lake. This was a bad day for the 86th so close to the end of the war as five men from H and M Companies were killed and about

fifty wounded in a tunnel from an unlucky
German artillery round, and nine men from B
Company were killed by bombs from a German
plane.

30 Apr 45   Colonel William Darby and Master
Sergeant John Evans are killed by an air burst
in the main square of Torbole well after our
infantry had secured the town.

01 May 45   All advances are made without significant
resistance.

02 May 45   The German Army in Italy surrenders.

08 May 45   Germany surrenders.

13 May 45   The II Corps orders the 10th Mountain
Division to move to the vicinity of the Ghedi
Airport in the Po Valley.

14 May 45   The move is started and completed by
the 15th.

17 May 45   The Division is given a 48 hour alert for a
move to Udine.

19 May 45   The Division move to the Yugoslav border
is started.

20 May 45   The move is completed and the Regiments
are deployed along the north half of the Yugoslav
border called the Morgan Line. Much of it is
along the Isonzo River. The 2nd New Zealand
Division holds the south half of the line.

26 May 45   The border region has settled down. The
Division ends active patrolling and resumes
regular training.

24 Jun 45   10th Division Ski races are held on Grossglockner.

15 Jul 45   The 86th moves by train to Florence.

26 Jul 45   The 86th sails from Livorno on the *Westbrook Victory.*

30 Jul 45   The 85th leaves from Naples on the *Marine Fox.*

07 Aug 45   The *Westbrook Victory* docks at Hampton Roads.

11 Aug 45   The *Marine Fox* docks at New York, and the *Mount Vernon* docks at Newport News with the rest of the Division.

14 Aug 45   Japan surrenders unconditionally and signs the formal surrender documents on 2 Sep 45.

20 Oct 45   The 10th Mountain Division and the 87th Mountain Infantry are deactivated at Camp Carson, Colorado. The Division had been activated as the 10th Light Division (Alpine) on July 19, 1943 so it lived to an age of 27 months.

23 Nov 45   The 86th Mountain Infantry is deactivated.

26 Nov 45   The 85th Mountain Infantry is deactivated. The first unit of the Division to be activated was the 1st Battalion of the 87th Mountain Regiment on Nov. 15, 1941. Thus elements of the Division lived for a 48 month period.

APPENDIX B

HONOR ROLL OF OUR WAR DEAD

Under the harsh conditions of World War II we referred to them as KIAs for Killed In Action. In the fighting in Italy we did not have time to mourn them. Our regrets were deep for these losses, but we were always thankful one day at a time for the gift of life. Now more than fifty years later these heroes live on in our hearts, and we resolve to do our best to see that memory of them will not fade from the mind of man and pray that they rest peacefully in the mind of God.

The 10th Mountain Division Foundation has gone to great effort to assign each of our dead to his wartime company or primary unit. Some names are listed at the ends of the 85th and 86th Mountain Infantry Regiments because information to assign them to their particular companies was not available. Names proceeded by an asterisk(*) designate men interred in the American Cemetery and Memorial at Florence, Italy.

We of the rest of the Division should pay special tribute to the men of our twenty-seven rifle companies. They numbered 35% of Division personnel, but they make up 75% of this roll of our dead which totals 992 men lost in the consuming flames of war.

10TH MOUNTAIN DIVISION

Headquarters and Headquarters Company

Darby, William O.
Edgecombe, Russell L.
Mack, Thomas F., Jr.

10th Mountain Cavalry Reconnaissance Troop

*Cox, Shelie D.

10th Mountain Police Platoon

Peterson, Leonard D.

10th Mountian Signal Company

Greene, John, J. A.
Rickenback, Theodore

10th Mountain Antitank Battalion

*Alexander, Selwyn T.
*Benn, Charles H.
DeSilvestro, John
Gordon, Walter T.
*Kennedy, William
Lish, Lyman D.
*Morgan, James P.
*Park, Norman E.
Thomas, Ned P.
*Willis, Paul M.
Wright, Robert E.

10th Mountain Medical Battalion

Anderson, Anton T.
*Cimelli, Frank F.
Cox, Fields C.
Ehleb, William H.
*Ruuska, Henry A.
Walker, Clark F.

Medical Detachment, 85th

*Hanson, Roy E.
*Lewin, John H.
Moraga, Alex

Medical Detachment, 86th

Malonas, Harry
*Parfitt, James H
*Stasko, Leo S.
Walter, William U.
Wilkins, James O.

Medical Detachment, 87th

Bajkan, Arel
*Buchanan, Paul J.
*Conner, William R.
Desorcy, Raymond V.
*Gay, Roy G.
*Harris, Harold S.
Heins, Rudolf W.
Lindsay, William M.
McMillan, Howard
Miller, William G.
Millman, William H.
*Morrison, Barton C.
*Perkins, Kenneth D.
*Piazza, Frank J.

10th Mountain Quartermaster Battalion

*Anderson, Herbert D.
Barbiere, August J.
Murchison, George A.
*Rawlings, John F.
Yourkoski, Joseph A.

126th Mountain Engineer Battalion

Allen, Alvie L.
Barrett, Melvin S.
Coleman, Oree
Filo, Nick J.
Lee, George E.
*Magallanez, Ynes
*McKelvey, Charles M.

Miller, Ralph K.
*Trople, Frait A.

10th Mountain Division Artillery 604th Field Artillery Battalion (Pack)

Carlson, Herbert T.
Craig, Thomas F.
Craig, Thomas S.
*Doiron, Raymond F.
*Drahos, Frank A.
Hazen, John L., Jr.
*Hutto, William J.
Koukol, Donald B.
Peters, Wayne O.
Scibek, Edmond
*Stepp, Walter J.
Wiemer, Wilbert A.
Wikstrom, Verner L.

605th Field Artillery Battalion

Armstrong, Walter J.
Armstrong, William R.
Britton, Merle
Champion, Max L.
Chapman, Willard E.
Dillard, Jerry T.
*Elmore, John D.
Hamilton, Emory E.
Harper, Howard
Harwell, James
Hilley, James
King, Leroy A.
Koskela, Edward E.
Lade, Stanley R.
Liska, John J.
Madara, William E.
Miller, Frank J.
Morrison, W. C., Jr.
Murray, Roger L.
Paulson, Elmer C.
Reynolds, Xwell X.
Russell, Gayle W., Jr.
Tame, Frank
Tannehill, Charles E.
Thalken, Francis R.
Wright, Richard

616th Field Artillery Battalion

*Carlson, Richard A.
Dutton, Jack W.
Kretzu, Walter V.
*Mantifel, Ralph J.
Sherman, Donald G.
Smith, Randolf C.
*Walker, James J., Jr.

85TH MOUNTAIN INFANTRY REGIMENT

Headquarters and Headquarters Company

Chafey, George H.
Dryka, Edward E.
*Taliaferro, F. T., Jr.

Service Company

Crooker, Coville G.

Headquarters Company 1st Battalion

Halford, Claude R., Jr.

Company A

*Buntele, William H.
Buskus, Albert A.
Bystrom, Arthur E.
Caprari, Lawrence R.
*Caulfield, Arthur H.
*Cobb, Daniel J.
Conner, William J.
*Emerson, Dudley R.
*Folger, Peter W.
Freebern, Carson G.
Garvey, Charles E.
*Hall, Walter P., Jr.
Hiney, Edmond L.
*Husted, Roy R.
Lewonski, Benjamin J.
*Luitink, William J.
Martin, James T.

Norman, Richard L.
*Polidoro, Anthony W.
Pridemore, Hughes P.
Sorenson, Axel W.
Stanley, Edward E.
*Vanboven, Walter E.

Company B

Baker, William H.
Barton, Russell A.
Beahm, Edward R.
Burdett, Howard J.
Cook, Samuel T.
Cullen, Terence J.
Devowe, Eugene C.
*Fleischman, Robert L.
Flost, John L.
*Geaniotis, Nicholas G.
Hansen, Marvin L.
*Haug, Robert M.
Haugh, Harvey E.
Hutchins, Emery T.
Jenkins, Paul E.
Jobe, Thomas M.
Johnson, Edwin A.
Jones, John D.
McDermott, Lester J.
Nusbaum, Joseph E.
*Phinney, James B.
Poling, Richard F.
St. Louis, Robert W.
Savage, Irving G.
Sellers, Arthur L.
Shaw, Frederick C.
Skinner, Thomas W., Jr.
*Smith, Warren F., Jr.
*Tabert, Joseph M.
*Thomason, Cleveland O.
Tsigris, Stamatios A.

Company C

Burkey, Norman L.
Danford, Thomas J.
Devenger, Delmas J.
Dubzinski, John E.
Fischer, Robert R.
Kellogg, Francis S.
*Kursinger, Frank T.
*Moore, Jessie H.
Norton, Francis P.

*Pakkala, Roy A.
*Parisey, Leonard F.
Pidsirkowny, John
*Polvrari, Geno J.
*Scott, Arthur M.
Taylor, Henry D.
Walker, Franklin W.

Company D

Delaney, Arthur L.
*Tomlinson, Robert B.

Headquarters Company 2nd Battalion

Blais, William G., Jr.
Craven, Hugh E.
Dolan, John J., Jr.
Nedosytko, Edwin R.
Radabaugh, Virgil P.
*Shepard, William M.

Company E

Altaha, Thomas
Anderson, Duane L. B.
*Burton, John C., Jr.
*Butts, John E., Jr.
Byrd, Melvin L.
Clendenin, Warren A.
Coiro, Joseph P.
Corrigan, James J.
Faulkner, C. R., Jr.
*Frost, Otto J.
Goodall, Robert A.
Greenberg, Jerome
Gross, Jesse W.
King, Edward J.
*LaBelle, Edward E.
Lewis, Harold J.
*Luth, William H., Jr.
Morrison, Joseph E.
Muir, James C.
Rivas, Lucilio F.
*Schlapkohl, Vernor
*Schmid, George H.
Spooner, Clyde S.
Tindall, Alan J.
*Wiren, Gerald A.
Yochum, Edmund A.

Company F

Brandt, Nesbur G.
Brezina, Harold W.
Briggs, William B.
Brown, William O.
Browne, William A.
Burrowes, Lawrence
Callahan, W. F., Jr.
Carson, Lorin J.
Creel, Tommie L.
*Dubois, Charles F.
Elmer, Richard J.
Faber, Otto C.
Fields, Lester B.
Gordon, Dean
Haines, Shapley H.
*Herrick, Roger W.
Hillard, Darwin D.
*Holtzman, Murray
Jensen, Harlan P.
Koski, John L.
Miller, Sol
Moses, Lawrence
Oman, Domer D.
*Paddock, Leonard W.
Pierce, Leonard W.
Pliseck, Michael S.
Rapp, Robert C.
Slaughter, Ned B.
Steiner, Warren C.
*Stepnowski, Edward
Struller, Albert F.
*Taylor, Arthur J.
*Vassar, Homer E.
Wagle, John E.
Watson, William E.
Wensel, Robert B.
*Westphal, Ruben A.

Company G

Billi, Remo J.
*Campbell, Jack R.
Condo, Richard C.
*Croke, Joseph P.
DeRose, Joseph L.
Dietrich, Vladimir
Doyle, John F.
Eden, Jesse H.
Epstein, Eugene A.
Farris, Virgil N.
Fiske, Gilbert H.

Halvorson, Otis F.
Ingram, Edward L.
Johnson, Jack H.
Jones, Robert L.
Kerekes, Lloyd J.
Lentz, J. L.
Lochiatto, Albert A.
Lopez, Andrew F.
MacKenzie, Lawrence S.
Magrath, John D.
*Mappes, Lee B.
Martin, Albert G., Jr.
*Mattison, Floyd L.
*Morgan, Elmer L.
*Newby, John L.
Novosad, Ludwig J.
Nygaard, Arthur M.
*Ratazzine, Tony F.
Reynolds, Warren C.
Sakowski, Joseph, Jr.
*Smith, James J.
*Soeder, Clyde E.
Thiede, Anton E.
*Tiesmaki, Hannu K.

Company H

Bennett, Ernest F., Jr.
Berry, Thomas W., Sr.
*Buoy, Mervin A.
Coons, William S.
Diener, Albert E.
Hunt, Albert W.
*Murphy, Jay G.
*Wikell, Bror H.
*Witte, Charles N., Jr.
Young, William O.
Zeigler, C. C., Jr.

Headquarters Company 3rd Battalion

Mautner, John, Jr.

Company I

Anthony, William L.
*Astuto, Angelo S.
*Augenstein, Cecil C.
*Beagan, John
Beauchamp, Sam T.
*Beaudoin, Lucien H.

Bohin, Steve, Jr.
Bornstein, Charles B.
Breese, Earl W.
Bridgewater, Horace A.
*Broderick, Vearl D.
*Dearborn, Edwin C.
Dolecki, Stanley J.
Eastman, Ernest
Hennessy, Norman S.
Hoey, Thomas
Hunnicutt, Charles J.
Isham, Robert H.
Jackson, James H.
*Johnson, Russel N.
Kvam, Keith L.
*Kynoch, William A.
Lapelle, Phillip B.
*Larsen, Racin W.
Larsen, Thomas W.
Leighton, Kenneth E.
Lupien, Henri J.
Luther, Walter A.
Martin, Homer R.
Mason, Robert V., Jr.
Mitchell, John D.
Payton, Delbert E.
*Pisani, William J.
Reinike, Joseph A.
*Richardson, O. B.
Romberg, Frederick A.
Rooney, James T., Jr.
*Schneider, Donald J.
Sims, William W.
*Skinner, William W.
Venetidy, Theodore
Williams, Joseph

Company K

*Arnold, Edwin H.
*Clancy, John P., Jr.
Cox, George O.
*Davy, Harry G., Jr.
Easley, Maynard L.
Edwards, William H.
*Fox, Everett E.
Jalkon, Joseph C.
*Johnson, Edward L.
Kolendek, Barnard J.
Mancuso, Anthony
Martin, Edgar F.
McCarthy, William P.

*Mergel, Henry
Morasco, Robert A.
*Peckham, Eben N.
Simon, Ted L.
Slight, Frank R.
Yost, James F.

Company L

Barker, James A.
Beckham, Vester G.
Bemis, William C.
Blake, Richard W.
*Clark, Cecil L.
*Davis, Robert H.
Dierolf, Richard C.
*Engle, Charles R.
Finn, Frederick J.
Fleming, Samuel A.
*Fryszkowski, Jerome F.
Impey, William F.
Jones, John P.
Kirk, Willis J.
*Koehler, Lorenz B.
*Letze, William P.
McKitrick, Thomas A.
Miskovich, Joseph G.
*Moorhead, David E.
Roeder, John O.
*Rosenberry, Eugene G.
*Ross, Clarence S.
Rost, Edward C.
*Smith, Donald L. B.
*Solomon, Sidney
Wolcott, Charles A.
Zimmer, Peter A.

Company M

*Bechini, Bertero
Cooley, Robert A.
England, Kenneth H.
Ersdale, Peter T.
Jessen, F. W., Jr.
Josten, Harold R.
Myers, Walter P.
*O'Brien, James P.
*Ozmun, Lyle M.
Pendleton, Ross L.
Roberts, Herbert E.
*Winter, Burdell S.

Company Unknown

*Bequeath, Garfield H.
Bowers, James A.
*Buger, Leroy C.
Calahan, Gerald F.
Campbell, Horace D.
*Clune, James E.
Coffey, Oscar R
Conway, Leonard M.
*Cronin, Elbert W.
Dudley, Joseph B.
*Everhart, Willie H.
*Gyori, Frank J.
Hayes, Millard
Hilyard, Glen D.
*Jones, William F.
Kimura, Paul T.
King, Wiley G., Jr.
Kramer, Willard J.
Kubica, John F.
*Lamere, Oliver J.
Laughman, Paul J.
*Lethco, Ralph R.
Maher, Thomas F.
Malik, John E.
Mallow, Clinton H.
Massey, Ralph M.
McCarty, Thruman P.
Meyers, Vincent F.
Moyes, James J.
Sodomora, Theodore
*Thorne, Wilbur S.
*Wilder, Lonnie C.
Wilder, Wilber E.
*Winget, Clifton

86th Mountain Infantry Regiment

Headquarters and Headquarters Company

*Evans, John T.
Hagens, Clarence J.

Headquarters Company 1st Battalion

*Matthews, James A.

Company A

*Bloom, Raymond W.
*Calhoon, Archie E.
Carey, Oscar C.
Cerepa, Richard A.
*Godwin, William G.
Griffin, Everett R.
Mermet, Leon J.
*Reed, Richard C.
Richardson, Neal M.
Tokle, Torger D.
Tokala, Arthur K.
Yammarino, John J.

Company B

*Brown, Marion W.
Casperson, Carl E.
Digitale, Edward H.
Faircloth, Woodrow A.
*Froelicher, Sangree M.
Garrison, Lewis E.
Goldstein, Andrew
*Good, Benjamin R.
Hall, Harold J.
Haughaboo, William S.
*Kovach, Norman
Masonis, Leo P.
Norton, Charles G.
Norton, Hershell
Pennebaker, John G.
Perez, David
Rank, John K.
Rand, Douglas L.
Roberge, Rosario D. D.
Ryan, William A.
Sbardella, Michael
Spiewak, Edwar F.
Whiting, Leroy
*Williams, Dwight C.
Wirkkala, Nillo A.

Company C

Cavanaugh, Russel H.
Clainos, Nicholas D.
Desmond, Morgan V.
Hengen, Henry W.
*Koon, Steeny L.
Lebrecht, Ferdinand
Lowery, Howell H.
Mallico, Charles D.

*Martino, Fred A.
*McGown, John A., III
Platten, Charles J.
Rietman, Albert C.
*Rodriquez, Fausto
Shafer, Al F.
Shaffer, Marion L.
Strickler, William H.
Thuness, Magnus O.

Company D

Boady, Lester L. Jr.
Bostonia, Michael G.
*Lentini, Robert M.
Smith, Robert G.
*Steele, Melvin C.
White, Lawrence A.

**Headquarters
Company
2nd Battalion**

(none)

Company E

Bruckelmyer, R. D.
*Carr, Paul
Coffin, Joel S., III
Crum, Roy E.
*Darrow, John A.
Duskey, Joseph P., Jr.
Ford, James C., Jr.
Freudenrich, Q. V.
Husband, Kenneth M.
Mix, Robert T.
*Murphy, Bernard J.
*Orsini, Leon
Posternak, Max
Riedell, Gerald E. N.
Schill, William J.
Smith, Edward F.
Sobocinski, John
*Staub, Earl W.

Company F

Bontempo, Peter A.
Colby, Jack R.
Crumbley, Lloyd E.
Cuoco, Joseph
*Fisher, Robert P.
Fuller, George W.

Hyatt, Michael L., Jr.
Lefand, Michael A.
*Martin, John D.
Poynor, Fred L.
*Sheppard, Harry M.
*Sherman, Felix A.
*Stage, Richard J.
*Thompson, Arnie L.
Tickell, Richard P., Jr.
*Vandeboncoeur, C. J.

Company G

*Austin, Jack R.
Carroll, Conrad F.
Cascella, Walter T.
*Compton, John P.
Crandall, Richard L.
*Dmythrow, William J.
*Donahue, James R.
Easley, Merle E.
*Foust, Ridgway
Freeman, Aaron G.
Garcia, Heriberto
*Goodwin, Eugene A.
Graham, Delmar
Ladue, Raymond G.
Larrabee, John W.
Madsen, Gilbert J.
*Peabody, Myron F.
Phipps, Charles R.
Shelby, James H.
Simpson, Donald G.
Vaccarino, Gregorie S.
*Vlasoff, Nicholas M.

Company H

*Ely, Lawrence B.
*Enright, James D., III
Hill, McKinley
Hooper, Elton L.
*Liegey, Marvin A.
Ligon, Elbert, Jr.
Naimen, Melvin H.
*Strohm, Howard E.
Wright, Alexander T.

**Headquarters
Company
3rd Battalion**

Bromaghin, Ralph B.

Company I

Bacon, James L.
Burbank, Charles W.
*Cherkassky, A. K.
*Cucci, Prospero M.
*Everingham, Frank R.
Fuller, Maynard A.
Gillick, Charles J.
Gunter, Clayton E.
Jack, William R.
Kuhnert, Robert L.
Luedtke, James E.
*Marrocco, Albert
Minturn, John C., III
Morrow, Robert H.
Mosey, Richard D.
*Ricken, Alfred
Riddle, James E.
*Roberts, Howard E.
Rogers, Richard A.
Sanwald, John W.
Schreiber, William
*Sellers, Arvil T.
Sorensen, Robert L.
*Stern, Horace A.
Thomas, Robert D.
Webb, Orville L.
*Wilcox, Jean A.
Wyckoff, Lyle E.

Company K

*Alex, Stratford G.
Anderson, Warren S.
Bordenave, Richard B.
*Burrows, John
*Espinosa, Dan
Ford, Claude S.
Garcia, Guillermo
*Gilleran, Alfred E.
*Gordon, Robert L.
Halcomb, Hoble
Howell, Thomas H., Jr.
Mitchell, W. R., Jr.
Nypaver, Kenneth J.
Rabe, Raymond E.
Ramirez, Pedro M.

Company L

*Abbott, Stuart E.
*Argiewicz, Arthur, Jr.

Clemens, Irvin W.
*Cronin, Robert J.
Enners, Edward H., III
Fowler, Roy A.
*Garcia, Jesus G.
Greene, Theodore S.
Gregory, Charles E.
*Grundter, Albert R.
Hertneky, Jack R., Jr.
*Katruska, Steve
*Kuhn, Archie F.
*Leto, Ralph T.
Patti, Thomas J.
Peterson, Ned O.
Piro, Robert H.
*Podborny, John S.
Reick, Wendell F.
Reiss, Henry
*Ruhlman, Robert G.
Strobel, James J.
*Sullivan, Horace L.
Trew, Jack E.
*Valentine, Lester L.
Wesley, Louis C.

Company M

*Hardy, Herbert V.
Ladd, Charles D.
*Naylor, Robert
Rush, Victor E.

Company Unknown

*Bazzell, Paul G., Jr.
Bentley, Arthur H.
*Brown, Wayne S.
Buxton, J. B.
*Callahan, Donald W.
Camire, Theodore J.
*Carbillano, Michael P.
Christensen, Frank B.
Clark, Joseph E.
Dullen, Thomas C.
Edminsten, John M.
*Fargus, Karl I.
Feith, Matthew W.
*Fisher, Joe S.
Flannery, Luther O.
Foster, Joseph C.
Gibson, Carl F.
*Jacobi, Robert W.

*Johnson, Glen C.
Little, James
Lopez, Cecilio
McGuire, Richard G.
Montgomery, Murl
*Moore, John S.
Moore, Roy T.
Morales, Robert F.
Mueller, Herman F.
Odden, Oscar P.
*Parker, James C.
Reid, Robert L.
Robinson, Merle H.
Stern, Joseph
*Stoneroad, Darwin H.
*Tressler, William H.
*Ward, Henry T.
Wieder, Jerry

87th Mountain Infantry Regiment

Headquarters and Headquarters Company

Contino, William S.
*Frank, Loren
*Montgomery, Harry
Van de Putte, John E.

Service Company

*Cochran, Walter R., Jr.
Davis, Kenneth
Irvin, Samuel L.
Self, Mack O.
Smith, George, Jr.

Headquarters Company 1st Battalion

Billings, Matthew
*Miller, Joseph C.
Schunk, Robert H.

Company A

*Abasta, Manuel G., Jr.
Aldahl, James A.
*Bennett, Sydney W.

Brietenbach, Roy R.
Carey, Mose
*Caudill, James R.
Chew, Lee H.
Creger, Harold M.
*Dean, Okey C.
Dunn, Harry H.
Farrell, Joseph C.
Forester, William H.
*Gordon, Edwin R.
Gorman, Lloyd A.
*Hall, Lee L.
Hamilton, Erik H.
Hoyt, David C.
Johnston, Richard D.
Kersting, Arthur L.
*Klein, Paul L.
Lewis, Luther P.
Murphy, John C.
Salazar, Jesus M.
Santoni, Abraham J.
Skomp, Anthony L.
Stanke, Edwin W.
Webb, William H.
*Woods, Grover P.

Company B

Bagneski, Eugene J.
Bettenberg, William J.
Clark, Wayne C.
Deeter, Lucien T.
Delgado, John P.
Diller, Walter W.
*Foley, Thomas A.
*Fotas, Beta
Frye, Paul N., Jr.
*Garfinkel, Harold E.
*Grabowsky, Robert W.
Haight, Donald G.
Hale, Marvin G.
Hermon, Wayne E.
Housley, Gilbert G.
*Kosa, Edward J.
LaBombard, Robert J.
Manchio, Albert
Nunnemacher, Jacob R.
Pantsari, Peter A.
Perkins, Marlin A.
Post, Robert M.
Rubins, Zale R.
*Santiesteban, F. L.

Schiller, Paul F.
Serakos, James C.
Shevchik, Harry M.
Stranger, Robert L.
*Tomich, John H.
Waldrip, Sylvan D.
Wells, William E.
Wilbur, John M.
Wilson, Paul T.
Wozencraft, Edward O.
Yarnell, Herbert G.

Company C

Bailey, Glen R.
*Barrientos, Juan
Brown, Louis O.
*Butler, Manfred
David, Prentis F.
*Dilkes, Herbert W.
*Ersland, Lester S.
Folse, Earl A.
Fristoe, Elmer
Heichel, John L.
Hemstreet, William E.
Hiner, Marvin E.
Huff, William D.
Kolkka, Larry
Lay, Marion F.
Leppek, Sylvester J.
*Norlin, Howard R.
*Ortwein, Carl H.
Pehr, Jack
*Poutiatine, Alexis
*Rainey, Horace H.
Ryberg, William S.
Steyert, William F.
Streumeyer, Joseph E.
Vest, Chester W.
Yupa, Charles
Zarlengo, Fred E.

Company D

Blocker, William B., Jr.
*Dorsey, Louis M.
*Fligg, Owen W., Jr.
Flowe, Walter O.
Floyd, Fred
*Goldberg, Jack
Leyman, Henry
*Merrill, William C.

Murphy, William F.
Sutherburg, Walfred F.
*Whyte, James C.

Headquarters Compny 2nd Battalion

Deane, David T.
Fanning, Gene
Huntley, Alan
*Miller, Leo J.
Trautwein, Lewis S.

Company E

Benjamin, Fedor H.
Bergendorff, Robert A.
Bruneau, Hector W.
Dickens, Freddie
Erickson, Gordon D.
Handwerk, Leo T.
Hathaway, Edmon E.
Hubbard, Ralph
Kasabuski, John A.
Kasabuski, Walter
Kenney, James P.
*Lathrop, Robert H.
*O'Neil, Thomas
*Pfusch, Robert B.
Sayer, Albert L.
Stice, Charles G.

Company F

*Benson, John P., Jr.
Campbell, Clarence E.
*Corn, Harvey F., Jr.
Garneau, Alfred A.
Haburne, Randolph
Hoffman, Marvin H.
Kennett, James C.
Konieczny, Rudolf W.
Kovar, Frank S.
*Krieger, Morris J.
*Lahti, Welsey E.
Largent, Ceceil D.
*Lawrence, George J.
Leinonen, Toivo H.
*Lunsford, Floyd H.
Malloy, Thomas J.
McCoy, Donald M., Jr.
Musick, Clarence K.

*Norton, Eugene A.
Ryan, James P.
Schaedler, Harry Y.
Simpson, Andrew E.
Strubel, Walter R.
Thomas, Lewis M.
Utter, Sidney B.
*Vukovich, Melo

Company G

*Bernstein, Melvin
Blaker, George J.
Connolly, Normand W.
Crisp, Lenard
Deschaine, Camille J.
Fantozzi, Aniceto
*Fritchie, Theodore J.
*Green, Charlie I.
Groeger, Albert F.
*Jazwinski, Stanley F.
Lowery, Francis E.
*Lynch, Brainerd F.
Main, Warren F.
Manthei, Everett G.
*Markson, Harry F.
Mathews, Nyeray O.
*McArdle, Lawrence E.
*McDonald, Alfred C.
Mootz, Robert D.
Mueller, Forrest N.
*Pierce, Burton E.
Redding, Wilbur D.
*Rose, Henry F., Jr.
Thaxton, Billy J.
Vanauken, Edwin G.

Company H

*Allison, Lester L.
Anetsberger, Fred J.
Baker, Frank P.
Dalton, Andrew W., Jr.
Hollingsworth, John
Linn, Clarence W., Jr.
Ringlein, Edward J.

Headquarters Company 3rd Battalion

*Berlin, Elmer A.
Corn, Wid R.

Davis, George T.
Felch, George A.
*Gusko, Alex
*Hemmer, Oscar W.
Heydenreich, George H.
Norgaard, George
Piotroski, Eugene J.
Stoner, Samuel H.
*Williams, Wayne

Company I

Cabezut, George E.
Campbell, William, Jr.
*Doane, Luther E., Jr.
Emerson, Roger D.
Funk, Wilfred J., Jr.
*Haines, John W., III
*Hance, Joseph G.
Johnson, Phillip O.
Levitt, Charles W.
Lindsey, Solon R.
Lowatti, John
*Lowe, Homer H.
Martinez, Joseph M.
*McBride, Roy L.
*McDaniel, Orval R.
Nevergall, James F.
*O'Hara, Gerard E
Ordaz, Louie A.
Prater, Carl C.
*Scuto, Anthony S.
Spreng, John G.
Stanley, George A.
Stevens, Earl H.
Strauss, Frederick B.
Tabbarracci, Jacob T.
Wenders, Theodore W.

Company K

Adkins, Charles W.
Aucoin, Maurice E.
Austin, Herman S.
Barr, Robert S.

Battiloro, Andrew
Camillo, John
*Campbell, Robert E.
*Dennis, David H. C.
*Erhard, Pierre B.
Fricke, William H.
*Gould, Harold R.
Hamill, Ralph
Hamilton, William L.
Hintze, Kenneth L.
Hujanen, Carl P.
Jilka, Casmir F.
Kalfin, Hyman
Lakeway, Walter F.
*Lutz, Marvin C.
Marrone, John C.
Mass, William C., III
Nylund, Evert L., Jr.
*Palmer, Fred M.
Perdue, Harold J.
Pfeiffer, Charles L.
Philp, William
Poirier, Joseph A., Jr.
Schall, Herbert M.
Schroeder, Claus
Seebade, Warren H.
Snyder, Edward
Spaulding, M. W. A.
*Stevens, James M.
*Thomas, Harry
*Tobis, Steve
Tomlinson, John E.
Welch, John J.
*Wentworth, William H.
*Wilson, Dan M.
Wyberg, Theodore A.
Yoder, Orlon J.

Company L

Baldor, Raphael, Jr.
*Blanchard, John B.
Burgess, Arthur H., Jr.
Chrysler, Glenn L.
Cochran, Thomas

Dora, Willard W.
Duncan, Joseph J.
Dunham, Dale W.
Foster, Egan L.
*Gallegos, Sam
Gustafson, Robert W.
*Hinshaw, Edward G.
Hodge, Walter W.
Jump, Homer P., Jr.
Kennedy, William M.
LaBonte, Lawrence J.
Lewis, Mervin H.
Luif, Frank J.
MacWilliams, R. L.
McNew, Roy
Meiser, Charles R., Jr.
*Nennig, Michael G.
*Nicosia, Michael
*Nocitra, Richard B.
Nokleby, Harvey J.
*Norris, Lee R.
Puskarich, Paul T.
Pydych, William S.
Reiche, Robert P.
*Reynolds, C. H., Jr.
*Rinfret, Alan H.
Rogers, James H., Jr.
Smith, Walter F., Jr.
Spaulding, Herbert C.
Stromer, Alan C.
Wall, Thomas E.
Wolfgram, William J.

Company M

*Day, George H., Jr.
*Floyd, William D.
*Horton, Palmer W.
*Huckabee, Walter R.
*Kearse, Mose
*King, Harrison H.
*Lafountain, F. A.
Ledbetter, Marvin D.
Raffety, Kenneth D.
Stromberg, Robert W.

In closing I reaffirm my dedication of this book to these valiant men who gave their lives for the United States of America and its great tradition of freedom under law.

"O LORD SUPPORT US ALL THE DAY LONG UNTIL THE SHADOWS LENGTHEN AND THE EVENING COMES AND THE FEVER OF LIFE IS OVER AND OUR WORK IS DONE THEN IN THY MERCY GRANT US A SAFE LODGING AND A HOLY REST AND PEACE AT LAST" *

*Quotation on Memorial Panel No. 4 at the American Military Cemetery, Florence, Italy from Cardinal Newman's Sermon XX included in the Episcopal Prayer Book

BIBLIOGRAPHY

The American Battle Monuments Commission. 1985.
Florence American Cemetery and Memorial.
Washington, D.C.: The American Battle Monument
Commission.

Bendini, Giancarlo. 1991. *Dagli "States" All Appennino.*
Bologna: Arti Grafice Giorgi.

Bounds, Lt. Col. Gary L. and Maj. Scott R. McMichael.
1985. "Counting Costs of Elite Forces." *ARMY*
(November).

Braly, James O. 1995. *Marching With Heroes.* Sherman,
Texas: Ann Jones.

Burton, Hal. 1971. *The Ski Troops.* New York: Simon
and Schuster.

Casewit, Curtis W. 1992. *Mountain Trooper! The Story
of the 10th Mountain Division.* New York:
Thomas Y. Crowell Co.

Dole, Minot (Minnie). 1965. *Adventures in Skiing.*
New York: Franklin Watts, Inc.

Dusenbery, Harris. 1991. *Ski The High Trail: World War II
Ski Troopers in the High Colorado Rockies.*
Portland, Oregon: Binford & Mort Publishing.

Earle, George F. 1945. *History of the 87th Mountain Infantry.* Denver: The 87th Mountain Infantry.

Fisher, Ernest F. Jr. 1977. *Cassino to the Alps.* Washington, D.C.: Center of Military History.

Harper, Frank. 1946. *Night Climb: The Story of the Skiing 10th.* New York: Longmans, Green & Co.

Hauptman, Charles M. 1977. *Combat History of the 10th Mountain Division: 1944-1945.* (Copy of major parts of the Division Narrative from Army records) Billings, Montana: Self-published.

Imbrie, John and Evans, Hugh W. 1995. *Good Times and Bad Times: History of C Company, 85th Mtn. Infantry.* Quechee: Vermont Heritage Press.

Krear, H. Robert. 1993. *The Journal of a U.S. Army Mountain Trooper in World War II.* Estes Park, Colorado: Desktop published by Jan Bishop.

Kohlman, Oley. 1985. *Uphill With The Ski Troops.* Walden, Colorado: Self-pusblished.

Lissy, David. 1988. *Colorado Ski!* Englewood, Colorado: Westcliffe Publishers, Inc.

Meinke, Albert H. Jr. 1992. *Mountain Troops and Medics: Wartime Stories of a Frontline Surgeon in the U.S. Ski Troops.* Kewadin, Michigan: Rucksack Publishing.

Motley, E. P. 1991."Memoirs of Six Months." *War, Literature and The Arts* (U.S. Air Force Academy) (Fall): 116 pages.

National Association of the 10th Mountain Division. 1994. *1994 National Roster.* Hernando, Florida: The National Association of the 10th Mountain Division.

Putnam, William Lowell. 1991. *Green Cognac: The Education of a Mountain Fighter.* New York: The AAC Press.

Skiing Heritage; Journal of the International Skiing History Association vol. 7, no. 2, (Fall 1995). New York.

U.S. Department of the Army. 1945. *19 Days from Apennines to the Alps: The Story of the Po Valley Canpaign.* Milan, Italy: Pizzi and Pizio.

Ware, Wilson P. 1946. "Italy: The Riva Ridge." *Journal of the American Alpine Club.* New York.

Wellborn, Charles. 1945. "History of the 86th Mountain Infantry." 63 page typewritten manuscript based on the Regimental Journal. Revised in 1989.

Whitlock, Flint and Bob Bishop. 1992. *Soldiers on Skis: A pictorial memoir of the 10th Mountain Division.* Boulder, Colorado: Paladin Press.

Williams, Lt. Col. Reginald L. 1945. *15th Army Group History, 16 December 1944–2 May 1945.* Reprint. Nashville, Tennessee: Battery Press.

Wilson, Ross J. 1991. *History of the 1st Battalion, 87th Mountain Infantry.* Kalispell, Montana: Self-published manuscript.